FUTURE CHURCH

All royalties from this book will go towards
the cost of further research for the church

Future Church

A global analysis of the Christian
community to the year 2010

DR PETER W BRIERLEY

MONARCH
BOOKS
Christian Research

Copyright © Peter Brierley 1998
The right of Peter Brierley to be identified
as author of this work has been asserted by him
in accordance with the Copyright, Designs
and Patents Act 1988.

First British edition 1998

ISBNs
Monarch Books: 1 85424 415 9
Christian Research: 1 85321 132 X

All rights reserved.
No part of this publication may be reproduced or
transmitted in any form or by any means, electronic
or mechanical, including photocopy, recording, or any
information storage and retrieval system, without
permission in writing from Monarch Books
in association with Angus Hudson Ltd,
Concorde House, Grenville Place,
Mill Hill, London NW7 3SA.

Editorial Office: Monarch Books,
Broadway House, The Broadway, Crowborough,
East Sussex TN6 1HQ.

Published jointly with Christian Research
Vision Building, 4 Footscray Road, Eltham
London SE9 2TZ.

British Library Cataloguing Data
A catalogue record for this book is available
from the British Library.

Designed and produced for the publishers by
Bookprint Creative Services
P.O. Box 827, BN21 3YJ, England
Printed in Great Britain.

To the Christian Research Team
who stood behind the hours of work
for the production of the
World Churches Handbook:

Boyd Myers, Pam Poynter, Jan Taylor,
and Heather Wraight

CONTENTS

	Acknowledgements and Introduction	9
	Foreword	11
1.	Revival? We've had it!	13
2.	The Church in the World	30
3.	The Catholic Church	56
4.	The Anglican Church	76
5.	The Other Institutional Churches (Orthodox, Lutheran and Presbyterian)	93
6.	The Charismatic Churches (Pentecostal and Indigenous)	120
7.	The Non-Charismatic Churches (Baptist, Methodist and Other Churches)	140
8.	Nominalism and its consequences	169
9.	Implications from Costa Rica	191
10.	Culture and Church Leadership	212
	Index	243

ACKNOWLEDGEMENTS AND INTRODUCTION

It was essentially through the weeks and months that I pored over the data in the *World Churches Handbook* that I realised that there was a story in the figures which somehow needed to be told. What was the best way to tell that story led to hours of discussion, but the result is here.

I have many people to thank for helping me in writing this book. First and foremost is Patrick Johnstone of WEC International, the author of *Operation World*. This book (and the *Atlas of World Christianity*) would never have happened without his generous agreement to let me use his world database for the compilation and production of the *World Churches Handbook*, on which this book is based. My thanks also go to John Marcus for his computer skills in allowing that database to become readily accessible, to Jan Taylor and Boyd Myers for hours of changing and correcting figures on the computer, and to Pam Poynter whose financial management enabled its publication to go ahead.

Even so, without the encouragement of my publisher, Tony Collins, this book would never have been written. Through numerous conversations he enabled me to define its shape. Then there was the tremendous encouragement of receiving Jorge Gómez' thesis from Dr John Kessler in Costa

Rica, my mounting excitement as I read it, and the realisation that in it was information important well beyond Central America.

How the two editors, Valerie Passmore, and my Assistant Director, Heather Wraight, had the patience to go through this text and make so many helpful comments I do not know, but I appreciate their help enormously. Many thanks to Heather also for being able to talk over the ideas in this volume on many occasions.

I sincerely hope that this volume will help readers to learn more about the church in all its varied worldwide phenomena, what are some of the current trends, and what might be some of the implications. Jesus said 2,000 years ago that He would build His Church – and He has, and He is still building it! It is a wonderful and complex piece of architecture. All we do here is to paint its outline on a piece of paper, and draw in a few brush strokes. Reader, may you be enthused to move with that church, and to encourage its growth in every way you can!

The first two Chapters give an overall introduction. Readers not wishing to read all the denominational detail may prefer to read the chapter or part chapter on their particular church, and then go to Chapters 8 and 9 which look at one consequence of the church community – nominalism. Chapter 10 is both a summary and a putting of the rest of the book in a church-cultural context, with implications for individual churches and church leaders. Do scan that too!

Peter Brierley
Eltham, London SE9
April 1998

FOREWORD

This amazing book *Future Church* is more important than perhaps the average Christian (whatever that is) realises. It needs to be read, prayed over and widely distributed.

Sometimes our evaluation of what God is doing around the world is based on exciting stories, some of which are not even true, rather than facts. People committed to godly research know that the facts are not easy to get and sometimes statistics can bring with them some distortion. I believe Dr Peter Brierley brings needed balance in this unique book.

The information on why people leave the church should drive all of us to repentance and prayer. Let's remember what our Lord said in Luke 15:4 – 'Suppose one of you has a hundred sheep and loses one of them. Does he not leave the ninety-nine in the open country and go after the lost sheep until he finds it?'

This book gives us vital information and challenging material about many different church movements in many different parts of the world. It will help us become more global in our thinking and praying. We all know that going to church is not enough and that being called a Christian might be more of a statistic than a dynamic, eternal reality.

The growth of nominalism is a major problem everywhere. At that same time, when we get to heaven, there may be a few surprises as to who is there.

My prayer, of course, is that this significant book will inspire us to be more realistic, prayerful, loving and evangelistic that we may see an even greater harvest in the years to come and into the millennium. I pray that all committed believers would become more grace awakened in their attitude towards people in other fellowships and churches and get a bigger view of God HIMSELF and all that HE is doing in the world today. I don't believe we should compromise the basic truths of God's Word, but we should realise that God's great programme of unity is in the midst of great diversity.

George Verwer

I

REVIVAL? WE'VE HAD IT!

This is a book about world Christianity – how is the church changing across the various continents?

Before we begin to look at that question, let me ask you one. Here is a graph – never mind what it is of for the moment. My question is: Where do you think the line will be by the year 2000? Mark it on the graph with a **X**.

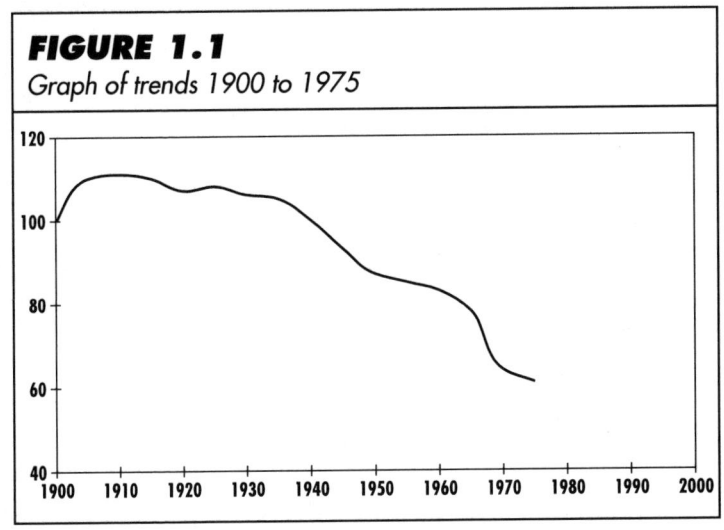

FIGURE 1.1
Graph of trends 1900 to 1975

Where did you put your **X**? What value did you give? If you worked from the original numbers and projected them mathematically the answer would be 36 by the year 2000. If you imagined a straight line from the high point in 1910 to the 1975 figure and continued it to 2000, the answer would be 40. What I did not tell you was that although the year 1970 was 64 and 1975 was 61, the 1980 figure was 64 and the 1985 figure was 66! If you'd known, you would probably have given a different answer!

So what does the graph show? The figures actually represent the membership of the Baptist Union of Great Britain since 1900. In 1900 they had 239,000 members and in 1905 262,000, an increase of 10%. The graph gives the 1900 figure as a base of 100, so the 1905 number is 110, and so on. You can see that the Union grew in the years before the First World War (along with most other denominations in Great Britain), and then slowly declined, dropping back to the 1900 level in 1940, and then continuing to decline in the years after the Second World War.

The unexpected

But something happened in the late 1970s which reversed the downward trend. Exactly what, except by the sovereign work of God, is not clear. In 1975 there were 146,000 members, but by 1980 there were 154,000 and by 1985 157,000. Sadly this increase didn't continue and subsequent figures are graphed below, with the year 2000 being an estimate.

I used to think that this was just an interesting but isolated case of church trends not always being predictable. However, something else happened in the late 1970s and early 1980s in the church in Britain. The New Churches, then called House Churches, had begun in the late 1960s and were really quite small in 1970. By 1975 it is estimated they had about 12,000 members[1]. By 1980 they had more than doubled to 25,000,

REVIVAL? WE'VE HAD IT! 15

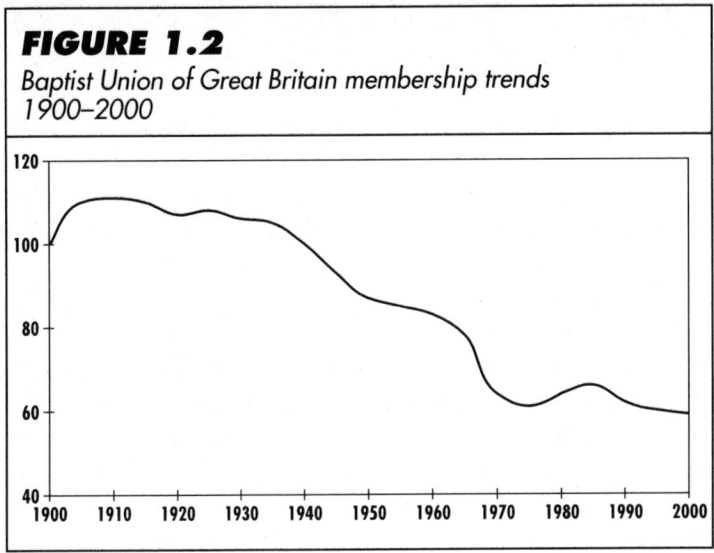

FIGURE 1.2
Baptist Union of Great Britain membership trends 1900–2000

and by 1985 they had not just doubled again but more than *trebled*!

In 1986 I did a survey of the existing New Churches in the UK asking how many members they had in 1980 and subsequent years. The first form I got back showed numbers had multiplied three-fold in those years and I can remember thinking, 'Wow, that's an exciting growth pattern.' The next day a couple more forms came in and they showed the same thing. I felt a buzz of excitement and couldn't wait for the rest. Imagine my astonishment when I listed all the results to find that every single stream[2] had grown about three times between 1980 and 1985 – a few a bit more but none substantially less. They have continued to grow since but never at such a rate. From 1985 to 1990 they increased by a further 50%, which is still high growth by any church standards, averaging 9% a year, but it is much less than the 26% a year between 1980 and 1985. You can see this spectacular growth very clearly in the graph below.

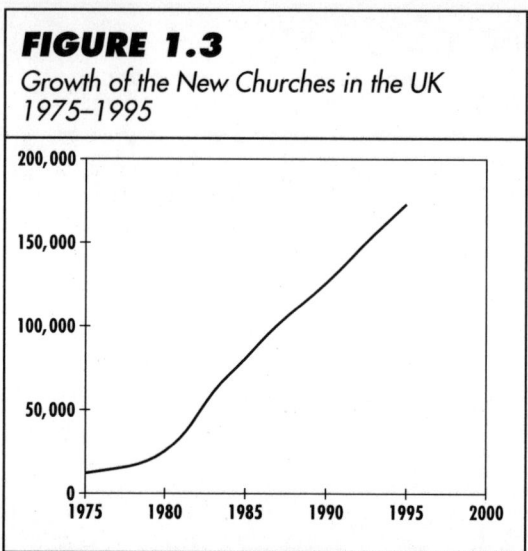

FIGURE 1.3
Growth of the New Churches in the UK
1975–1995

Here then are two examples from church life in Britain of growth between 1975 and 1985 which was different from the trends of the early 1970s and the late 1980s. Other churches in the UK did not have a similar experience and I did not think these results particularly special until the opportunity came to look much more widely.

Some History

Operation World

Before we plunge into the detail of this book, it is worth looking at how it came to be written. Patrick Johnstone is a man with a deep passion to see the world won for Christ. He knows that prayer is a significant component of the work to be done, and in the 1970s was concerned to give Christian people specific items for prayer for each of the many countries in the world. To stimulate such prayer, information is needed, including data on the Christian church in each land. For the latter Patrick used the 1968 *World Christian Handbook*[3] for church membership figures. The result, *Operation World*, was published in 1974[4].

Enter George Verwer, the charismatic founder and Director of Operation Mobilization, now a worldwide organisation seeking to bring the gospel of Christ in many lands through literature, education programmes, two ships which travel the world, and direct preaching and explaining of the good news of Jesus. George saw the first edition of *Operation World*, liked it, and wrote enthusiastically to Patrick, inspiring him to produce a second edition in 1978.

World Christian Encyclopedia

Another key person in this story is the Rev Dr David Barrett who was a missionary in Kenya in the 1970s. There he established and ran the Anglican Church's Research Centre. Encouraged by Ed Dayton, the founder of MARC[5], he took the membership data in the 1968 *World Christian Handbook* and computerised it. David then added to this mass of information much more data derived from a vast research exercise which quite literally went to every corner of the world. He gathered the latest details from thousands of people on denominations and churches in every country, and incorporated it all into his magnificent *World Christian Encyclopedia,* published in 1982[6]. Ever since, this has been a highly valuable source of information for all who want to know the nuts and bolts of the Christian world. He has since updated selections of the totals and published them each year[7].

Patrick Johnstone proceeded to expand and modify his database. He used the *World Christian Encyclopedia* for the 1986 and 1993 editions of *Operation World*[8], updating the material in the process. His updated database is now being used by David Barrett in *his* updating of the *World Christian*

Encyclopedia, to be published in three volumes, hopefully in 1999[9].

World Churches Handbook

After many requests Patrick Johnstone made *Operation World* available on computer diskette and decided also to release his database in the same way. While the diskette version of the book sold well, that of his database did not, and even those who did buy it found it difficult to use because the associated software to manipulate and display the data could not be sold with the raw files without greatly raising the price[10]. This is when I came in to the picture. I asked Patrick if he would allow his database to be published in book form, and he graciously gave permission.

The resulting book was the *World Churches Handbook*, published in 1997[11]. It is based on Patrick's database, updated and amended for publication. In addition the data was forecast through to the year 2010[12], assuming that current trends will continue.

The many denominations were organised into 10 major groupings: Anglican, Baptist, Catholic, Indigenous, Lutheran, Methodist, Orthodox, Pentecostal, Presbyterian and Other Churches.

The 'Catholic' group includes a few other than Roman Catholics, like the Uniates. The Uniate Churches are 'Eastern Christian churches in communion with Rome who have retained their own liturgies, liturgical language, and ecclesiastical customs and rites.'[13] They fall into five groups: The Antiochenes, Chaldeans, Alexandrines, Byzantines and Italo-Greek-Albanians.

The 'Pentecostal' churches are the worldwide main line Pentecostal denominations plus other smaller groups.

Independent churches, which may or may not be charismatic, are included under 'Other Churches'. They differ from the very similar Indigenous churches as many of these Independent churches operate in more than one country (and some, like the Seventh-Day Adventists, are worldwide).

'Indigenous' churches are frequently individual churches which have formed within the culture of one particular country. They do not always group together into recognised denominations and rarely form congregations outside their own locality. There are none in Europe.

'Other Churches', which are mainly the smaller denominations, including for example the Salvation Army, Mennonites or Christian Brethren, which always occur in more than one country. They are thus different to the Indigenous Churches.

What information does the *World Churches Handbook* give? Primarily for every country in the world and the majority of denominations within each country, there are three pieces of data:

The size of the church community, or the number of adherents

The number of church members, roughly half the community figure

The number of individual churches or congregations.

The number of members is frequently derived from an appropriate percentage of the community, so we limit ourselves mostly to looking at the size of the church community, sometimes abbreviated to 'Christendom', and to the supporting congregations.

Future Church

Built on the United Nations six continents of Africa, North America (including Central America and the Caribbean), South America, Asia, Europe and Oceania (Australia, New Zealand and territories in the Pacific), this present book is based entirely on the statistics in the *World Churches Handbook*[14], updated where later information is available.

In 1992, the United Nations changed its definition of nine of the constituent countries of the old USSR. Previous to 1992 the entire USSR was included within Europe, but after 1992 only those six countries in the western part of the old USSR were deemed part of Europe – Belarus, Estonia, Latvia, Lithuania, Moldova and the Ukraine. The rest were classified as being in Asia. This move, especially of Russia from Europe to Asia, has created a numerical jump between 1990 and 1995.

Church Growth Worldwide

Now I can return to the examples of growth with which I started the chapter. The absolutely fascinating thing about an analysis of the data in the *World Churches Handbook* is that it shows that growth in the 1970s and 1980s was not limited to the United Kingdom. For example, in Africa

In the 1960s the churches grew by 41 million
    1970s   50 million
    1980s   63 million
    1990s   50 million

In other words the numbers joining the church peaked between 1980 and 1990.

The same is true of growth in the churches in Asia. The growth figures are given below:

In the 1960s the churches grew by 24 million
    1970s   49 million
    1980s   71 million
    1990s   48 million

The peak in the 1980s was not just due to the giant expansion of the church in China, massive though that was. However, take China's growth out of the Asia figures above and you still get 24 million, 28 million, 37 million and 20 million for the four decades. So the growth in Asia took place across many countries in the 1980s, not only China.

In the other continents the changes have been less pronounced. In North America the churches grew by 30 million in the 1960s and by 41 million in the 1970s, but they have maintained that level of growth, so that the period of the 1980s was not especially large. In South America the growth has been continuous and while higher in the 1980s (at 51 million) than the 1970s (at 46 million) it was not a very great difference.

Oceania and Europe regrettably did not experience such overall changes as a whole, but, as in the United Kingdom, there were similar changes in some denominations in various countries.

Increase per day

The numbers are so large that they are easier to grasp if we translate them into the increase to the church on a *daily* average basis. The Table on Page 22 uses that to show the growth of the churches worldwide in the 50 years from 1960 to 2010.

These figures are graphed in Figure 1.4, and the high in the 1980s is immediately obvious. The *rate* of increase in the number of Christians was significantly greater in the period 1975–80 and increased again between 1980 and 1985. Since then it has decreased, although it seems to have levelled off at present, and looks like staying that way for the first part of the 21st century.

TABLE 1.1
Average daily increase in the church community

Period	Christendom
1960–1965	+40,000
1965–1970	+45,000
1970–1975	+48,000
1975–1980	+61,000
1980–1985	+67,000
1985–1990	+62,000
1990–1995	+56,000
1995–2000	+53,000
2000–2005	+51,000
2005–2010	+51,000

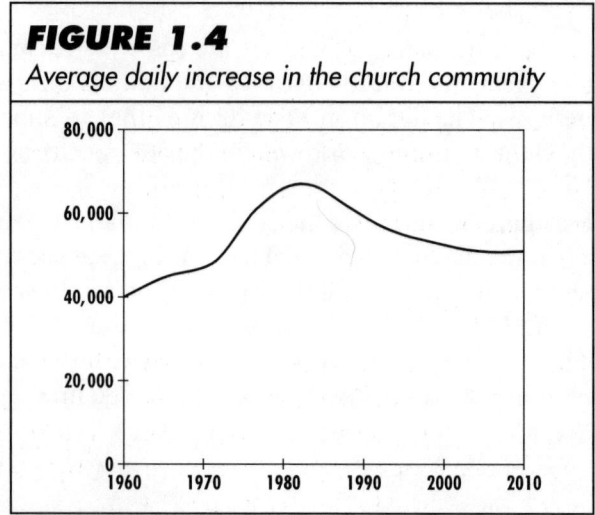

FIGURE 1.4
Average daily increase in the church community

We've had revival!

If revival is defined as the rapid increase in the number of people who become Christian, then the world had a revival in the early 1980s – and no-one noticed it!

There are of course other more theological definitions of revival, such as conviction of and repentance for sin (as espoused for example by Dr Clifford Hill, editor of *Prophecy Today*)[15], the Spirit of God falling on people who become Christian (as espoused for example by Gerald Coates, leader of the Pioneer group of the New Churches)[16], and so on. There are also the interesting events which many called revival which began on 20th January 1994 at the Vineyard Christian Fellowship by Toronto, Canada, Airport. I visited the Church in August that year, and much enjoyed the preaching of the leader, John Arnott, and saw many 'drunk in the Spirit'.

Then there are the happenings at Pensacola in the United States at Brownsville Assembly of God Church which began in 1996, and again which many describe as Revival. Steve Hill, the Senior Minister, seeks to preach 'with a great sensitivity to what the Holy Spirit is saying'[17]. Some 125,000 people had been converted by the middle of 1997, described as 'very strong repentance, a lot of screaming out at the altars, a lot of weeping and wailing'[18]. These definitions and experiences are equally valid demonstrations of revival. I have simply used a numerical one!

Net not gross figures

The figures given previously for average daily increases are net figures: that is, the difference between the number joining the church and the number leaving. There has been no worldwide research on why people join or leave the church, though there is information for some countries.

FIGURE 1.5
Why people join the church

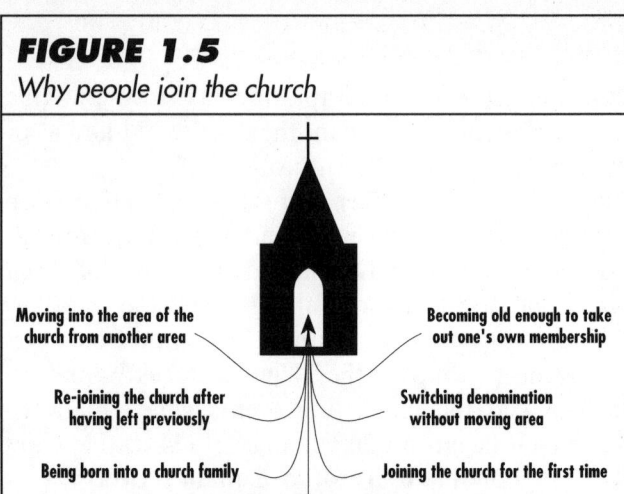

FIGURE 1.6
Why people leave the church

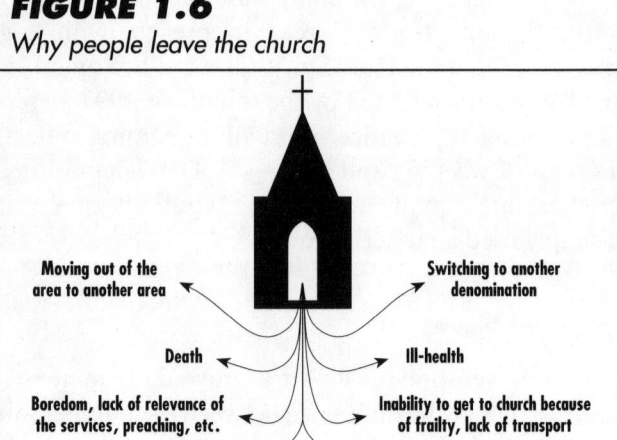

In Britain in 1992/93, 293,000 joined a church and 295,000 left[19]. The key reasons for joining were:

Transfers	42%
Conversions	27%
Children joining as adults	24%
Other reasons	7%

The main reasons for leaving were:

Transfers	42%
Loss of faith, etc	26%
Death	26%
Other reasons	6%

In addition there were 73,000 people who had left their church and were in the process of finding or joining another. A high proportion of these latter might find a church but not actually formally join it, thus adding to the transfer 'drain'.

Population comparison

Some might ask whether one of the reasons for an upsurge in the numbers joining the churches in the 1980s could be an increase in the world population? The answer is NO. In 1960 the world's population was 3,000 million, and it has been increasing at a fairly uniform rate of 1.7% a year since then. It is forecast to reach 7,000 million by 2010, more than doubling in 50 years. The rate of this increase varies, and is getting slightly faster in the 1990s than it was in the 1960s. In part this is a reflection of there being more people to help the reproduction rate! The average daily rates of increase are given below, and then graphed in Figure 1.7.

At the time when Christendom was beginning to increase, in the late 1970s, the world's population was increasing

26 FUTURE CHURCH

TABLE 1.2
Average daily increase in the world's population

Period	Population
1960–1965	+175,000
1965–1970	+199,000
1970–1975	+208,000
1975–1980	+201,000
1980–1985	+219,000
1985–1990	+231,000
1990–1995	+245,000
1995–2000	+240,000
2000–2005	+238,000
2005–2010	+239,000

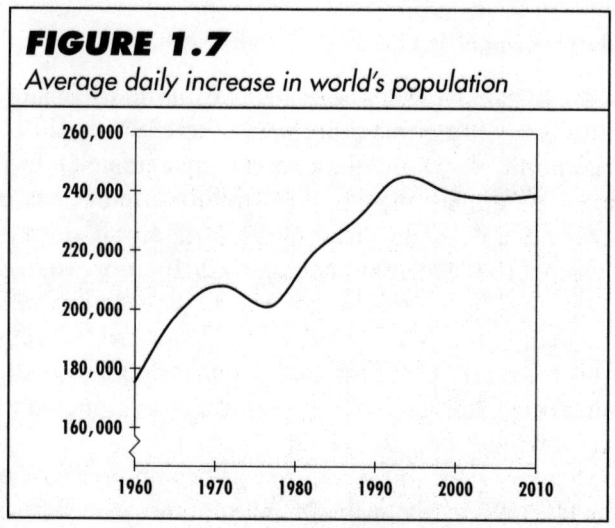

FIGURE 1.7
Average daily increase in world's population

slightly slower than it had been. This seems rather extraordinary, but they are the official United Nations figures! Although a detailed country by country analysis has not been undertaken, it would seem that population increase cannot be cited as the major reason for the church growth of the 1980s.

Church growth worldwide . . .

between 1960 and 1965 was equal to	23% of daily births
1965 and 1970	23%
1970 and 1975	23%
1975 and 1980	29%
1980 and 1985	31%
1985 and 1990	27%
1990 and 1995	23%

and will remain at about this level or a little less (21%) up to 2010. These percentages again reflect the peak increases of the late 1970s and early 1980s.

So where does all this take us?

This chapter has shown that there was a remarkable increase in the number of people joining the church in the 1980s: in the 1960s an average of over 40,000 people joined every day, but in the 1980s this increased to 65,000 people – averaging 45 people every minute. Since then the number has dropped to just over 50,000 people a day.

When church leaders want to know how the church around the world is changing, one key answer is that it is growing. This is encouraging, especially if our piece of ministry or our particular congregation or denomination is not doing so well.

The increase was not due to variations in the population growth in the world. Currently the population is growing at almost a quarter of a million people every day – 165 people per minute – considerably more quickly than the church. Whatever else we are doing, there remains much work to be done for the People of God to extend the Kingdom of God by the knowledge of the Word of God.

The total numbers joining the church are actually much greater than given, but are offset by those leaving. Unfortunately the total numbers joining are not known, only the net difference between them and those leaving.

What this chapter does is to look at the rate of growth, but does not give any feel as to the total size of the church or how it is spread around the world. That's the next chapter!

NOTES

1. *UK Christian Handbook*, 1996/97 edition, edited by Dr Peter Brierley and Heather Wraight, Christian Research, UK, 1995.
2. New churches whilst generally independent often associate together in groups, or associations or 'streams', usually under the banner of a particular leader or location. In 1995 there were some 21 such streams in the UK.
3. Published by Lutterworth Press, London, UK, 1968, edited by Sir Kenneth Grubb (who had also edited volumes published by the World Dominion Press in 1949, 1952, 1957 and 1962) and H Wakelin Coxill.
4. Published by the Dorothea Mission, Bristol, UK.
5. The Missions Advanced Research and Communications Centre was established in 1967 in Monrovia, Los Angeles, USA and became part of World Vision International shortly afterwards.
6. Published by the Oxford University Press, UK, 1982.
7. Published in the January issue each year of the *International Bulletin of Missionary Research,* Overseas Ministry Study Centre, New Haven, Connecticut, USA.
8. Published by STL and WEC International, Gerrards Cross, UK, 1986 and by OM, Carlisle, UK, 1993.
9. Also to be published by the Oxford University Press, UK.
10. The original database is in a subsequent CD-ROM of the 20:21 Project of Global Mapping International, Colorado Springs, USA.
11. Published by the Lausanne Committee for World Evangelization and Christian Research, London, UK, 1997.

12. A linear regression model was used which effectively fits a straight line to the existing data. Other models were tried but were found to be less satisfactory. Where figures are steadily growing or declining the linear regression method works well. Where figures go, say, initially up and then decline, this method is less good. Every single forecast for every denomination in every country was inspected and changes made where necessary.
13. Taken from *The New International Dictionary of the Christian Church*, General Editor J D Douglas, The Paternoster Press, then in Exeter, Devon, United Kingdom, 1974, Page 994.
14. So also is the *Atlas of World Christianity*, edited by Dr Peter Brierley and Heather Wraight, Hunt & Thorpe through Paternoster Publishing, Carlisle, and Christian Research, London, UK, 1998, which graphs in full colour many of its statistics.
15. As stated in the *News Review*, Christian World, Manchester, UK, December 1997, Page 8.
16. Ibid.
17. Article 'My extraordinary time in Pensacola' by Tony Black in *Renewal* magazine, Crowborough, East Sussex, UK, January 1998, Page 47.
18. Article 'The Pensacola Outpouring: still flowing' by Clive Price in *Christianity* magazine, Worthing, West Sussex, UK, November 1997, Page 9.
19. Op cit (Item 1), Introductory article, Page 27. This is a summary of a longer document, Leaders Briefing No 3, *Changing Churches*, an analysis of some of the movements of the contemporary church scene, Peter Brierley, Christian Research, 1996.

2

THE CHURCH IN THE WORLD

In 1995 the estimated number of Christians around the world was 1,615 million, 28% of its total population, or two in every seven people in the world.

FIGURE 2.1
2 in every 7 people are Christian

The purpose of this chapter is to consider what this number really means in terms of the denominations and continents across the world, as well as how it compares with the population. It hopefully sets the context for the rest of the book when we will discuss questions such as what this number means for the different denominations and for our overall world view.

Other religions

This 28% is the number of adherents, or the Christian community. It is the people who, if asked, would describe themselves as Christian, perhaps because their parents were, or they were baptised as babies, or live in a country with a Christian heritage. It therefore includes many nominal Christians.

It is measured on the same basis as Muslims count adherents to Islam, which David Barrett estimated at 1,057 million[1], or 18% of the world's population, in 1995. Figures for both religions include many who are nominal. The third largest group are the Hindus, assessed by Dr Barrett in 1995 at 777 million[2], or 13% of the world's population. This means that three-fifths (59%) of the world's population are either Christian, Muslim or Hindu. They are not, of course, equally spread across all the continents.

Different figures for Christians

You may have been surprised at the *World Churches Handbook* figure of 28% for the number of Christians. It is indeed lower than the better known 34% given by David Barrett in the article from which the figures for other religions were taken. This is for five reasons:

- He counts more Orthodox. The Russian Orthodox Church claim 150 million Orthodox people in Russia[3], in effect the entire population. David Barrett takes just under half this figure, 70 million. Patrick Johnstone bears in mind the huge number of those who were formerly atheist in the country and gives a much lower figure, 26 million, the figure used in the *Handbook*. The truth is that no-one knows! A difference of 44 million is equivalent to 0.8% worldwide.

- He counts more Catholics. Catholics are the largest single Christian group in the world. Many who move to another denomination may still continue to be included in the Catholic Church's numbers. How one adjusts for the resulting double counting is a matter of judgement. David Barrett has a world figure in 1995 of 999 million Catholics; the *World Churches Handbook* has 913 million; this difference of 86 million is equivalent to 1.5%.

- He counts more charismatics. The *World Churches Handbook* does not have a figure for charismatics, since these are not a separate denomination. David Barrett's 1995 total of what the *Handbook* calls 'indigenous' and other Protestants is 578 million, against the *Handbook* total of 509 million, a difference of 1.2%.

- David Barrett includes the Jehovah's Witnesses and Mormons as 'Marginal Protestants' which the *Handbook* does not. Although it does list and number such non-Trinitarian groups as these it excludes them from the totals. In 1995 these groups collectively totalled 26 million worldwide, a difference of 0.5%.

- David Barrett gives a total Christian community of 1,995 million, but the various parts he identifies only add up to 1,880 million. The 115 million he does not explicitly identify are omitted in the *World Churches Handbook,* a difference of 2.0%.

Increasing or decreasing percentage?

There is another difference between David Barrett's figures and those in the *World Churches Handbook.* He predicts a growth from 34% Christian population in 1995 to 37% by 2025, whereas the *Handbook's* 28% in 1995 is predicted to go down to 27% by 2010 and is not forecast to 2025.

How do you choose between these two trends? Professor Andrew Walls founded and for many years directed the Centre for the Study of Christianity in the Non-Western World at the Aberdeen and then Edinburgh Universities in Scotland. In 1996 in a conversation with my colleague, Heather Wraight, he stated that he believed the decreasing trend was correct. This comment is not in print, however. The *Atlas of World Christianity*[4], however, includes an article by the futorologist Tom Sine in which he quotes, and agrees with, Bryant Myers, Vice-President of Mission and Evangelism at World Vision International, that the world Christian percentage is declining.

Growing number

Which way is the trend going? If world Christendom was 28% of the population in 1995 what was it 1960? The answer is 30%, so in real terms it has fallen behind and not kept pace with the rapidly growing world population. This percentage is projected to fall to 27% by the year 2010, as mentioned above, but this drop has not been uniform across the 50-year period. Because of the 'revival' described in the previous chapter, Christendom's percentage rose in 1980 to 29% and stayed at that level till 1990, as follows:

TABLE 2.1
Size of Christendom and as a percentage of the world's population

Year	Community	Percentage
1960	920,000,000	30%
1965	1,000,000,000	30%
1970	1,080,000,000	29%
1975	1,170,000,000	28%
1980	1,280,000,000	29%
1985	1,400,000,000	29%
1990	1,510,000,000	29%
1995	1,615,000,000	28%
2000	1,710,000,000	28%
2005	1,800,000,000	27%
2010	1,900,000,000	27%

As this book is based on the *World Churches Handbook*, we take the decreasing percentage. But this should not be confused with the fact that the number of Christians worldwide is definitely *growing*! In 1960 there were 920 million Christians worldwide, and if present trends continue this will more than double by 2010, to 1,900 million. The number is unquestionably increasing; it is just that the world's population is growing faster!

Christianity by continent

The Bible describes the church as in the world, meaning that it is part of society. But geographically how is it distributed across the world? This can be looked at in several different ways:

FIGURE 2.2
Growth of Christendom and the world population

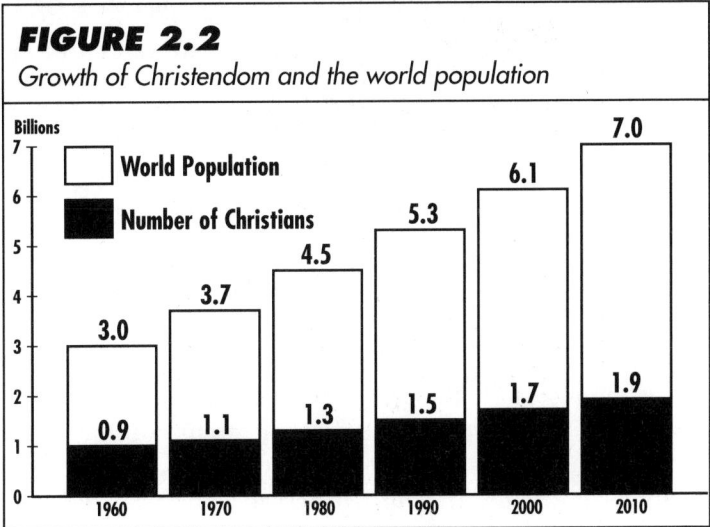

- the number of Christian people in each continent
- the percentage in each continent of all Christians
- the percentage in each continent of that continent's population

The next Table gives all three:

TABLE 2.2
Christian Community by continent in 1995

Continent	Christian Community	% of total	% of population
Europe	434,900,000	27%	60%
North America	347,200,000	22%	76%
South America	308,100,000	19%	96%
Asia	262,700,000	16%	8%
Africa	243,800,000	15%	33%
Oceania	18,700,000	1%	65%
Total	1,615,400,000	100%	28%

Now let us take these three groups one at a time. In total numbers of Christians it is immediately obvious that Europe has the most, but these numbers don't mean very much unless we look at the other two columns.

The percentage of all Christians shows us that just over a quarter of Christendom (27%) is in Europe, followed by a fifth in each of North (22%) and South (19%) America, with about a seventh in each of Asia (16%) and Africa (15%).

The Table also shows that the proportion of a continent's population which is Christian varies very greatly. Overall 2 people out of every 7 in the world are Christian but there is almost nowhere in the world where it applies! Africa is nearest with 33% or 1 in 3, but four of the six continents are far more Christian, and one is very considerably less! Virtually everyone in South America would say they are Christian (96%), and 3 out of 4 (76%) of those in North America. Oceania comes next with 2 in 3 (65%), followed by Europe with 3 in 5 (60%). It is in Asia, which has by far the largest population (60% of world total) that the Christian percentage is lowest at 1 in 13 (8%).

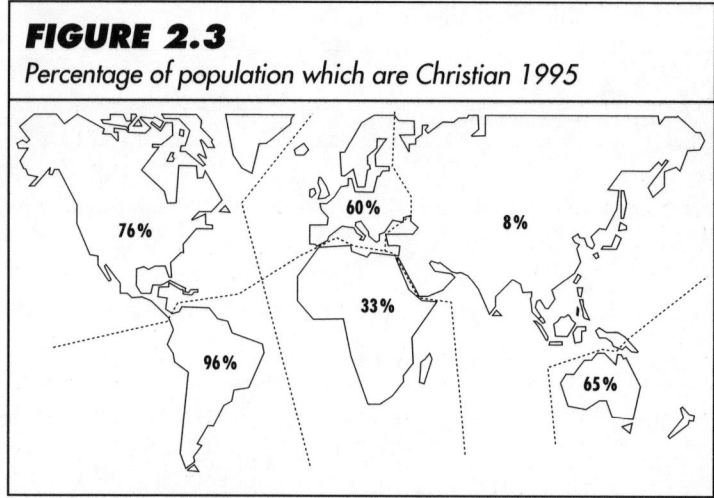

FIGURE 2.3
Percentage of population which are Christian 1995

Continental trends

The figures we have just considered are a snapshot of 1995. But how are they changing in the different continents?

TABLE 2.3
Proportion of Christendom by continent 1960–2010

Continent	1960 %	1995 %	2010 %
Europe	46	27	22
North America	23	22	22
South America	16	19	20
Asia	7	16	18
Africa	7	15	17
Oceania	1	1	1
Total (=100%)	0.9bn	1.6bn	1.9bn

(% of total Christians)

These figures show the rapid advance of Christianity in both Africa and Asia in this 50-year period, the latter at least partly due to the enormous increase in Home Meetings (the secret churches) in China. It shows it by looking at the Christian Community not the number of churches; we look at the latter in Chapter 10.

The plummeting drop in Europe is obvious; it is the only continent where the number of Christians *decreases* over this period, from 426 million in 1960 to an estimated 422 million by 2010, against a population increase from 657 million in 1960 to an estimated 731 million by 2010. However, this drop is not what it first appears. In 1992 the United Nations changed their definition of what area Europe covers by moving some of the countries of the former Soviet Union from Europe to Asia. This accounts for some of the decline in Europe, as well as some of the growth in Asia. However, churches in other continents are sending increasing numbers of missionaries to Europe, seeing it as a continent where the church needs help!

The following Table is in a format I shall use for every denomination in the following chapters. So let us look at all the continents in the same way. The 1960 total in each continent is taken as the starting base (=100) and each subsequent decadal year is shown as a percentage of the 1960 figure except that the number is multiplied by 100 and has no percentage sign! For example, Africa in 1970 could have been written as +59%. The 1960 and 2010 figures in millions are given at the foot of the Table. The final line gives the percentage each continent is of the 2010 total.

TABLE 2.4
The growth of Christendom by continent 1960–2010

Year	Africa	Europe	Oceania	North America	Asia	South America	World
1960	100	100	100	100	100	100	100
1970	159	104	123	114	138	130	117
1980	235	106	123	134	216	162	138
1990	330	108	141	153	327	198	164
2000	405	101	154	173	460	232	185
2010	484	99	171	192	550	262	205
1960	67m	426m	13m	213m	63m	143m	924m
2010	324m	422m	22m	408m	348m	376m	1,898m
% of total	17%	22%	1%	22%	18%	20%	100%

FIGURE 2.4
Growth of Christendom by continent 1960–2010

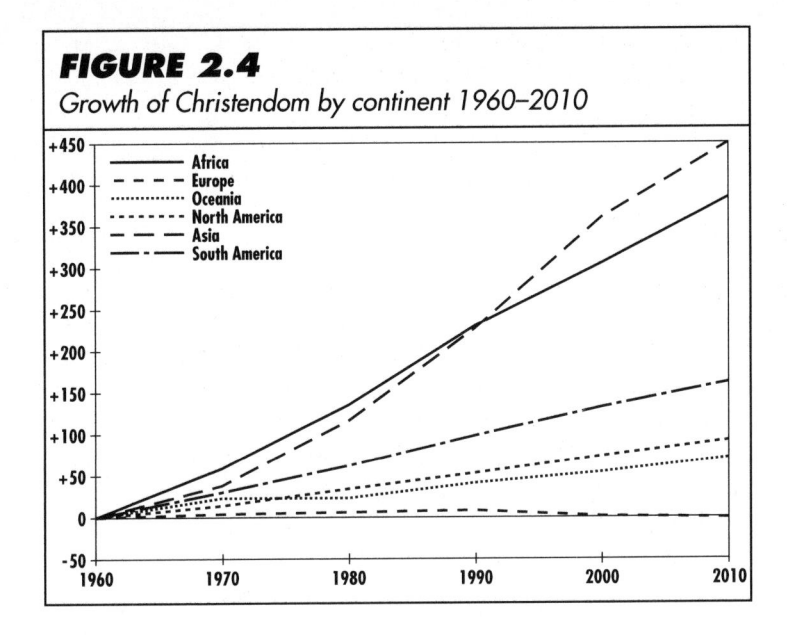

World Christianity is projected to double in these 50 years, but it has grown much faster in Africa and Asia, where the growth has been five-fold, slightly faster in South America, less fast in North America and Oceania and has slowed in Europe. The reasons for these different changes will emerge as we look at individual denominations.

Christianity by denomination

The *World Churches Handbook* collates the many Christian denominations in the world into 10 broad groupings, details of which were given in the previous chapter. We need to consider these in the same ways as we looked at continents.

So, again, let us begin with the number of Christians in these denominational groups in 1995, and the percentage that number was of total world Christianity as well as of the world's population:

TABLE 2.5
Christian Community by denominational grouping in 1995

Denomination	Christian Community	% of total	% of population
Catholic	912,600,000	56%	16%
Other Churches	142,500,000	9%	2%
Orthodox	139,500,000	9%	2%
Pentecostal	105,800,000	7%	2%
Lutheran	84,500,000	5%	2%
Baptist	67,200,000	4%	1%
Anglican	54,500,000	3%	1%
Presbyterian	48,000,000	3%	1%
Indigenous	35,200,000	2%	½%
Methodist	25,600,000	2%	½%
Total	1,615,400,000	100%	28%

As with the continents, the total numbers are interesting, but the percentages tell us much more. This table shows that 5 in every 9 (56%) Christian people in the world are Catholic. The Orthodox and Other Churches account for a further 9% each, or 1 person in every 11, followed by 7%, or 1 person in 14, who are Pentecostal.

A complication in understanding these Community figures is that they are defined differently for the various denominations. Anglicans and Catholics seek to represent the number in a country who have been baptised. Unfortunately few countries have reliable national figures, so they are nearly always the best estimates that can be given.

Table 2.5 shows that the Catholic Church is by far the largest. Not only is it just over half of Christendom, but it represents 1 person in 6 across the world (16%). When Cardinal Hume, the leader of the Roman Catholic church in

Britain, speaks on television he typically says, 'The Church believes . . .', even though he has been introduced as 'The head of the Roman Catholic Church', reflecting his consciousness of representing the largest church in Christendom.

The next largest churches are the Other Churches, Orthodox, Pentecostal and Lutheran, though each of these consists of several denominations.

Denominational trends

Just as the proportions in each continent are changing, so are the proportions for each denomination, as the following Table shows:

TABLE 2.6
Proportion of Christendom by denomination 1960–2010

Denomination	% of total Christians		
	1960 %	1995 %	2010 %
Catholic	61	56	56
Other churches	4	9	10
Orthodox	10	9	8
Pentecostal	1	7	8
Lutheran	9	5	4
Baptist	4	4	4
Anglican	4	3	3
Presbyterian	3	3	3
Indigenous	1	2	3
Methodist	3	2	1
Total (=100%)	0.9bn	1.6bn	1.9bn

The Pentecostal denomination is growing the fastest. It increases dramatically from 12 million in 1960 to an estimated 154 million by 2010. Indigenous churches are also increasing, as are Other Churches, largely due to the emergence of many new denominations, especially in Asia.

Baptists and Presbyterians hold their own, the first by their growth in the United States, the second by their growth in South Korea. Anglicans and Orthodox decline slightly. Lutherans decline most proportionately, though the Catholics also lose out.

Institutional or Non-institutional

The ten denominational groups can be sub-divided into two groups of five – institutional and non-institutional churches. The definition used here for an institutional church is that it is the State Church in at least one country in the world. On that basis we have the following:

Institutional	*Non-institutional*
Anglican	Baptist
Catholic	Indigenous
Lutheran	Methodist
Orthodox	Pentecostal
Presbyterian	Other Churches

On this basis the institutional churches account for 1,239 million Christians, or 77% of the total, and represent 22% of the world's population. The Non-institutional can claim 376 million Christians, 23% of Christendom, but just 6% of the world's population. But the important thing about these numbers is how they are changing.

Institutional culture

In 1960 the institutional churches accounted for 87% of Christendom, but by 2010 they will account for only 74%, as is shown in Figure 2.5:

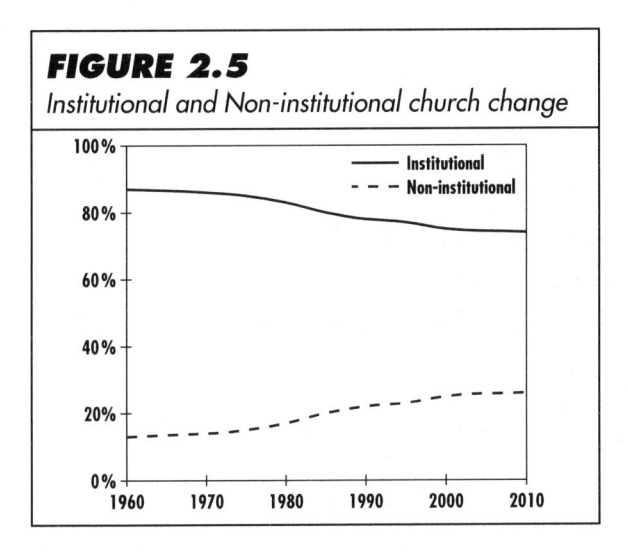

FIGURE 2.5
Institutional and Non-institutional church change

It is very clear from this graph where the growth is taking place! Note also that the decline occurred especially in the early 1980s. In 1980 the institutional churches represented 83% of Christendom; by 1985 it was down to 80%, this 3% drop being the biggest over 5 years in the whole 50 year period. (It went down 2% in 1975 to 1980, and from 1985 to 1990.) Why this big change in the early 1980s? This was when the 'revival' was at its height, and it shows that its impact was greater in the non-institutional churches.

There are several reasons why the Institutional churches lose out from 1960 to 2010.

- They find it hard to change quickly, and adapt to the current culture in society. Today this is usually labelled 'post-modern', a term which describes some of the distinctives in the late 20th century western societies.

- They have local structures which have been established for decades, sometimes for centuries, and which therefore cannot easily be altered. It would be difficult, for example, to change the parish system of the Church of England without radically changing the nature of the church itself.

- They often have buildings or other property which cannot be readily altered, sold off, or used for other purposes. For example, in 17 out of the 46 counties in England in 1992 80% or more of the churches of the Church of England were listed buildings[5], and protected from change by law!

- Their legal responsibilities *vis-a-vis* the State cannot be dropped or amended without lengthy discussions. There may be financial responsibilities as with many of the Lutheran state churches, or governmental like the 26 Bishops who sit in the British House of Lords.

- They are more likely to see themselves as guardians of a Christian heritage. This may result in leadership which does not want to change, though this is probably becoming less common, as many leaders of institutional churches are very concerned with current trends and are pushing for change in various ways.

- They are often broader theologically than the non-institutional churches, and therefore have to take care to include a wider range of people in any change.

- They often have a hierarchical bureaucracy which can inhibit radical decisions.

We have so far looked at the spread of Christianity by continent and by denomination separately, so now we need to draw these two major criteria together.

Denominations by continent

The way each denomination is spread across the continents is interesting because there are some fascinating dominances, as the following Table shows:

TABLE 2.7
The proportions of each denomination in each continent in 1995

Denomination	Europe %	North America %	South America %	Asia %	Africa %	Oceania %	Total (=100%) million
Catholic	28	22	28	11	10	1	912.6
Other Churches	3	15	4	55	22	1	142.5
Orthodox	54	6	0	19	21	0	139.5
Pentecostal	3	28	36	12	20	1	105.8
Lutheran	67	17	2	6	7	1	84.5
Baptist	4	66	4	12	13	1	67.2
Anglican	48	7	0	1	34	10	54.5
Presbyterian	26	17	2	30	23	2	48.0
Indigenous	0	1	0	26	73	0	35.2
Methodist	6	51	1	12	28	2	25.6
Overall	27	22	19	16	15	1	1,615.4

What does this Table tell us?

- The Catholics are the only truly 'world church' in that they are spread across all continents without any one dominating.
- Over half (55%) of those belonging to Other Churches are in Asia, with 70% of these being the estimated 55 million in Home Meetings in China.
- Just over half the Orthodox (54%) are in Europe. This figure was much higher in 1990 (70%) and the difference

reflects the UN's reallocation of most of the constituent countries of the old USSR from Europe to Asia.

- The Pentecostals are also well spread across the world but are relatively weak in Europe. More than a third (36%) are in South America, and 81% of these are in Brazil.

- Two-thirds (67%) of the world's Lutherans are in Europe, with 59% of them in Germany.

- Almost two-thirds (66%) of the world's Baptists are in North America, with 96% of these in the United States.

- A third (34%) of the world's Anglicans are in Africa, 10% in Oceania and virtually half (48%) in Europe. Over 99% of those in Europe are in the United Kingdom. There are virtually none in South America.

- Nearly a third (30%) of the world's Presbyterians are in Asia, 45% of whom are in South Korea. A further quarter (26%) are in Europe, found mainly as the Reformed Churches in the Netherlands (29%) and Hungary (16%), or the Church of Scotland and other Presbyterian churches in the United Kingdom (21%).

- Almost three-quarters (73%) of the Indigenous Community are in Africa, and of these 29% are in Nigeria and 23% in Zaïre.

- Just over half (51%) the world's Methodists are in North America, of which 96% are in the United States.

These figures reflect the European origins of Anglicans, Lutherans and the Orthodox church. The table shows the continental nature of many of the world's big denominations, almost their 'parochialism' or 'nationalism' if one can use these words in a continental setting. This is an important finding, which we need to return to in a moment.

In the 1990s the areas for growth are the increasing proportions of:

Anglicans in Africa (at the expense of Europe)
Baptists in Asia (at the expense of North America)
Methodists in Africa (at the expense of North America)
Other Churches in Asia (also at the expense of North America).

Each of these movements represents a two or more percentage point change between 1990 and 1995.

Denominations by continents

Now we look at the denominational mix within each continent. Percentages which are close to zero are given as '<1' but are counted as zero in the totals.

TABLE 2.8
The proportions in each continent of each denomination in 1995

Denomination	Europe %	North America %	South America %	Asia %	Africa %	Oceania %	Overall %
Catholic	58	58	84	40	36	40	56
Other Churches	1	6	2	30	13	11	9
Orthodox	17	2	<1	10	12	3	9
Pentecostal	1	9	12	5	8	4	7
Lutheran	13	4	1	2	2	5	5
Baptist	1	13	1	3	4	2	4
Anglican	6	1	<1	<1	7	27	3
Presbyterian	3	3	<1	6	4	5	3
Indigenous	0	<1	<1	3	11	1	2
Methodist	<1	4	<1	1	3	2	2
Total (=100%) in millions	434.9	347.2	308.1	262.7	243.8	18.7	1,615.4

Table 2.8 shows that the major denominations are present in every continent except South America, and that each denominational group except the Methodists and Presbyterians is especially strong in at least one continent.

- European Christianity is dominated by the Catholics (over half the community) and the Orthodox (a sixth), leaving only a quarter for all the others put together.

- In North America the Catholics and the Baptists together account for over two- thirds (71%) of the church community.

- South America is dominated by the Catholic Church (84%) and the Pentecostals.

- In Africa the Catholics account for over a third (36%), their lowest proportion in any continent, and the Indigenous Churches have their highest proportion (11%).

- In Asia, beside the Catholics, the Other Churches are especially strong.

- The Anglicans account for over a quarter (27%) of Oceania's small church community.

Table 2.8 is represented by two maps. Figure 2.6 takes the numbers in Table 2.8 and puts them on to each continent but reducing them to just three figures for simplicity: the Catholic percentage, the Other Institutional churches, and the five Non-institutional denominations. Figure 2.7 shows the proportions in each continent of the Catholic church, and then the major church(es) in that continent whatever that denomination(s) might be.

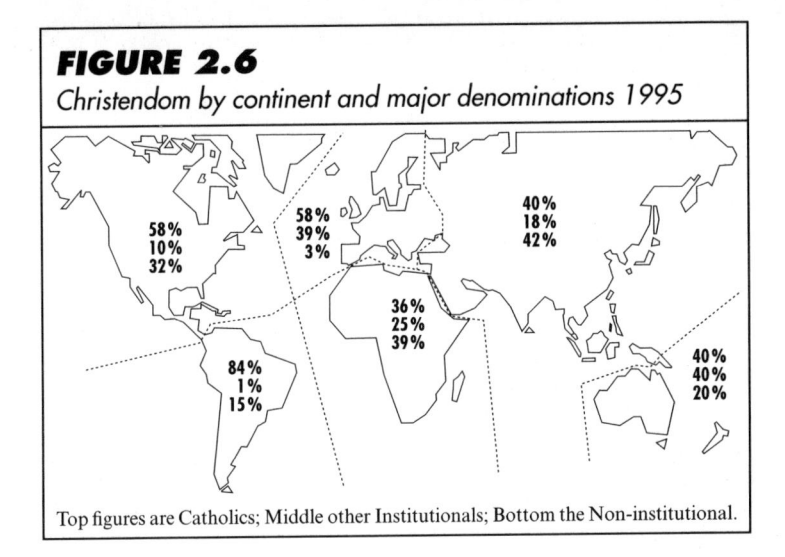

FIGURE 2.6
Christendom by continent and major denominations 1995

North America: 58% / 10% / 32%
Europe: 58% / 39% / 3%
Middle East: 40% / 18% / 42%
Africa: 36% / 25% / 39%
Latin America: 84% / 1% / 15%
Asia/Oceania: 40% / 40% / 20%

Top figures are Catholics; Middle other Institutionals; Bottom the Non-institutional.

Denominational/continental culture

The relationship of denomination to continent is not often discussed, but the numbers in Table 2.8 and Figures 2.6 and 2.7 especially do show a correlation. As far as I am aware this finding has not previously been highlighted so strikingly, even though it inevitably reflects the history of each continent and the colonial heritage within it, if any.

It suggests that the cultures implicit in different continents are drawn to different forms of church life or in some cases that the form of church life may have affected the culture of the continent.

As has been shown, each continent has a large number of Catholics. It is the denomination which is next in size *after* the Catholics which is considered here. In North America, for example, the Baptists are the major non-Catholic denomination representing 30% of the non-Catholic community. No wonder the Baptists can say to Disney Corporation 'We want you to reinforce your traditional

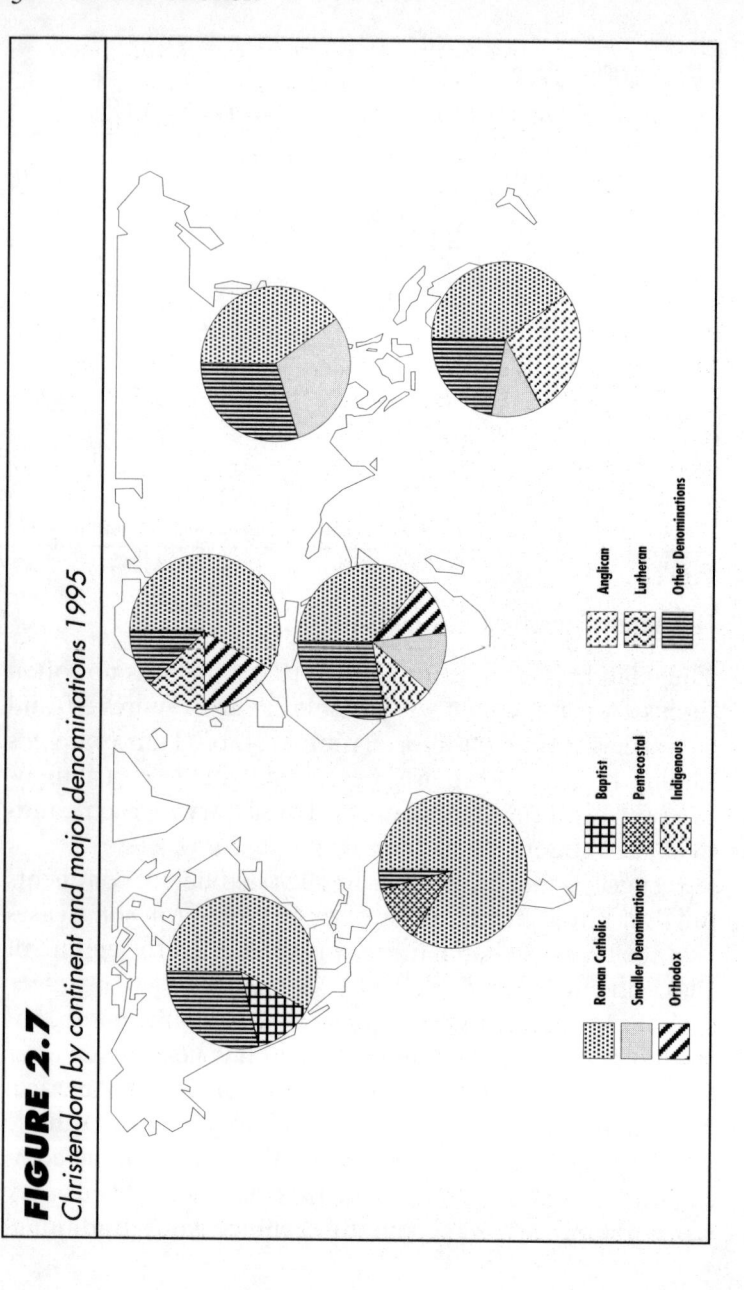

FIGURE 2.7
Christendom by continent and major denominations 1995

family values' as the Southern Baptist Convention did in its annual meeting in 1995. Whether Disney wishes to listen is another matter, given the many visitors to their theme parks who are either outside church or from overseas and thus from a different culture.

North America

I was once driving down the main road of a town called Wears Valley in Tennessee approaching the Great Smoky Mountains in the eastern United States. It had a population of perhaps 10,000 people including those in outlying areas. It was essentially a town on two sides of the road as you drove through. I was amazed at the number of churches, and decided to take a photo of each one.

There was the Wears Valley Independent Baptist Church, a nice modern building with a big car park. Right next door was the Wears Valley Independent Missionary Baptist Church with its congregation clearly bidding you a big welcome. Then there was the First Baptist Church with its rusty tin roof, followed by Valley View Baptist Church, and Covemont Baptist Church. The one that appealed most to me was the Friendship Baptist church with its neat wooden display board. Oh, and there was also the United Methodist Church and finally Headrick's Chapel with its roadside cemetery. Eight churches for this town, and *six* of them Baptist. Baptist thinking is very much part of the culture!

One person in 6 in North America is Baptist (compared to 1 in 220 in the rest of the world). Maybe the American flair for independence and individualism fits the Baptist ethos of independence and it's theology of individual responsibility. Is it accidental that so much of North America is Baptist?[6]

South America

In South America the scene couldn't be more different. If you are not a Catholic you are Pentecostal. While other denominations do exist, they are very small and mostly struggling. Pentecostals are charismatic, often in small congregations, with an emphasis on evangelism, and the gifts of healing and speaking in tongues.

If you move from an independently-minded North America to become a missionary in an institutional Catholic country where Pentecostalism is the only alternative, you're in for a theological shock, to go with all the other culture shocks!

Europe

Europe is baked in institutionalism! After institutional Catholicism, come institutional Orthodox Churches, followed by institutional Lutheran churches. One delegate to the second European Ecumenical Assembly in Graz, Austria in June 1997, later wrote, 'What a massive tapestry of opinion, tradition, history and culture to reconcile.'[7]

Non-institutional churches take much less account of these factors, so it is no wonder the Pentecostals have a smaller proportion in Europe than anywhere else in the world! Europe is not 'the land of the free' church, but the 'land of the organised'. The Romans gave it to us, the Holy Roman Empire and the Ottoman Empire all followed.

In what other continent do people have a history of *empires*? Only Asia, but with China so dominant it is a different story.

Asia

Asia is dominated by small denominations. There are hundreds of denominations in Japan for example, with its small Christian presence. Smallness here enables people to identify with their locality, or to belong to a small, almost secret, group. In China this has made it possible for the underground church to survive in its many Home Meetings. As the authorities close down one, another small group can begin.

Africa

Africa is in some ways similar to Asia. It has the smallest proportional Catholic presence of any continent, as well as a flavour of Orthodoxy in its northern states. However it has many smaller denominations and indigenous churches.

In Johannesburg in 1987 Professor Oosthuizen, Director of the Research Unit for New Religions and Independent/Indigenous Churches in the University of Zululand, showed me a computer print out which listed over 4,000 separate Zionist denominations in South Africa alone! I asked him why there were so many micro denominations, with an average size of just a dozen or so people? He replied that black people wanted status, and in a small fellowship everybody was something – the Preacher, the Prophet, the Worship Leader, the Ladies Leader, the Prayer Leader, the Assistant Prayer Leader, the Interpreter, the Reader, and so on for a long list.

Smallness in Africa is for a different reason to Asia, not to help everyone identify with a local group, but to give people status. Each individual counted in their church – a totally different philosophy from Europe or Latin America.

Oceania

Oceania displays yet another pattern. After Catholicism comes the Anglican church. Archbishops in Australia are especially influential. Sydney is known as being an evangelical *Diocese*, not, as in England, where a *parish* church would be known as evangelical. Why is Anglicanism important in Australia? Partly because it is the historical church, literally taken out with the convicts. That has less relevance today, but has been re-inforced by many later immigrants coming from Britain. Is the concern over territory exhibited by the various Australian States but a reflection, at State level, of its Anglican theology? Are the two related? Is this suggestion too preposterous?

All this shows that there is a link between the major denominations and the temperament, history and culture of different parts of the world. A theological culture which is imbedded in some way with national identities. It also raises practical questions, for example, in these days when missionaries go from as well as to almost every country how do we prepare people to cross not only social but also theological cultures?

Hopefully it will be fun to work some of this out as we look at these ten denominational groupings in subsequent chapters. Whatever denomination you happen to be, you'll be included in one of them. Don't read only about your own, but also about the others. What is happening on a global scale is also relevant to the local scale, in the practical ecumenism that we embrace at street and town level where we live.

NOTES

1. 'Status of Global Mission' by Rev Dr David Barrett in *International Bulletin of Missionary Research*, Overseas Missions Studies Centre, Connecticut, USA, January 1995. This article is updated each year in the January issue.
2. Ibid.
3. *Orthodox News*, London, UK, Volume 10, Number 5, Autumn 1996, Page 2.
4. *Atlas of World Christianity*, Dr Peter Brierley and Heather Wraight, Hunt & Thorpe through Paternoster Publishing, Carlisle, and Christian Research, London, UK, 1998.
5. *UK Christian Handbook: Religious Trends,* No 1, 1998/99 edition, Dr Peter Brierley, Christian Research and Paternoster Publishing, London and Carlisle, UK, 1997, Figure 2.9.5. A 'listed building' in the UK is designated as such by local or national planning authorities, often with little or no consultation with the building's owners.
6. The majority of Baptists are evangelical. See Dr Alister McGrath's discussion of the cultural nature of the evangelical approach to theology in North America in *A Passion for Truth*, Alistair McGrath, Apollos, Leicester, UK, 1996, Pages 11–20.

7. 'Globalisation from Below: The Challenge of Graz for Mission in Europe' article by Simon Barrow in Connect*ions*, Issue Number 1, September 1997, The Churches' Commission on Mission, Council of Churches for Britain and Ireland, Page 2.

3
THE CATHOLIC CHURCH

One person in six in the world is a Catholic. When the Pope speaks on behalf of the church he represents more people than anyone except the Premier of the State Council in China and the President of India – in 1995 India's population (953 million) exceeded the Catholic population (913 million) for the first time.

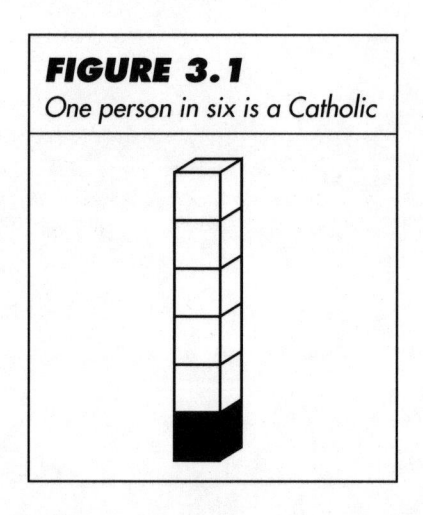

FIGURE 3.1
One person in six is a Catholic

Large number, spread worldwide

913 million people is a huge number, although, to be fair, not all would acknowledge the headship of the Pope even while calling themselves 'Catholic'. To give an idea of the size of the number, it is equivalent to the number of seconds in 29 years, or the number of miles you would travel if you went to the sun and back five times over!

Catholics represent 56% of the world's 1,615 million Christians, or 5 in every 9. Catholics form a huge slice of world Christianity. They are six times larger than the next largest church, the Orthodox.

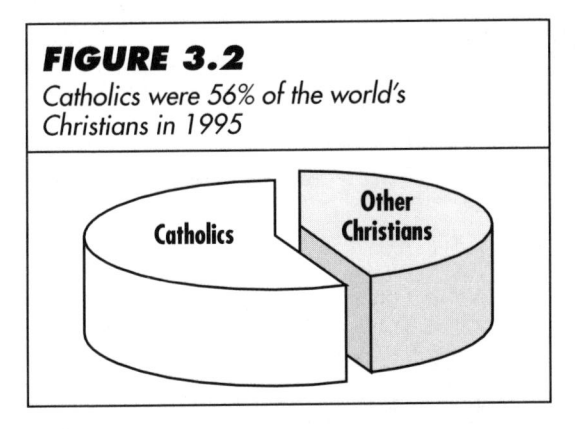

FIGURE 3.2
Catholics were 56% of the world's Christians in 1995

A second major factor is that they are well spread *across the world*. The Catholics are 84% (5 in every 6) of the Christians in South America, 58% (3 in every 5) in Europe and North America, 40% (2 in every 5) of those in Asia and Oceania, and 36% (3 in every 8) of those in Africa. No other church is so uniformly spread across the continents.

Growth and decline

During the 1990s the Catholic church around the world grew

at an average rate of almost 40,000 people a day. The large majority of these would have been natural growth, that is babies born into Catholic families. This number represents 72% of the net growth of Christianity in the world, or in other words, for every 4 new Christians in the 1990s, 3 were Catholic. These are *net* figures, that is, the difference between total gains and total losses, but even if we knew the total gain and loss figures the Catholics would still dominate, as their number is so huge.

Table 3.1 shows the growth of the Catholic population alongside the growth of world Christianity and the world population. The ratio figures are graphed in Figure 3.3.

TABLE 3.1
Catholic and Total Christian Population and World Population 1960–2010

Year	Catholic Population Number Ratio	Total Christendom Number Ratio	World Population Number Ratio
1960	561 million 100	924 million 100	3,041 million 100
1970	661 million 118	1,079 million 117	3,724 million 122
1980	763 million 136	1,276 million 138	4,471 million 147
1990	865 million 154	1,513 million 164	5,292 million 174
1995	913 million 163	1,615 million 175	5,740 million 189
2000	1,009 million 180	1,712 million 185	6,178 million 203
2010	1,055 million 188	1,898 million 205	7,048 million 232

FIGURE 3.3
Growth of Catholicism, Christendom and World Population 1960–2010

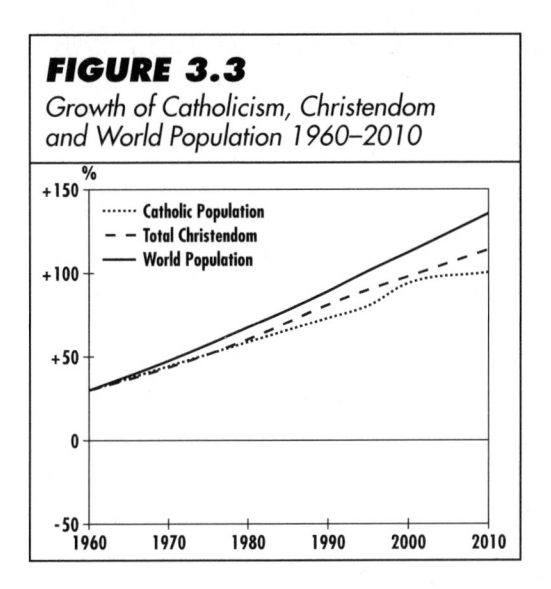

Figure 3.3 shows that the Catholic church has not kept up proportionally with the growth of Christendom, nor with the world's population. It fell behind Christendom as a whole in the 1980s and early 1990s, though, if the forecast proves correct, it will make up some ground in the late 1990s, before falling behind again in the first decade of the twenty-first century.

What this suggests is that in the:

- 1970s the Catholics were unable to change sufficiently when the falling behind first became evident
- 1980s this continued in the years when the non-institutional churches especially grew considerably
- 1990s the situation has not deteriorated markedly further, even if it might do so after that.

Much the same is true as far as the world's population is

concerned: Catholics dropped behind in the 1970s and in the 1980s in particular, largely kept pace in the 1990s, but again are likely to drop behind between 2000 and 2010.

Catholics by continent

Growth by continent is shown in Table 3.2. To make comparison easier, the ratio numbers are given for each decade; these are the numbers used in Figure 3.5. The 1960 and 2010 figures in millions are given at the foot of the Table, and the final line puts these figures as percentages of the 2010 total (used in Figure 3.4).

TABLE 3.2
The growth of the Catholic population by continent 1960–2010

Year	Africa	Europe	Oceania	North America	Asia	South America	World
1960	100	100	100	100	100	100	100
1970	154	104	144	123	129	126	118
1980	213	106	163	148	166	153	136
1990	292	107	200	169	222	175	154
2000	351	105	231	196	274	200	180
2010	420	104	267	220	320	220	188
1960	27m	241m	3m	110m	42m	137m	561m
2010	116m	251m	9m	244m	134m	302m	1,055m
% of total	11%	24%	1%	23%	13%	28%	100%

FIGURE 3.4
Proportions of Catholicism by continent 2010

- 23%
- 24%
- 13%
- 11%
- 28%
- 1%

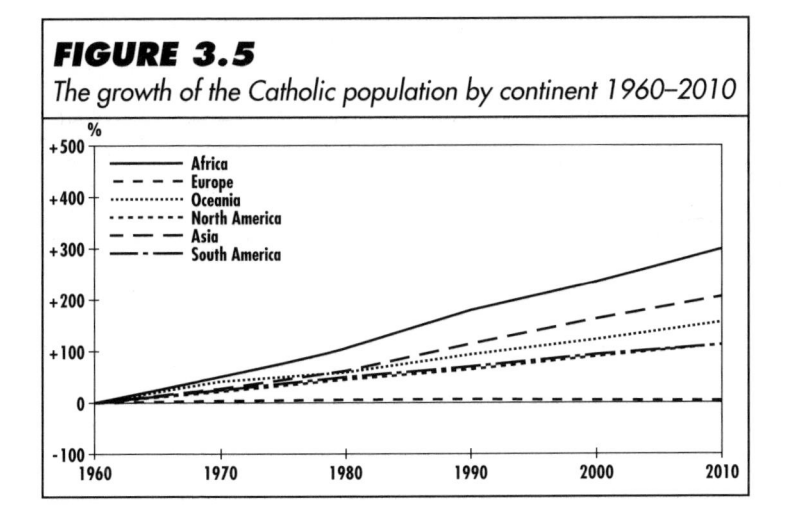

FIGURE 3.5
The growth of the Catholic population by continent 1960–2010

- Africa
- Europe
- Oceania
- North America
- Asia
- South America

The Catholic population will quadruple in Africa in the fifty years 1960 to 2010, if present trends continue, which is a staggering increase, but still only half the rate of the Anglican church, and is slower than the Lutheran growth. It might appear that Africans preferred the Anglican form of institutionalism to the Catholic form, but 'it is probably more to do with numbers of priests available to evangelise'[1].

Catholic growth exceeded Anglican growth in North America over the same period. It was also greater than the Anglicans in Asia and Oceania, but less than the Lutherans in both continents, and behind the Presbyterians in Asia. In South America Catholics and Anglicans grew at about the same rate, although not in the same numbers. The Presbyterians grew faster, perhaps suggesting alternative types of institutionalism attract if someone does not wish to join the Pentecostals.

The situation in Europe is different from the other continents. This was partly because there will be only 4% growth over 50 years, an increase averaging just 550 persons per day, against a population increase of 4,100 a day. If Europeans' proportion in the world population, 19%, was applied to these births, one would have expected a Catholic growth of 800 per day. Had European Catholicism grown at the same rate as in other continents worldwide Catholicism would be about 200 million more, that is about 20% more or about the size of the Chinese population.

Africa

In 1995 there were 86.7 million Catholics in Africa. 17 countries had more than a million. The largest ten, collectively accounting for 74% of the total, are given in Table 3.3. The largest is Zaïre, which since the *World Churches Handbook* was published has changed its name to the Democratic Republic of Congo. For simplicity in this volume we retain the use of the old name.

TABLE 3.3
Catholics in Africa 1995

	Millions		Millions
Zaïre	18.0	Angola	5.1
Nigeria	9.1	Cameroon	3.6
Uganda	8.3	Burundi	3.3
Tanzania	5.6	South Africa	3.1
Kenya	5.5	Madagascar	2.7

FIGURE 3.6
Catholicism in Africa – countries with a million or more in 1995

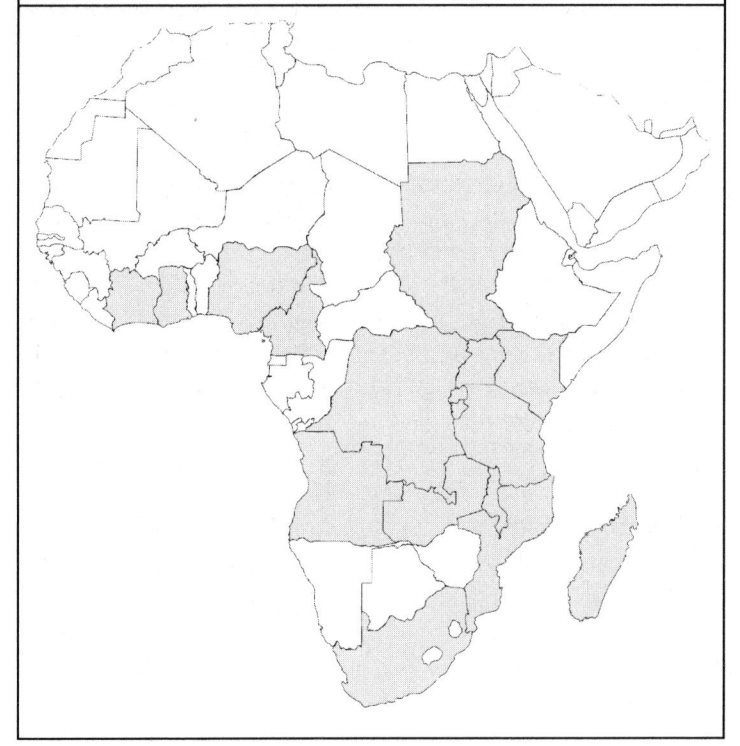

The *Religions . . . in Africa*[2] booklet gives the total religious composition of all African countries as estimated at the year 2000. When the Pope went to Uganda in February 1993 he told the Diplomatic Corps, 'Africa can never consent to being colonised anew. Her nations are independent and must remain so. This does not mean that help from other members of the family of nations is not necessary and desirable. Far from it, help is needed more than ever now. But to do any real good, it must not reflect a relationship of subjection, but of interdependence.'[3] The general importance of interdependence is taken up later.

North America

In 1995 there were 201.9 million Catholics in North and Central America and the Caribbean. Two countries accounted for 71% of these – Mexico and the United States. 11 other countries had more than a million, as given:

TABLE 3.4
Catholics in North America 1995

	Millions
Mexico	84.7
United States	59.2
Canada	12.1
Guatemala	8.1
Dominican Republic	6.4
Haiti	4.9
Honduras	4.9
El Salvador	4.5
Cuba	4.4
Nicaragua	3.4
Costa Rica	2.9
Puerto Rico	2.4
Panama	2.1

FIGURE 3.7
Catholicism in North America – countries with 2 million or more in 1995

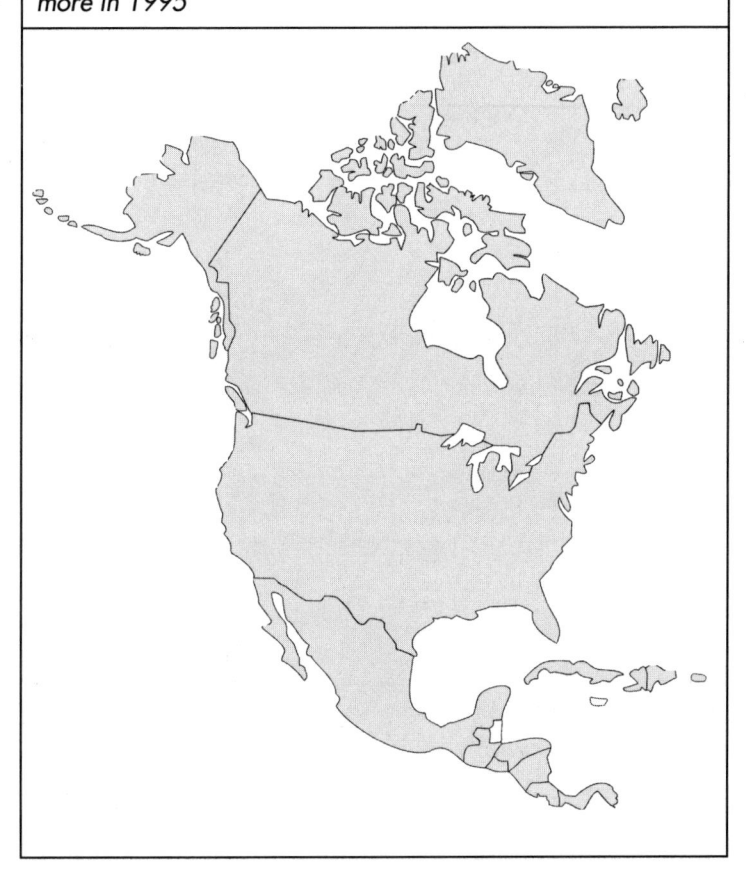

Many of the 4.4 million in Cuba greeted the Pope during his 8 day visit there in January 1998. These 13 countries account for 99% of the Catholics in the region.

South America

In 1995 there were 258.4 million Catholics in South

America. One country accounts for half (47%) of that figure – Brazil, and the top five listed in Table 3.5 account for 7 in every 8 (87%).

TABLE 3.5
Catholics in South America 1995

	Millions
Brazil	120.2
Columbia	33.4
Argentina	30.3
Peru	21.1
Venezuela	19.1
Ecuador	10.6
Chile	9.8
Bolivia	6.6
Paraguay	4.4
Uruguay	2.5

THE CATHOLIC CHURCH 67

FIGURE 3.8
Catholicism in South America – countries with 2.5 million or more in 1995

This huge dominance may be looked at another way. Brazil may account for 47% of Latin America's Catholics, but Catholics account for three-quarters (76%) of Brazil's Christians. In the other countries the dominance of the Catholics is even greater – 96% of the Christians in Columbia in 1995 were Catholic, 95% in Venezula, 93% in Peru and 92% in Argentina. This indirectly points to something important – it is mainly in Brazil, with its large population, that the non-Catholic denominations are making most headway.

Europe

In 1995 there were 253.6 million Catholics in Europe, almost the same number as in South America, though the proportions are very different (58% to 84%). 21 countries had more than a million Catholics, accounting for 99.9% of the total. Five countries however account for 71% – the main Catholic countries of Europe – Italy, France, Poland, Germany, and Spain (although it is not totally fair to the Lutherans to list Germany here). These and the next 7 largest (all with at least 5 million) are:

TABLE 3.6
Catholics in Europe 1995

	Millions		Millions
Italy	46.7	Portugal	9.1
France	44.2	Belgium	8.9
Poland	34.8	Hungary	6.4
Germany	27.8	Austria	6.0
Spain	26.4	Czech Republic	5.9
		United Kingdom	5.7
		The Netherlands	5.4

FIGURE 3.9
Catholicism in Europe – countries with 5 million or more in 1995

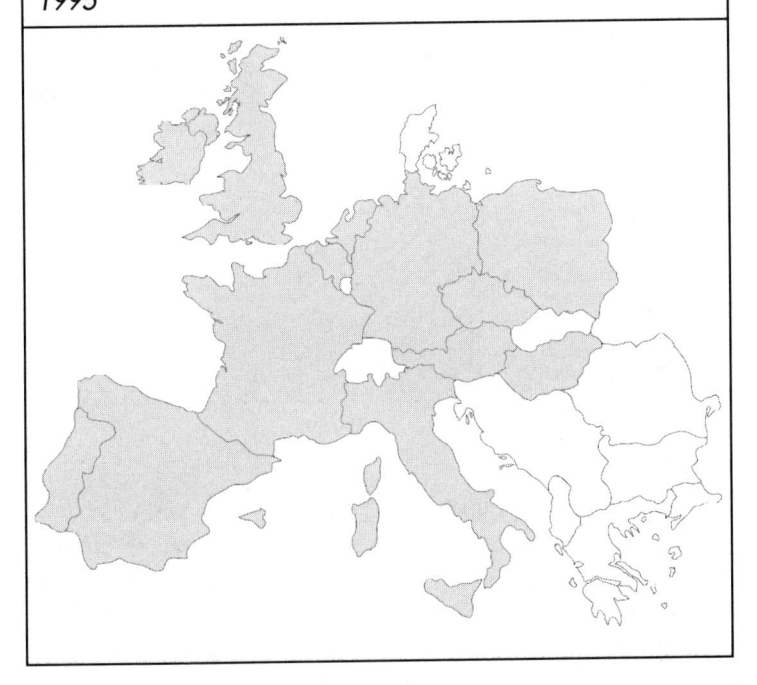

European Catholicism has not increased as in the rest of the world, and furthermore has lagged behind population growth in Europe. Therefore it may be instructive to look at how Catholicism has fared in the five countries with the highest numbers of Catholics. The final line in Table 3.7 is the percentage of the 2010 number.

TABLE 3.7
The growth of the Catholic population in Europe 1960–2010

Year	Italy	France	Poland	Germany	Spain	All others	Europe
1960	100	100	100	100	100	100	100
1970	101	102	110	107	104	104	104
1980	98	102	120	108	105	110	106
1990	96	102	132	105	97	113	107
2000	97	101	134	104	90	108	105
2010	98	96	137	101	85	111	104
1960	48m	44m	26m	26m	28m	68m	241m
2010	47m	42m	36m	27m	24m	75m	251m
% of total	19%	17%	14%	11%	9%	30%	100%

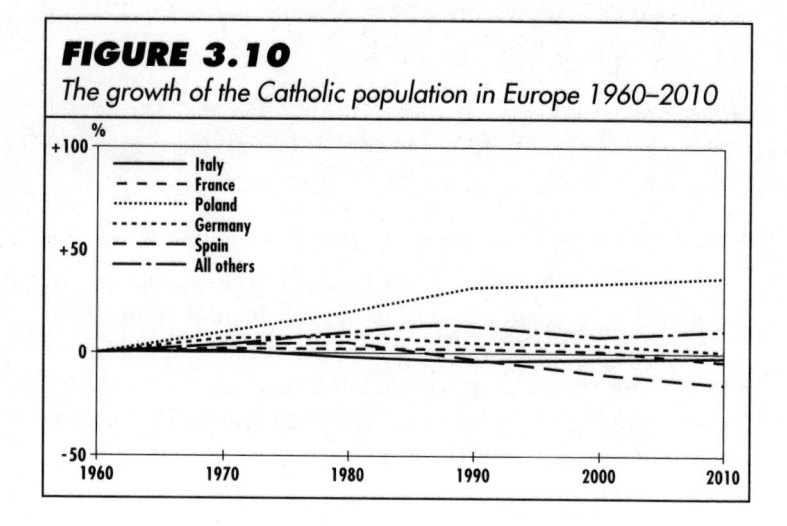

FIGURE 3.10
The growth of the Catholic population in Europe 1960–2010

Catholicism grew throughout Europe during the 1960s. But in the 1970s it remained static in France, and began to decline in Italy. In the 1980s it continued static in France, kept on declining in Italy, began to decline in Germany and

Spain, but continued to grow in Poland and elsewhere in Europe.

In the 1990s the existing pattern continued except in Italy where there was a slight growth. In the rest of Europe there was decline, perhaps partly because of the United Nations reallocating much of the old USSR from Europe into Asia. Such a change has made previous estimates of the individual component countries very difficult. In the coming decade, if trends continue, the existing patterns will remain, with growth in Italy, Poland and other parts of Europe.

It is clear that the traditional Catholic countries are finding the going difficult, with the exception of Poland, where undoubtedly the new social and religious freedom have made a great impact. It is in other parts of Europe that the main growth is currently taking place.

Asia and Oceania

There were 104.6 million Catholics in Asia in 1995 and 7.4 million in Oceania. Just over half (52%) of the Asian Catholics were in the Philippines, and the next six largest countries also given in Table 3.8. These 7 countries account for 91% of all Catholics in Asia.

TABLE 3.8
Catholics in Asia 1995

	Millions
Philippines	54.3
India	15.7
China	9.6
Indonesia	5.8
Vietnam	5.8
South Korea	2.6
Sri Lanka	1.0

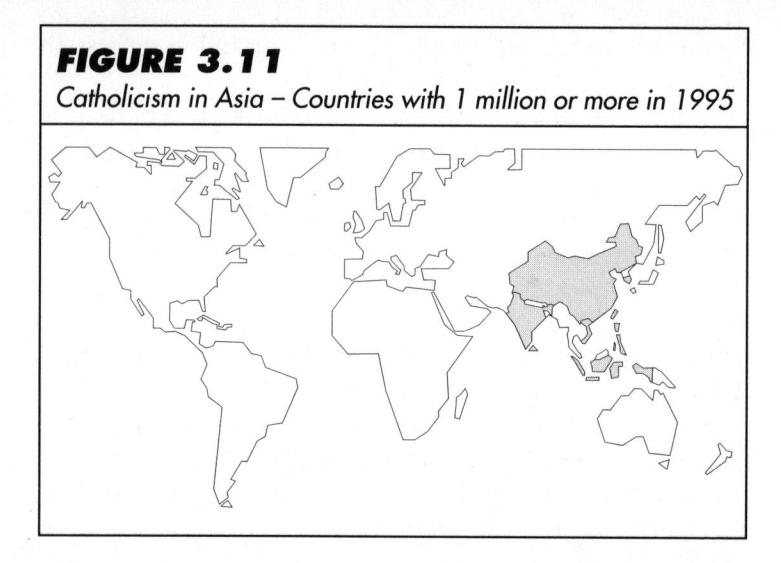

FIGURE 3.11
Catholicism in Asia – Countries with 1 million or more in 1995

In Oceania two-thirds (66%) of the Catholics were in Australia (4.9 million), with a further 1.4 million in Papua New Guinea and half a million in New Zealand, leaving 8% elsewhere.

Catholic churches are LARGE!

The average Catholic church represented a Catholic population of 2,400 people in 1995, a figure which hasn't changed since 1960 and isn't forecast to change by 2010.

This does, however, vary in different continents. A Catholic church represents only 900 people in Africa, 1,200 in Asia, 1,700 in Oceania and 1,800 in Europe but 4,600 in North America! In South America each church has an average population of 10,600, a huge figure which explains the need for many priests per church, but also helps explain some of the nominalism in South America, perhaps caused in part by the inevitable lack of pastoral care such a large number represents.

These figures ultimately come from the *Statistical Yearbook of the Church*, published by the Vatican, although we have used these as computerised by Patrick Johnstone. To get the average population, the number has to be divided by the number of churches. However the *Statistical Yearbook* includes parishes, mission stations (with and without priests) and other centres as if these were independent of each other. In reality many mission stations and other centres are contained within the parishes. On this basis, the average Catholic church has 4,500 per parish[4]. This figure varies widely: in Uganda, for example, it is closer to 25,000. Such a large number is not supported by just a few priests, but by a network of catechists who live in the villages, take Sunday services and so on, and are just visited occasionally by a priest.

So what does all this mean?

The figures in this chapter show that the Catholic church is a BIG church. Big in its overall numbers (5 in every 9 Christians are Catholic), big in the size of its churches, and as a result big in other ways too.

Its influence around the world is huge; the numbers count for something, especially as there are so many in every continent. Its hierarchical structure means that the writings and theology of the Pope, for example, have a big impact, although the Catholic church has a very wide range of theologians. If, for example, Pope John Paul II embraces the Blessed Virgin Mary as a Co-Redemptrix, as some reports suggest[5], that will have a profound impact around the world. He is a powerful influence, and is often credited as being a factor behind the fall of Communism[6].

The Catholic anti-abortion stand is well known, and their opposition to birth control was important enough to be taken very seriously at the 1995 World Population Summit in Cairo[7], partly because of the numbers they represent.

However, its numbers are not increasing as fast as other churches, and its natural growth is not as fast as its worldwide strength would suggest. It has historically been strong in Europe, but although there is still a massive residual presence it is now its weakest continent in growth. The Catholic structure is almost certainly very difficult to change because of its huge size, quite apart from the outlook and awareness of the Church's leaders. The worldwide travels of the Pope will enable him to have many insights, but he has to carry other leaders with him. The basic numbers (and this is but one factor on which to judge) suggest that the Church is not coping as well as it needs to for the next century. Although the Second Vatican Council 1962–64 brought great freedoms, it is likely that different kinds of freedom are needed for the years ahead. The lack of ordinations in Europe must be a continuing worry[8], and this also has implications for its structure. In the Third World however ordinations are significantly increasing[9].

It is rethinking its mission in many countries, and its Renewal[10] programme is one manifestation of this. Ultimately it has the same problem as other churches – a huge number of nominal Catholics who need to be reached in an evangelisation process. Its success in finding an answer to the nominal issue will probably be key for the way the church moves in the coming decades.

NOTES

1. Personal correspondence with Father Joe Brankin, General Secretary, Catholic Missionary Union of England and Wales, London, UK, March 1998.
2. Available from the Catholic Missionary Education Centre, Holcombe House, The Ridgeway, Mill Hill, London NW7 4HY, as is a list of all their publications. The second edition of this booklet was published in June 1997.

3. *Agenda for the Third Millennium*, His Holiness Pope John Paul II, Fount, HarperCollins, London, UK, 1996, Page 189.
4. Op cit (Item 1).
5. Article 'Hail, Mary', by Kenneth L Woodward, *Independent on Sunday* magazine, London, UK, 1997, Page 39.
6. *Atlas of World Christianity*, edited by Dr Peter Brierley and Heather Wraight, Hunt & Thorpe with Paternoster Publishing, Carlisle and Christian Research, London, UK, 1998, article by Rev Canon Michael Bordeaux.
7. See for example the article 'A personal interpretation of Roman Catholic teaching on population', by John Smeaton, in *Transformation*, Oxford Centre for Mission Studies, UK, Volume 13, Number 3, July- September 1996, Page 4.
8. See for example *Europe Without Priests*, edited by Jan Kerkhofs, SCM Press Ltd, London, UK, 1995.
9. Op cit (Item 1).
10. See for example the article 'Reaching Out to Nominal Christians', by Archbishop, now Cardinal, Tom Winning, in *Catholic International*, USA, Volume 2, Number 1, 1–14 October 1991, Page 832.

4

THE ANGLICAN CHURCH

'17 million Anglicans go missing!' was the rather startling headline of the *Church of England Newspaper* when it reported the publication of the *World Churches Handbook* in March 1997[1]. The reason was the apparent discrepancy between the figure of 53 million Anglicans worldwide given in the *Handbook* (although now revised upwards to 55 million in Table 4.1) and the 70 million figure more commonly accepted. So where did the larger figure come from?

Rev Dr David Barrett helped prepare information for the 1978 Lambeth Conference[2] which was published as a booklet[3]. This gave the strength of the Anglican Communion in 1968 as 58.9 million and in 1978 as 63.9 million[4]. These figures have been loosely extrapolated to reach the suggested 70 million for the mid 1990s.

However, since then David Barrett has revised his figures downwards, both in his *World Christian Encyclopedia*[5], and in his annual updates of these figures[6]. The 1982 *Encyclopedia* gave a 1970 Anglican Communion figure of 47.6 million, increasing to 48.5 million in 1975 and an estimated 51.1 million in 1985. In his updated figures he gave a 1996 figure of 54.1 million, and 1997 as 54.4 million, which is very similar to the 1995 *Handbook* figure of 54.5 million.

The problem comes mainly in measuring the degree of *overlap* between those who are regarded as members of the Anglican Communion (having been baptised in the Anglican Church) but who are now part of another Christian denomination. In the *Handbook* they are taken as having transferred and are therefore no longer counted as part of the Anglican Communion. If these transfers are not allowed, then the Anglican Communion worldwide might well be closer to the notional 70 million.

Number and location

In 1995 there were 26.1 million Anglicans in the UK, by far the largest church grouping. This figure refers, as others in the *World Churches Handbook*, to the community in the UK, or the overall number of adherents including the many baptised as infants. The number of actual church members is much smaller, 1.8 million.[7]

These 26.1 million are a significant part of the 54.5 million Anglicans across the world, 3% of all Christendom and 1% of the world's population. In 1960 the 40.9 million Anglicans were 4% of the world's Christian community, so while their numbers have increased they have not grown as much as other sectors of Christendom.

As shown in Chapter 2, a third of the world's Anglicans are in Africa, 10% in Oceania and virtually half in Europe. Over 99% of those in Europe are in the United Kingdom. There are virtually none in South America. This geographical spread reflects the dominance of the old British Empire rather than a true worldwide distribution, hence the continuation of the name 'Church of England' for the Anglican Communion's largest denomination. The term 'Anglican' itself reflects the church's roots in England.

Growth and decline

In the 1990s the Anglican Communion worldwide was growing at an average rate of about 900 people per day, just under 2% or 1 in 50 of the total growth of Christianity. It is estimated that worldwide Anglicanism will grow to 59 million by the year 2010, a growth of 45% from the 1960 total. This compares with a decline in numerical terms in the Lutheran church in the same period, and a growth of 18% in the Methodist church.

It is, however, a smaller growth rate than other denominations' – the Orthodox grew 50%, the Presbyterians 76%, the Catholics 88% and the Baptists 123%. Some grew much faster: the Other Churches grew four fold (442%), the Indigenous churches six fold (592%), and the Pentecostals twelve fold (1,162%) in this 50 year period.

In growth therefore the Anglican church comes eighth in the ten denominational groups being considered and in size it comes seventh. Its 55 million in 1995 is greater than the 48 million Presbyterians, the 35 million Indigenous church community, and the 26 million Methodists.

The next Table shows the growth of the Anglican Community worldwide since 1960 with projections to 2010; these figures are graphed in the following figure. The column headed 'ratio' shows the proportion by which the figure for the particular years has increased, using 1960 as a base and equal to 100. 1995 has been added to show a more contemporary figure.

TABLE 4.1
Anglican and Total Christian Community and World Population 1960–2010

Year	Anglican Community Number	Ratio	Total Christendom Number	Ratio	World Population Number	Ratio
1960	40,892,000	100	924,263,000	100	3,040,955,000	100
1970	45,246,000	111	1,078,384,000	117	3,724,393,000	122
1980	50,283,000	123	1,276,028,000	138	4,471,080,000	147
1990	53,009,000	130	1,513,405,000	164	5,292,427,000	174
1995	54,530,000	133	1,615,382,000	175	5,739,642,000	189
2000	56,112,000	137	1,711,695,000	185	6,177,996,000	203
2010	59,121,000	145	1,898,333,000	205	7,047,971,000	232

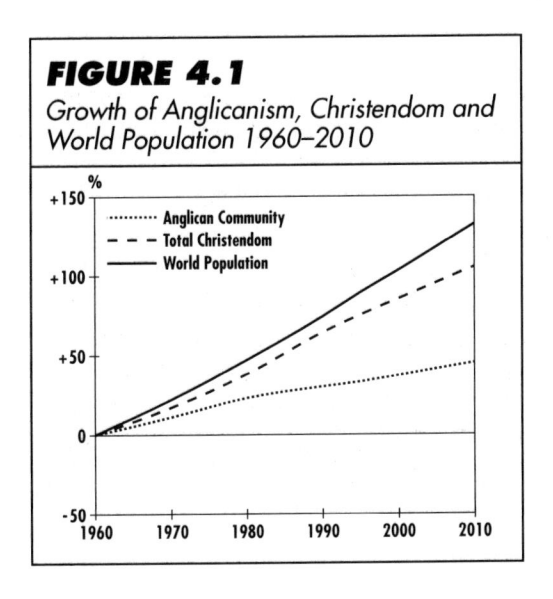

FIGURE 4.1
Growth of Anglicanism, Christendom and World Population 1960–2010

The figure for 1980, 50 million, is considerably less than the figure of 64 million for 1978 suggested in the *Preparatory Information* booklet issued for the Lambeth Conference that year. However, that larger figure was more comprehensive: 'all who claim to be Anglicans: baptized Anglicans, plus nominal Anglicans not known to the Churches nor on its rolls'[8].

The Anglican Community grew less between 1980 and 1990 (7 points) than in earlier decades or are projected to do so between 2000 and 2010. The ratio figures for Christendom grew most in the 1980s (26 points) showing that the competition between denominations was very intense in the 1980s. The fastest growth was by the non-institutional churches.

The Anglican Communion by continent

Table 4.2 shows the growth of the Anglican church by individual continent, with 1960 as a base of 100, in the same way as in the previous Chapter.

TABLE 4.2
The growth of the Anglican Communion by continent 1960–2010

Year	Africa	Europe	Oceania	North America	Asia	South America	World
1960	100	100	100	100	100	100	100
1970	261	100	108	110	146	136	112
1980	395	97	106	117	195	161	123
1990	529	94	111	104	223	183	133
2000	679	90	112	92	254	197	137
2010	823	87	114	82	283	218	145
1960	3.0m	27.9m	4.6m	5.1m	0.2m	0.1m	40.9m
2010	24.7m	24.1m	5.3m	4.2m	0.6m	0.2m	59.1m
% of total	42%	41%	9%	7%	1%	0%	100%

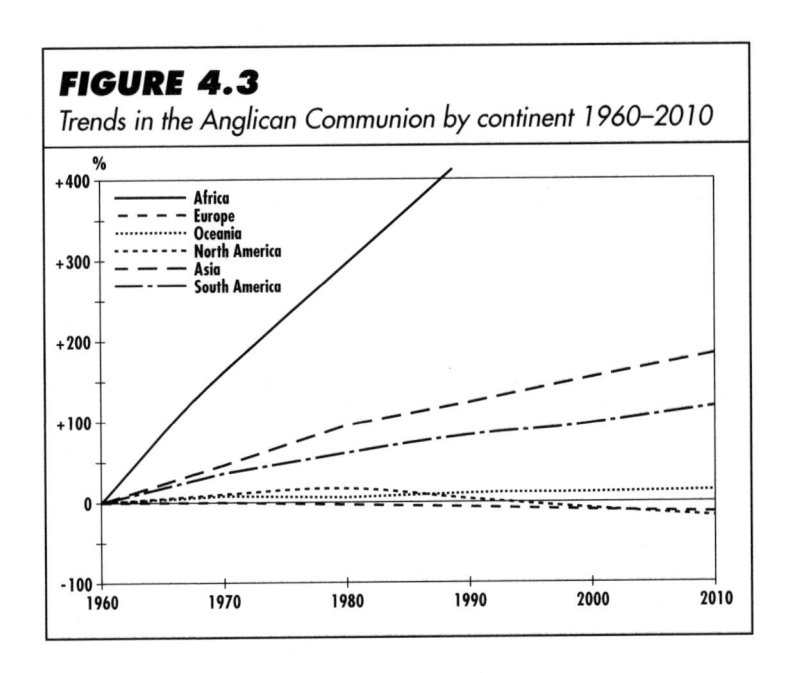

FIGURE 4.2
Proportions of the Anglican Communion by continent 2010

- North America: 7%
- Europe: 41%
- Asia: 1%
- Africa: 42%
- South America: 0%
- Oceania: 9%

FIGURE 4.3
Trends in the Anglican Communion by continent 1960–2010

- Africa
- Europe
- Oceania
- North America
- Asia
- South America

It is obvious that the growth of the Anglican church in the latter part of the twentieth century, and projected into the twenty-first, is almost entirely because of the huge expansion in Africa. This is true on both counts: both the speed of increase (no other continent has a ratio as high as Africa in 2010) and the size of increase (no other continent has achieved a 21 million person growth).

Anglicanism is losing out in North America, where the Baptists are the second largest denomination, in South America where the Pentecostals are the second largest denomination and in Asia where the smaller non-institutional Other Churches are the second largest. This suggests that in these continents non-institutional Christianity is specially attractive.

Anglicans have also grown quite quickly in South America and Asia, but the numbers are relatively small. In Oceania they have grown proportionally more slowly but with larger actual numbers. Anglicans have decreased in both North America and Europe, although at a slower pace in Europe than in North America.

Africa

Africa is important for the Anglican Communion, so it is worth looking at the detail of the six countries where the *World Churches Handbook* forecasts at least 1 million Anglicans in 2010. They are given on the next page, again using ratios, with the remaining countries given in composite.

TABLE 4.3
The growth of the Anglican Communion in Africa 1960–2010

Year	Kenya	Nigeria	South Africa	Sudan	Tanzania	Uganda	All Others	All Africa
1960	100	100	100	100	100	100	100	100
1970	261	448	153	365	470	168	195	261
1980	455	889	186	600	769	339	308	395
1990	675	1039	248	974	1108	497	415	529
2000	890	1483	274	1145	1717	648	417	679
2010	1100	1811	311	1242	2180	795	517	823
1960	0.2m	0.4m	0.9m	0.1m	0.1m	0.8m	0.5m	3.0m
2010	2.2m	7.8m	2.7m	1.0m	1.8m	6.6m	2.6m	24.7m
% of total	9%	32%	11%	4%	7%	27%	10%	100%

These figures show the huge growth of Anglicanism in Nigeria and Uganda, and the huge percentage increases in Tanzania, Nigeria, Sudan and Kenya. The importance of encouraging the church in Sudan, as typified by two visits of the Archbishop of Canterbury, can be seen from this Table. It is the second largest church in the country after the Catholics, and growing very quickly (actually faster than any other major denomination). The many conflicts and civil wars in Africa in the 1990s (Mozambique, Angola, Somalia, Liberia, Congo, Sudan, etc.) are not likely to explain the virtually static figure for 'All others' between 1990 and 2000, since few of these countries have a large Anglican presence, except Sudan which has seen much growth despite (perhaps because of) the fighting.

The Table shows that there was almost an explosive growth of Anglicanism in Nigeria, Tanzania and Sudan in the 1960s, when numbers quadrupled. Presumably in Tanzania this is partly the impact of the East African Revival. In Nigeria it reflects the requirement for everyone to register their religion, the forerunner of the Muslim/ Christian tensions today, and one of the underlying causes of the Biafran War.

Oceania and Asia

The Anglican Community in both these continents has grown since 1960, faster in Asia though the number of Anglicans there is much smaller than in Oceania. The two major contributing countries in Oceania are detailed in the Table below, together with the two countries with the largest Anglican Communities in Asia: Malaysia and the Philippines.

TABLE 4.4
The growth of the Anglican Communion in Oceania and Asia 1960–2010

Year	Australia	New Zealand	All Others	Oceania	Malaysia	Philippines	All Others	Asia
1960	100	100	100	100	100	100	100	100
1970	108	107	127	108	175	125	145	146
1980	104	97	245	106	286	195	167	195
1990	110	88	326	111	377	204	184	223
2000	111	82	410	112	475	214	202	254
2010	112	76	499	114	570	223	219	283
1960	3.7m	0.8m	0.1m	4.6m	0.04m	0.05m	0.13m	0.22m
2010	4.1m	0.6m	0.5m	5.3m	0.23m	0.10m	0.29m	0.62m
% of total	78%	12%	10%	100%	36%	17%	47%	100%

The decrease in the ratio between 1970 and 1980 in Australia, and consequently in Oceania, is due to the formation of the Uniting Church in Australia in June 1977 from the Methodist, Presbyterian and Congregational Churches. Although this grouping excluded the Anglicans, the total

Australian Census figures (from which the figures are taken) showed almost a million *decrease* nationally between 1970 and 1980 as different groups re-aligned. Many more than usual did not record themselves as belonging to any denomination, some of which affected the Anglican church. The Anglican church has been growing steadily since then, if only slowly.

In New Zealand the reverse applies, with constant decline since the high water mark of 1970. The striking growth in 'All Others' comes from the highly contagious Anglicanism in the many Pacific islands. The Anglican Community sometimes involves a substantial majority of the population. However, these populations are very small; Papua New Guinea is the largest (59% in 2010) with a projected Anglican Community of over 300,000 by 2010.

The Anglican church has grown throughout Asia, and especially in Malaysia, where over a third of the continent's Anglicans can be found. It was already strong (and therefore an opportune situation in which to work) when the Overseas Missionary Fellowship made Malaysia their 'Anglican field'. This was when the Mission spread into other countries of Asia after being forced to evacuate from China in 1952.

North America and Europe

The Anglican church is declining in the continents of North America and Europe; details are in the following Table, where the last line is the percentage of the 2010 figure.

TABLE 4.5
The decline of the Anglican Communion in North America and Europe 1960–2010

Year	United States	Canada	All Others	North America	United Kingdom	All Others	Europe
1960	100	100	100	100	100	100	100
1970	102	138	94	110	100	102	100
1980	93	189	93	117	97	105	97
1990	79	170	93	104	93	113	94
2000	68	150	93	92	90	116	90
2010	60	131	93	82	86	119	87
1960	3.1m	1.3m	0.7m	5.1m	27.6m	0.2m	27.8m
2010	1.9m	1.7m	0.6m	4.2m	23.9m	0.2m	24.1m
% of total	45%	41%	14%	100%	99%	1%	100%

The decline in the United States has not been uniform; Anglicanism grew there in the 1960s, but since then has declined, and particularly so in the 1980s. In Canada the 1970s and the 1980s saw a growth in the Anglican church. This turned from growth to decline in the early 1980s, and has continued to fall subsequently. The 1980s was a decade of decline for many denominations in Canada, though the Catholics, Lutherans and Pentecostals all grew. The static numbers reflected in the 'All Others' category show the steady contribution the Anglican church makes to the spiritual life of the many islands in Central America and the Caribbean.

In 2010 99% of Anglicanism in Europe will be the Church of England in England. The Anglican Church in the United Kingdom has slowly declined and is projected to fall further. This is partly due to the decreasing number of baptisms which fell from 266,000 in 1980 to an estimated 172,000 by 2010[9]. As a percentage of births, the 1980 baptisms represent 40% of the total, and the 2010 figure 30%.

The Anglican Church in the rest of Europe, though small numerically, has been slowly growing since 1960 and is projected to continue doing so. This is partly due to the work of organisations like the Intercontinental Church Society. Another factor is that many more English people are at least temporarily resident in Europe because of increasing business in the European Union and may attend English-language church services on a Sunday.

The largest Anglican countries

There are just a few countries which account for the majority of the world's Anglicans, as follows:

TABLE 4.6
The key Anglican countries in 2010

Country	Community millions	% of total %	Cumulative millions	Cumulative %
England	23.9	41	23.9	41
Nigeria	7.8	14	31.7	55
Uganda	6.6	11	38.3	66
Australia	3.7	6	42.0	72
South Africa	2.7	5	44.7	77
Kenya	2.2	4	46.9	81
United States	1.9	3	48.8	84
Canada	1.7	3	50.5	87
Other 137 countries	8.6	13	59.1	100
Total	59.1	100	59.1	100

FIGURE 4.4
The eight key Anglican Countries

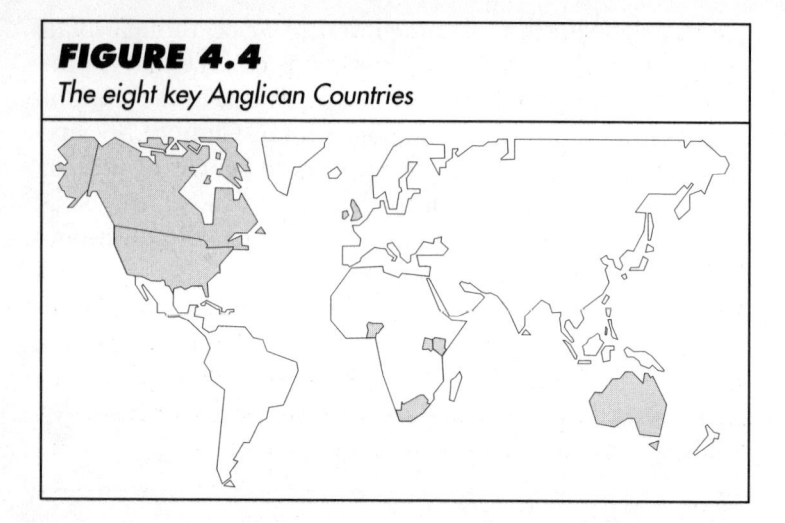

Six Anglicans in 7 (87%) live in one of the eight countries listed in Table 4.6, all of which have been British colonies. Two in 5 of the world's Anglicans reside in England. The four countries of Africa listed, account for 1 in 3 (33%) of the Anglican Community. The Table also shows how relatively thinly spread Anglicanism is in the remaining countries listing Anglicans in the *World Churches Handbook*.

Anglican membership

The discussion thus far has centred around the Anglican *Community*. However, many are neither practising Anglicans, nor members of an Anglican church. The *World Churches Handbook* does not give information on the number attending Anglican churches. The *Handbook* however does give the numbers of church members. In 1995 they totalled 10.6 million across the world, or 19% of the community figure. Just 1 'Anglican' in 5 belongs to a local Anglican church. If practice worldwide follows the pattern in England, then only 58%[10], or 3 in every 5 members, actually attend church.

The 19% worldwide membership proportion varies by

continent. It is 48% in North America, 42% in Asia, 37% in South America, 28% in Africa, 20% in Oceania and 7% in Europe. This suggests a huge amount of nominalism in the Anglican church, especially in Europe, something not unique to Anglicanism, and to which we return in greater depth in Chapter 8.

Anglican churches

According to David Barrett, there are about 25,000 Christian denominations[11] worldwide. The *Handbook* gives the number of churches for many of these denominations each year. It indicates that in 1995 there were just over 80,000 Anglican churches worldwide, almost 4% of the 2.2 million churches.

The Anglicans thus have proportionately slightly more of the world's churches than of the world's Christian community, meaning that the number of people per church, 660, is lower for Anglicans than for most of the other institutional churches. The Catholics with 2,400 per church, the Orthodox 1,600, and the Lutheran with 780 are all higher; only the Presbyterians with 440 are lower. This gives an average institutional community of 1,600 per church, more than 6 times the non-institutional average of 250 people per church.

It is worth looking at how the Anglican figures vary by continent, and these are given in the next Table.

TABLE 4.7
The number and size of Anglican churches by continent in 1995

Feature	Africa	Europe	North America	Oceania	Asia	South America	Total
Number	42,500	19,500	12,300	4,200	1,200	600	80,300
% of total	53%	24%	15%	5%	2%	1%	100%
Average size	420	1,310	300	1,230	420	350	660

Anglican culture

This Chapter has shown how Anglicanism is moving across the world, and its relative size compared with other parts of Christendom. The question that hasn't been answered is, 'What is Anglicanism?' This could obviously be answered historically, but it can also be answered pragmatically.

Bill Pickering describes the Communion as '[not] a unified Church or even a number of Churches controlled by an authoritative body. It is made up a loose federation of Churches which are in communion with the see of Canterbury.'[12]

The Anglican Communion 'holds to the centrality of the scriptures, the doctrines of the two great creeds, [and] . . . the *Book of Common Prayer*'.[13] It is a church which has given birth to many mighty mission movements, and which today can still take bold steps. The Archbishop of Canterbury does not have the same authority as the Pope; the ordination of women in England followed a move which had already been taken in many other parts of the world, such as by Bishop Festo Kivengere of Kigezi in Uganda in December 1983.[14]

It is a church with differing theological traditions, evangelical, broad or central, and Anglo-Catholic or Tractarian. The Rev John Leach, when newly appointed as Director of Anglican Renewal Ministries, summed up the flexibility of the Anglican church when he wrote, 'Most Anglicans probably live in something of a love/hate relationship with the Church of England. We love her funny little ways, her wonderful liturgies, all those nice bishops, and so on. Yet we weep over the deadness, the nominalism, the immovable bureaucracy, the sheer *respectability* of it all. That God should give prophetic revelation, move people around, and appoint someone to work full-time promoting charismatic renewal in the Anglican church says one thing loud and clear; He hasn't given up on the C of E yet!'[15]

So what does all this mean?

The Anglican church is significant in its virtual worldwide coverage, and is especially of key importance in Africa, Oceania and the United Kingdom. Its growth is slower in those continents where non-institutional denominations flourish (the Americas and Asia). This suggests that it may be important to identify the primary characteristics of an Anglican church – what does it mean to be Anglican? Even, what are the benefits of being Anglican? Alternatively, should the Anglican church consider becoming less 'Anglican' and more 'national' in non-English cultures?

Anglicanism is growing in some countries but declining in others. What are the reasons for both changes, and what can those in the latter countries learn from those in the former? This suggests that increasing research is needed both locally and worldwide. Should the Anglican Communion appoint a Research Officer?

Anglicanism has followed similar trends to other worldwide institutional churches, so it is not alone in its problems. Working with other churches is therefore likely to be of increasing importance.

The huge amount of nominalism in the Anglican Community highlights the importance of tackling the problem. While most obvious in England, the same issues are being found across the world, and suggests that this could be one of the key challenges for the twenty-first century.

NOTES

1. *Church of England Newspaper*, Friday, 14 March 1997.
2. The Lambeth Conference is a gathering of senior Anglican clergy from around the world, called by the Archbishop of Canterbury. It usually takes place very 10 years. One was held in 1998.

3. *Preparatory Information*, Statistics: Documentation: Addresses: Maps:, The Lambeth Conference 1978, CIO Publishing, London, UK, 1978.
4. Ibid, Table 4, Page 14.
5. *World Christian Encyclopedia*, edited by Rev Dr David Barrett, published by Oxford University Press, UK, 1982, Global Table 4, Page 6.
6. January edition each year of the *International Bulletin of Missionary Research*, Overseas Missions Studies Centre, Connecticut, USA.
7. *UK Christian Handbook: Religious Trends*, No 1 1998/99 edition, edited by Dr Peter Brierley, Christian Research, London, and Paternoster Publishing, Carlisle, UK, Tables 2.4.1 and 2.8.2.
8. Op cit (Item 3).
9. *UK Christian Handbook*, 1996/97 edition, edited by Dr Peter Brierley, Christian Research, London, UK 1995, Table 11, Page 244.
10. Op cit (Item 7), Tables 2.12.1 and 2.8.2.
11. Op cit (Item 5).
12. *Study of Anglicanism,* SPCK, London, UK, 1985, Page 364.
13. *The Anglicans in Australia*, by 'Tricia Blombery, Australian Government Publishing Service, Canberra, 1996, Page 20.
14. *Festo Kivengere*, Mrs Anne Coomes, Monarch Publications, Crowborough, UK, 1990, Page 427.
15. Article 'God hasn't given up on the C of E yet!' by Rev John Leach, in *Renewal* magazine, Monarch Publications, Crowborough, UK, January 1998, Page 27.

5

THE OTHER INSTITUTIONAL CHURCHES: ORTHODOX, LUTHERAN AND PRESBYTERIAN

The Orthodox Churches are historically the second main strand of Christianity: the Catholics are the first and Protestants the third. Collectively they were the second largest group in Christendom in 1960, but are only one-sixth the size of the Catholic Church. In 1960 they were 10% of the total. If present trends continue, by the year 2010, they will be in third place with 8%, having been overtaken by the collective 'Other Churches'. The Lutheran churches were the third largest grouping around the world in 1960, but in 2010 will be only the sixth. On the other hand, the Presbyterian churches have remained in the same respective position throughout these years, at eighth.

THE ORTHODOX CHURCHES

A substantial total

Altogether in 1995 there were 140 million Orthodox Christians worldwide. This total depends critically on what number is used for the size of the Russian Orthodox Church in Russia. In one issue of *Orthodox News*[1], the Russian leader claimed there were 150 million Orthodox Christians in Russia. Since the population of Russia is 147 million people, this was effectively saying that the entire Russian population is Orthodox. Given the 70-year period of atheistic Communist rule which ended in 1988, he is perhaps optimistic to say that the whole population are still Christians at heart, and that all are Orthodox Christians.

David Barrett uses a figure of 70 million Orthodox, but this is for the whole of the former USSR, and his figure for Russia alone is not known. Patrick Johnstone had a 1990 figure of 49 million for the former USSR, so his estimate is considerably less than David Barrett's. For the purpose of analysis here, his figure of 26 million in Russia in 1995 is used. Obviously if the number of Orthodox in Russia were greater the worldwide total of 140 million will be likewise increased.

24 million of the 26 are Russian Orthodox, but the rest are 1.6 million Old Believers and 0.4 million Armenian Apostolic Church. In addition there are 2 million other Christians in Russia (0.7 million Baptist, 0.4 million Catholic, 0.3 million Pentecostal, and 0.3 million Lutherans being the main groups).

Worldwide growth

The Orthodox Churches are growing worldwide. In 1960 they numbered 96 million, and by 2010, if present trends continue, will be 143 million, an increase of almost exactly half. This compares with an increase of 88% in the Catholic Church, 105% in total world Christianity, and 132% in the world's population. Thus its growth rate is not as strong as other denominations.

The Orthodox community by continent

This growth has occurred across all continents: in Oceania it grew 163% in this 50-year period (although starting from a very small base), in Africa it grew 134%, and in South America 91%. In North America its growth has only been 26%.

The situation in Asia and Europe is complicated by the fact that the United Nations changed their continental definitions in 1992, primarily because of the collapse of the USSR. Therefore we get a fairer picture if we add together Asia and Europe. This shows that in 1960 there were 75 million Orthodox on these two continents (2.5 million in Asia and 72.2 million in Europe), and in 2010 101 million, a growth of 35% (28.0 million in Asia and 73.2 million in Europe).

The details of this growth, using ratios, are given in Table 5.1, merging Asia and Europe.

TABLE 5.1
The growth of the Orthodox Community by continent 1960–2010

Year	Africa	Asia+ Europe	Oceania	North America	South America	World
1960	100	100	100	100	100	100
1970	125	110	131	120	119	113
1980	163	119	152	125	138	126
1990	191	128	210	126	156	138
2000	211	135	234	126	173	146
2010	234	135	263	126	191	150
1960	14m	75m	0.2m	6.3m	0.3m	96m
2010	33m	101m	0.6m	7.9m	0.5m	143m
% of total	23%	71%	0%	6%	0%	100%

This Table shows that nearly three-quarters (71%) of the world's Orthodox are in Asia and Europe, and a quarter (23%) in Africa, with a small proportion (6%) in North America.

FIGURE 5.1
Proportion of Orthodox Community by continent 2010

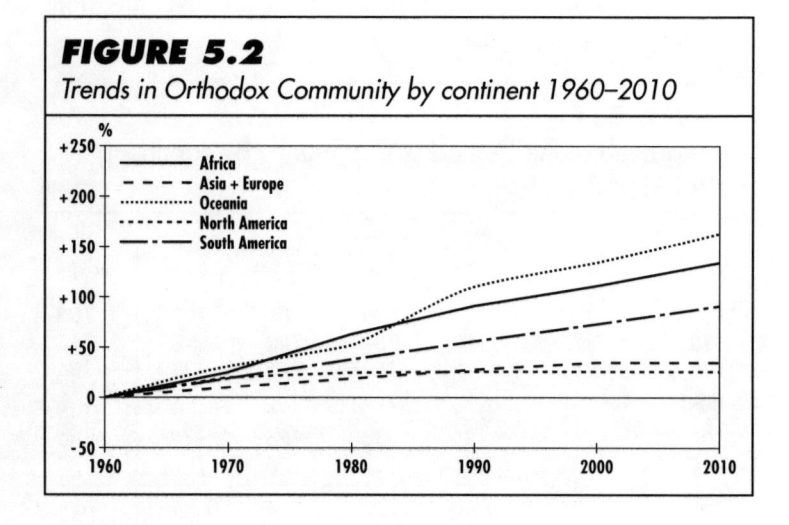

- North America: 6%
- Asia/Europe: 71%
- Africa: 23%
- South America: 0%
- Oceania: 0%

FIGURE 5.2
Trends in Orthodox Community by continent 1960–2010

- Africa
- Asia + Europe
- Oceania
- North America
- South America

There is a unique part of the Orthodox Church in Europe: the Lord's Army in Romania. It started in the 1920s, has a six-figure membership, and it encourages lay participation and the use of spiritual gifts. Its main meetings are in Sibiu at Pentecost, and it is guided by 'the impressive leadership'[2] of Father Mihoc.

Two-thirds (65%) of the African Orthodox are in Ethiopia, with a further 28% in Egypt. There are just under 2 million throughout the rest of Africa (7%). In Ethiopia all but a handful (less than 0.01%) are members of the Ethiopian Orthodox Church; and virtually the same is true of the Coptic Orthodox Church in Egypt (99.7% are members).

In North America 91% of the Orthodox are in the United States, and are spread across more than 20 Orthodox Patriarchates, which are equivalent to Catholic or Anglican Dioceses. The largest is the Greek Orthodox (24%), but no other group has more than a million adherents.

Church size

Orthodox Churches, like the Catholics, are large – an average 1,600 people (or community) per church worldwide. However, this varies by continent: in Africa these churches have 1,700 each, in North America 1,900, in Oceania 2,600, and in Asia larger still – an average of 3,700 each. But in Europe and South America they are much smaller, just 1,300 and 300 people per church respectively.

So what does this all mean?

The situation in the UK where Orthodox Christianity is growing perhaps gives us a clue. Along with the Pentecostals and New Churches, it is going against the trend of decline, with a growth of 58% in the 20 years 1980 to 2000. What causes that growth? Some of it comes through immigration, but others are over the issue of the ordination of women. This is especially true for those who moved from the Church of England, because the Orthodox Church represents stability.

'It would be unthinkable to start redefining the dogmas of

the church,' said Father Alban in an interview in the *Independent on Sunday*[3]. The Orthodox liturgy also has not been altered since the early centuries of the church. 'What would cause the church to grow faster?', the journalist asked Father Alban. Uniting the varying Orthodox factions, he replied, or at least the main ones, and having more leadership – the number of priests is small in Britain. The Orthodox church 'appeals primarily to thoughtful people who have an unsatisfied need for God. It does not have the mass public appeal of, say, evangelicalism. We feel that Christianity goes far deeper than being cheered up by joyful music.'[4]

THE LUTHERAN CHURCH

The Lutheran Church in effect began when Martin Luther, aged 34, nailed his *Ninety-Five Theses upon Indulgences* to the doors of the castle church in Wittenberg, Germany, on 31st October 1517. He stood before the emperor and the estates of the empire in the Diet of Worms in 1521, and refused to recant unless so persuaded by Scripture. He was not just the Professor of History at the University, but the leader of a movement, subsequently called the Reformation. His greatness can perhaps be judged by the fact that since his death over 450 years ago, more books have been written about him than any other figure in history, save Jesus of Nazareth[5].

A declining church

The Lutheran church is in a unique and unenviable position in the world. If present trends continue, it will have fewer members in 2010 than it had in 1960! In between the church has grown, declined very slightly, grown again, but declined again. Figure 5.3 shows how essentially static the church has been over these 50 years.

FIGURE 5.3
The Lutheran Community 1960–2010

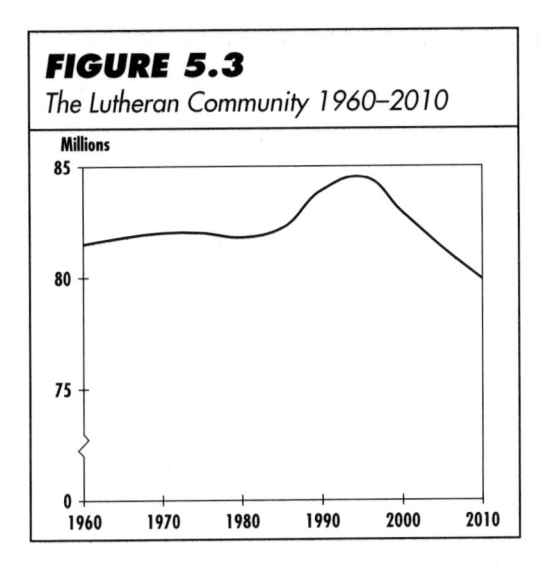

Whilst this graph shows a decline in numbers, the effect has also been a decline in respective position. It has gone from third largest denomination in the world to sixth largest in 50 years, quite a drop. No other denomination has fallen so much relatively, and no other denomination has fallen in real terms, with fewer adherents in 2010 than in 1960.

Lutherans by continent

Although the majority of the world's Lutherans are in Europe, they are spread around the world, as Table 5.2 illustrates.

TABLE 5.2
Changes to the Lutheran Community by continent 1960–2010

Year	Africa	Europe	Oceania	North America	Asia	South America	World
1960	100	100	100	100	100	100	100
1970	161	97	176	102	149	114	101
1980	240	93	233	103	203	123	100
1990	370	91	283	101	268	141	103
2000	480	85	326	99	315	155	102
2010	577	77	376	97	358	170	98
1960	1.4m	62.9m	0.3m	14.1m	1.8m	0.9m	81.5m
2010	8.3m	48.6m	1.2m	13.7m	6.6m	1.5m	79.9m
% of total	10%	61%	2%	17%	8%	2%	100%

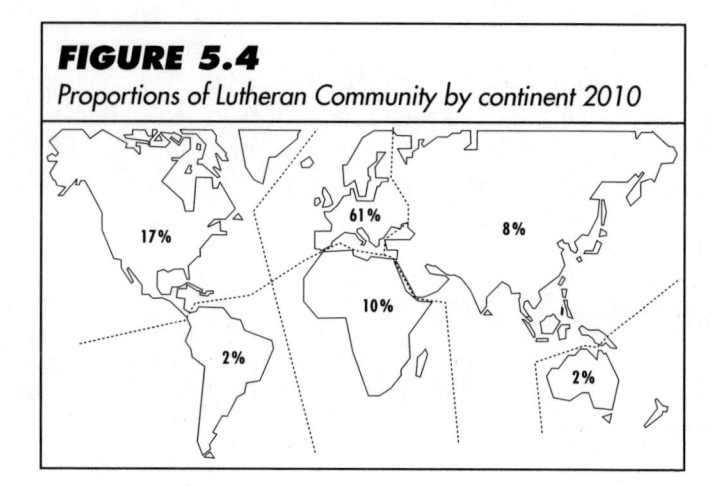

FIGURE 5.4
Proportions of Lutheran Community by continent 2010

- North America: 17%
- Europe: 61%
- Asia: 8%
- Africa: 10%
- South America: 2%
- Oceania: 2%

FIGURE 5.5
Changes to the Lutheran Community by continent 1960–2010

[Graph showing percentage changes from 1960 to 2010 for: Africa, Europe, Oceania, North America, Asia, South America. Y-axis ranges from -100% to +500%.]

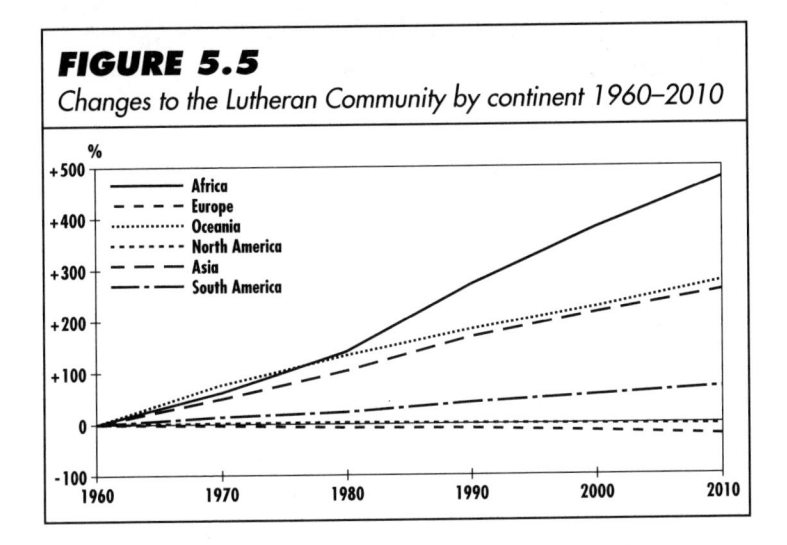

This Table shows that the Lutheran Church *can* expand, but it's just that in its heartlands it hasn't. Outside Europe and North America the Lutheran Church has more than tripled in Asia and Oceania, and expanded six-fold in Africa. It expanded particularly fast in Africa and Asia in the 1970s and the 1980s, part of the growth world-wide in these decades. It has not expanded world-wide simply because in its mother country and mother continent, the numbers have fallen.

Africa

Three-quarters (74%) of Africa's 6.2 million Lutherans in 1995 are in 5 countries: Tanzania (1.9 million), Ethiopia (1.0 million), South Africa (760,000), Namibia (560,000), and Nigeria (400,000). These five countries are responsible for three-quarters (73%) of the Lutheran growth in Africa over the period 1960–2010. Tanzania and Ethiopia are the key countries, both having many Scandinavian missionaries serving in them. For example, in 1988 80% of Swedish missionaries served in Africa, as did 68% of Danish and 51% of Finnish.[6] Namibia shows the strong German connection.

Oceania

In Oceania the Lutheran church is essentially just in two countries, which together account for 99.5% of the total: Papua New Guinea had 700,000 Lutherans in 1995, and Australia had 280,000. Australian Lutherans are growing, unlike their counterparts in most other Western nations. This is partly because they have 60 primary and 17 secondary schools in Australia[7]. 70% of them were born in Australia, and a further 14% in Germany[8]. However, almost half (46%) Australia's Lutherans live in just five cities: Adelaide (34,400), Brisbane and Melbourne (25,700 each), Sydney (22,100) and Perth (7,600)[9]. Lutherans spread widely but concentrate in particular places when they get there, as it were.

North America

The Lutherans in North America are spread over 14 different denominations. In 1995 they totalled 13.7 million, 97% of the continent's total. The largest, the Evangelical Lutheran Church, had a community of 5.2 million in 1995, followed by the Lutheran Church with 2.7 million, the Lutheran Church (Missouri Synod) with 2.6 million, and the American Lutheran Church with 2.4 million, these 4 accounting for 94% of the total.

Asia

Nine Lutherans in ten (91%) in Asia are either in Indonesia (3.7 million out of Asia's 5.5 million in 1995) or India (1.3 million). Again, Indonesia has been the host of many German and Scandinavian missionaries. In relation to the size of their churches, Scandinavia has the highest percentage of overseas mission workers in the world. This is partly because the theological training, especially in Norway, integrates home and overseas mission. If someone wants to serve overseas they do a course on home mission; if a person wishes to be a minister at home, they will do a course on overseas ministry. Consequently overseas mission endeavour becomes a natural focus in the life of the church.

South America

Five Lutherans in every six (85%) in South America are in Brazil, which had 1.1 million in 1995. Again this is mainly the result of mission endeavour from the strongly Lutheran countries in Europe.

Lutherans in Europe

In 1995 two-thirds (67%) of the world's Lutherans were in Europe, and in Europe three-fifths (59%) were in Germany. So German Lutherans constitute two-fifths (39%) of the world's number. The Lutherans in Europe are concentrated essentially in Germany and Scandinavia:

TABLE 5.3
The Lutheran church in Europe 1995

Country	Total (millions) Lutherans	Lutherans as % of Church	Lutherans as % of population
Germany	33.3	53%	41%
Sweden	7.0	90%	80%
Denmark	4.6	98%	89%
Finland	4.5	96%	88%
Norway	3.9	94%	89%
Iceland	0.3	98%	95%
Rest of Europe	2.7	0.6%	0.4%

In Scandinavia the Lutheran church is the state church, and its dominance is profound with of the order of 90% of the *population* belonging to it. The mores of Lutheranism become the mores of the State, or vice versa. Lutherans make less impact in that sense in Germany because of the huge number of Catholics in the country, 34% of the population, 44% of the Christians.

Elsewhere only in Estonia and Latvia does the Lutheran church make a significant impact. Its 374,000 community in Latvia is 37% of the total church community and its 210,000 in Estonia 36%. Everywhere else the Lutherans form a small minority amongst all the other churches.

The plight of Lutheranism in Europe is typified by the changes in Germany. The figures used relate to the community. Lutheran membership in Germany is counted by those paying additional tax (through the income tax mechanism) for church purposes. This tax pays for the many social institutions for which the Lutheran Church is responsible, which in other countries might well be covered by the State. But with increasing disillusion about the church, a number are opting out of paying the extra tax, and thus ostensibly the right to be married or buried by the church.

In addition, and more seriously for the church, are the many immigrants Germany accepts to help keep its industry and commerce going. In 1992, almost half the 6 million foreign workers in Europe were in Germany[10], one in 14 of its work-force, but most of these are not Lutheran and do not pay the church tax.

The two factors of declining population and opting out of the church tax makes dismal reading. In the mid 1980s an official publication[11] of the Evangelical Lutheran Church of Germany (the EKD) forecast that Lutheran church membership could fall by almost half in the years 1980 to 2030 (Figure 5.6). How much this is affected by the re-unification of Germany is not known. Figure 5.7 shows the changing population profile in West Germany, where dotted lines indicate forecast figures.

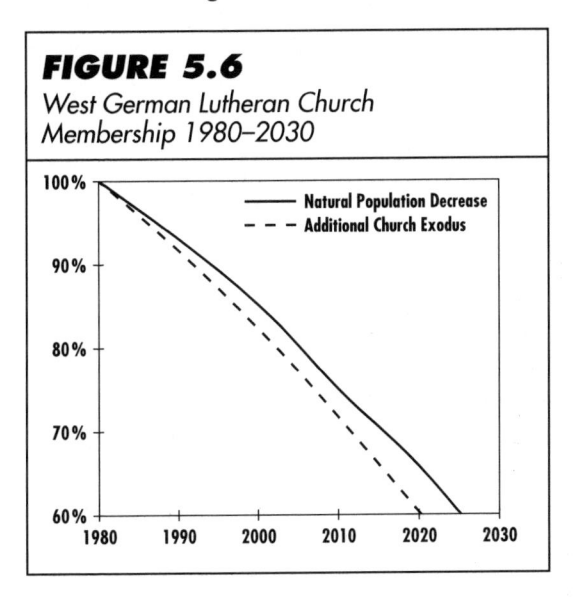

FIGURE 5.6
West German Lutheran Church Membership 1980–2030

— Natural Population Decrease
– – Additional Church Exodus

The reason this is important is that the actual number of German Lutherans could significantly fall if these population forecasts are fulfilled. They extend beyond the year 2010 used in this book, but because Germany accounts for such a significant number of Lutherans worldwide, a major change in German Lutheranism would affect the worldwide denomination considerably, and could cause it to decrease further in the decades ahead.

Lutheran churches

The average size of a Lutheran church in 1960 was 1,000 people. By 2010 it will be down to 700. In other words, although Lutheran membership may be static or slightly declining, the number of Lutheran churches around the

106 FUTURE CHURCH

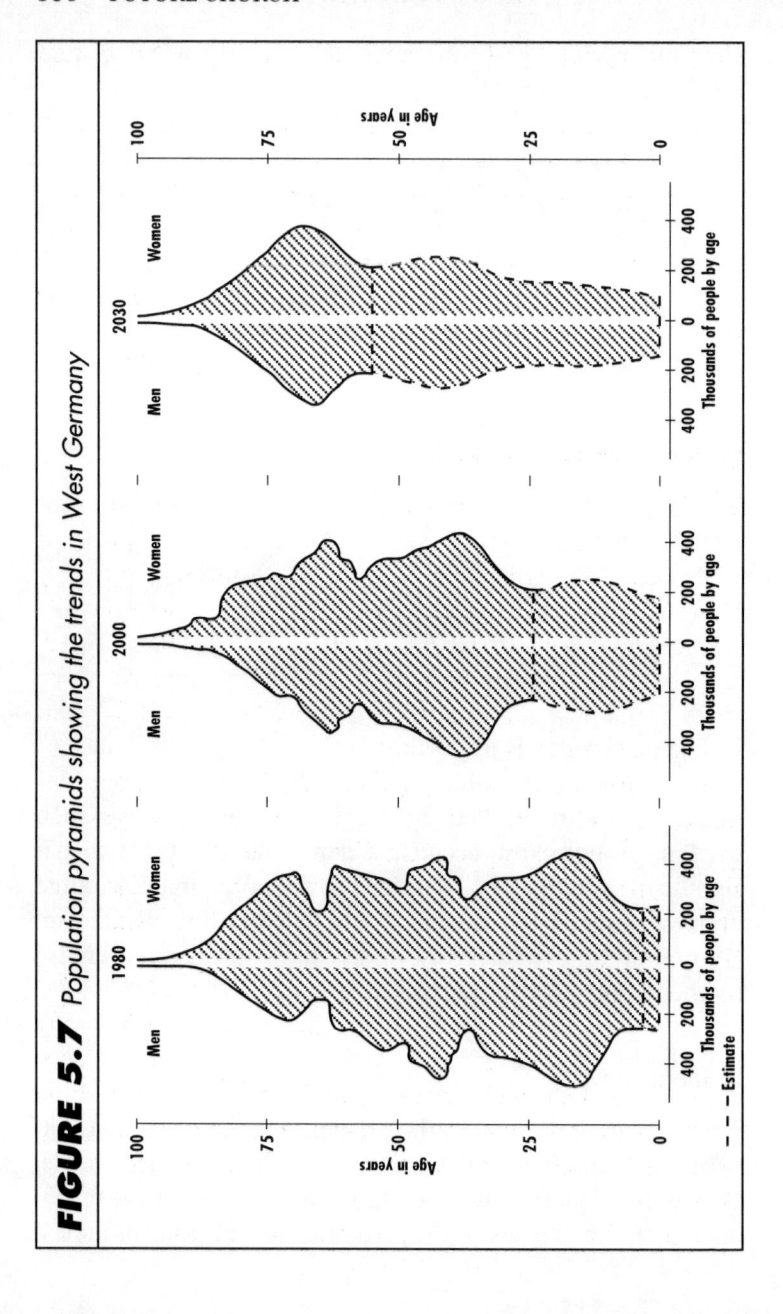

FIGURE 5.7 *Population pyramids showing the trends in West Germany*

world is increasing. This reflects the growth in Africa and Asia.

For example, there were 5,200 Lutheran churches in Africa in 1960 (average size 300); if present trends continue, by 2010 there will be 26,000 (average size still 300). In Asia there were 8,600 Lutheran churches in 1960 (average size 220); by 2010 there will be 25,000 (average size 260).

To put these numbers in perspective – in Europe in 1960 there were 33,000 Lutheran churches, average size 1,900; by 2010 there will be 27,000 churches, average size 1,800.

So what does all this mean?

The Lutheran Church globally is at best static. But this is not a fair assessment overall because the figures could suggest that Lutheranism is dying. But this is not so, primarily because the mission endeavours by German and especially Scandinavian workers in Indonesia, Tanzania, India, Brazil, Ethiopia, Papua New Guinea, South Africa and Namibia (in order of Lutheran population) have laid a firm foundation which is growing.

The Lutheran church in mother Germany has grave problems, some of which are internal. But one of its greatest problems is demographic – the Church needs to persuade its members to have lots of children in the hope they'll join the church later on! Likewise in the strong Lutheran Scandinavian countries, the church is under financial and structural pressure, but nothing like as acute as in Germany.

North American Lutheranism follows Europe in being static or just declining. South American Lutheranism is concentrated in the Brazilian church, and the Church in Oceania in Australia and Papua New Guinea. Unlike other areas of Western Lutheranism, Australia's Lutheran churches are growing.

Although there are many countries with a small presence

(the *World Churches Handbook* gives details of congregations in 70 countries) the main impact of Lutheranism is in just a few countries where they are especially strong. As with Australia, they have spread into many places, but just a few cities have a large presence. It is this breadth of presence on the one hand, and concentration to make a particular impact on the other which is a key feature of Lutherans today. Where they are concentrated, their leadership will thus become especially important.

Lutherans will probably continue to decline because of the problems in Germany, and because North America is not growing. But don't write Lutheranism off! They have a mission tradition, a strategy of concentration, and of making a difference where they are. You can almost hear the echo from Martin Luther, 'Here I stand! I can do no other' in much of what Lutheranism is at the end of the twentieth century. And if that spirit doesn't die, nor will Lutheranism.

THE PRESBYTERIAN CHURCH

The term derives from the word 'presbyter', and signifies a church which is governed by presbyters, usually elected by the congregation. Presbyterian churches are the general title given to the English-speaking Reformed or Calvinistic churches emerging from the Reformation, and their derivatives in many lands. The first such church was formed in Geneva in 1555 under the direction of the Scottish preacher, John Knox, who was unwilling to accept the Anglican *Book of Common Prayer*. The primary supposition of Presbyterianism is that the risen Christ is the only head of the church[12].

Church numbers

In 1995 these were 48 million Presbyterians worldwide. This

was 3% of Christendom, and 1% of the world's population. These proportions were the same in 1960 and will remain so by the year 2010, if present trends continue, showing that the Presbyterian church is keeping pace with world trends but neither beating them nor losing to them. This means that they will grow from 30 million in 1960 to 52 million by 2010.

The Presbyterian community by continent

Unlike other denominations, Presbyterians are evenly spread across the world's continents, with 30% in Asia in 1995, 26% in Europe, 23% in Africa, 17% in North America, and the remaining 4% spread equally between Oceania and South America (2% each). This last hides, however, a rapid growth in South America and an almost equivalent decline in Oceania.

TABLE 5.4
The growth of the Presbyterian Community by continent 1960–2010

Year	Africa	Europe	Oceania	North America	Asia	South America	World
1960	100	100	100	100	100	100	100
1970	137	101	106	109	157	125	117
1980	183	101	55	135	235	181	138
1990	220	98	58	151	313	239	159
2000	237	94	58	154	356	274	167
2010	261	92	60	156	394	304	176
1960	4.9m	13.1m	1.5m	5.4m	4.3m	0.3m	29.5m
2010	12.7m	12.0m	0.9m	8.4m	17.0m	1.0m	52.0m
% of total	24%	23%	2%	16%	33%	2%	100%

110 FUTURE CHURCH

FIGURE 5.8
Proportion of Presbyterian Community by continent 2010

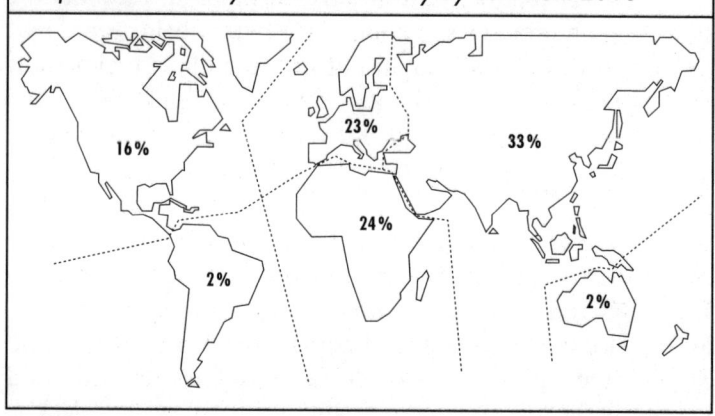

- North America: 16%
- Europe: 23%
- Asia: 33%
- Africa: 24%
- South America: 2%
- Oceania: 2%

FIGURE 5.9
Growth of Presbyterian Community by continent 1960–2010

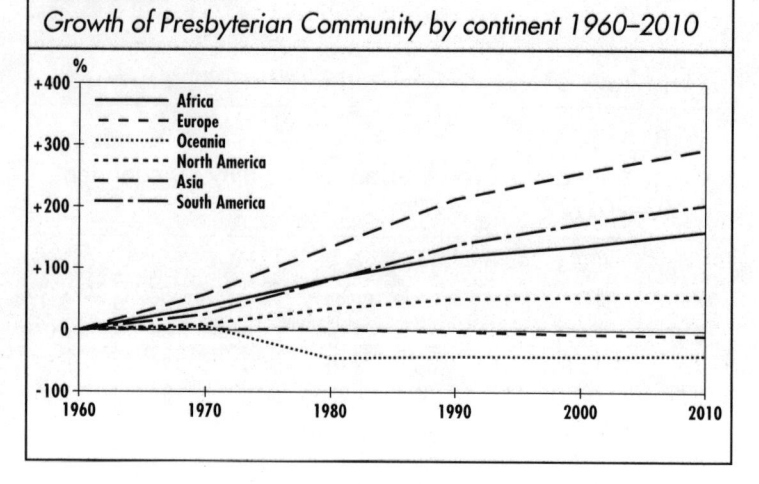

Europe and Oceania

The Presbyterian church will have declined in both Europe and Oceania between 1960 and 2010. Presbyterianism is reasonably well spread throughout Europe, with its main countries are The Netherlands, Switzerland, the United Kingdom and Hungary, and to a lesser extent Romania. In 1995 these countries respectively had 29%, 22%, 21%, 16% and 6%, in total 93% of the continent's Presbyterians. The decline in Europe is mainly due to the drop in the number in the Netherlands, which lost half a million in the community from 1970 to 1990.

The decline in Oceania comes through the merging in Australia of the Methodist, Presbyterian and Congregational Union churches into the Uniting Church in June 1977. Before the merger the Presbyterian Church had 964,000 adherents in 1975, afterwards the Presbyterian Church of Australia Continuing had 152,000 in 1980. The Uniting Church is included among 'Other Churches' in the *World Churches Handbook*, so the fall in the Presbyterian numbers in Oceania is largely one of changed definition.

Africa

The Presbyterian church grew particularly fast in the 1970s and 1980s generally, although in Africa the growth was especially strong early in the 1970s. Half this 1970s growth occurred in four countries: the main branch of the Dutch Reformed Church in South Africa, the NGK, and other Reformed Churches in that country, and the Presbyterian Churches in Ghana, Kenya and Zaïre.

North America

The main growth in the Presbyterian Church in North America also occurred in the 1970s: it doubled in the United States from 1.1 million in 1970 to 2.8 million by 1980, although this was partly offset by the decline of the United Presbyterian Church from 3.3 million to 2.9 million in the same period.

South America

In South America the growth happened equally in the 1970s and the 1980s. The small Presbyterian Church in this continent is dominated by its presence in two countries – Brazil and Peru: in 1970 three-quarters (77%) of the 390,000 Presbyterians were in Brazil and 8% in Peru. By 1980, however, the proportions (out of total of 570,000) were 75% and 14% respectively, but by 1990, out of 750,000 South American Presbyterians 63% were in Brazil and 27% in Peru, a very rapid eight-fold growth from 25,000 in 1970 to 200,000 by 1990 in Peru.

Presbyterians in Asia

However, the major growth in Presbyterianism is in Asia, which in the 50 years 1960 to 2010 multiplied four-fold. This growth was largely because the two dominant Presbyterian countries in the continent both grew very fast. In 1970 there were 6.8 million Presbyterians in Asia. A third (31%) were in the Republic of (South) Korea, and nearly three-fifths (56%) in Indonesia. Only three other countries had a Presbyterian presence in six figures – India and Pakistan with 300,000 each, and Taiwan with 200,000. These five countries account for 99% of Asia's Presbyterians.

By 1980 the South Korean numbers had doubled to 4.3 million, now 43% of the continent's 10.1 million, while Indonesian Presbyterians had grown to 4.6 million or 46%. In the next ten years the Korean growth increased by a further 2 million to 6.3 million, reaching 47% of the continent's 13.5 million Presbyterians, overtaking Indonesia which by then had reached 5.7 million or 42%. India and

Pakistan's 300,000 grew to 500,000 over the same 20 years, a similar proportional increase to Indonesia.

The growth of Presbyterianism in these two countries, and the rest of Asia is given in Figure 5.10, along with the growth of Presbyterianism in the other five continents.

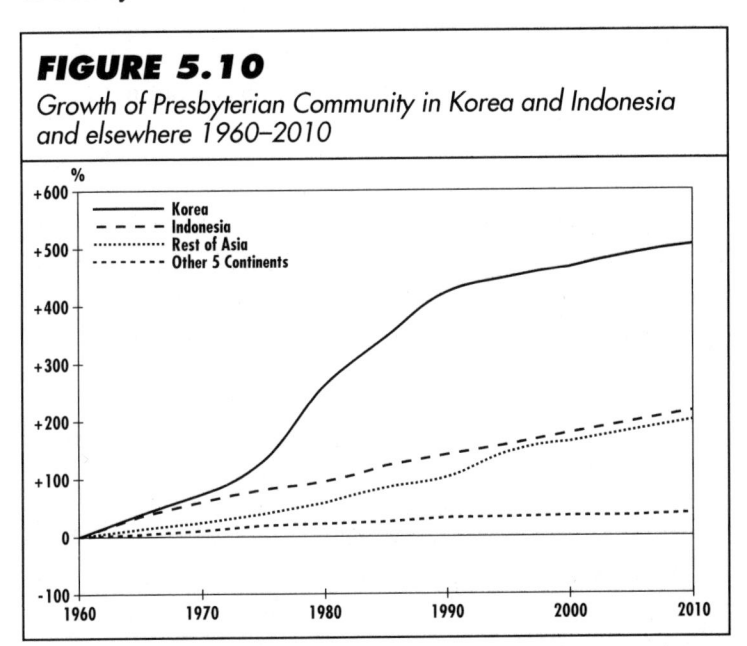

FIGURE 5.10
Growth of Presbyterian Community in Korea and Indonesia and elsewhere 1960–2010

This shows the phenomenal increase in the South Korean Presbyterian churches in the late 1970s, which continued with slight abatement in the 1980s. However, it has slowed down considerably in the 1990s, and is forecast to remain at this lower rate of growth in the first decade of the twenty-first century. It may also be seen that Asian Presbyterianism has grown much faster than in the rest of the world.

South Korean growth

Why the huge growth in South Korea? Many books have written on the Korean Church Growth explosion, which occurred not just in the Presbyterian Church. But as the 24 or more Presbyterians denominations account for about half the nation's Christians, clearly what happens to Presbyterians in Korea is critical for other denominations.

1. One of the key features of the Korean church has been their outstanding *prayer life*. I will never forget my visit to the Prayer Mountain belonging to the Yoido Full Gospel Church in 1989, with its myriad of small cells, which you had to kneel to enter. It also has a huge meeting arena where thousands met for united prayer, either in small groups, or together as a grand assembly. Such prayer was encouraged during the main services of Yoido when everyone stood to pray out loud simultaneously when it came to intercession time.

    I also had the privilege of attending the 4,000-strong Global Consultation on World Evangelisation (GCOWE) held in May 1995 in Seoul, Korea. This was based in the magnificent Korean Centre for World Mission, aptly called the Torch Centre[13]. This Centre had on its top floor a whole series of prayer rooms, with no furniture except a prayer stool; they were constantly in use.

2. But prayer, while vital, is not the only key feature of Korean Christianity. Their *vision* has been outstanding. Dr David Yonggi Cho, the senior minister of the largest church in the world, the 750,000 member strong Yoido Full Gospel saw his church grow in stages, as the Lord gave him direction. He described the Lord's words to him about the new size of the church as 'incubating'[14] until he felt able to share it with his elders, and they then planned how it might come about.

At the GCOWE event I visited the Kwang Lim Methodist church, the largest Methodist church in the world, with 74,000 members. It was a huge building, and would in other countries and denominations be called a cathedral. It seats 5,000 people several times over every Sunday, and was built in the late 1970s when the congregation was 'just' 3,000 people. Why did a group of people that size build such a large building? Answer in part is 'their vision'.

3. A third factor has played a vital part in Korea's great growth. This is their *missionary involvement*. The numbers have rocketed from 100 missionaries in 1979 to 1,200 in 1989 and 3,300 in 1994[15]. These missionaries need supporting. And support requires generous giving. The Korean people have dug deep in their pockets to help evangelize the world. They made a very significant contribution for the 1995 GCOWE by providing free accommodation for all delegates from Third World countries. However, in contrast, the second main cause of missionary attrition by Korean mission workers was the lack of support from home, according to a 1995 study[16]. (The main cause was problems with their peers).

4. Whilst the sending of missionaries is an obvious way to count numerical overseas evangelistic endeavours, it should be noted that the Korean churches *continuously engage in evangelism*. Integral to the latter is an elaborate mechanism in most churches for incorporating people into cell groups, right from their first interest in Christianity. Indeed many of these home groups are evangelistic in focus. In one group I learned that they regularly pray for families living in the same blocks of flats as church members, especially if they are ill. They also call on these families and tell them they are being prayed for. When those prayed for recover they often

come to the cell group to express their thanks. This frequently leads to them coming regularly and being converted. In Yoido Full Gospel Church there are 50,000 such home groups meeting every week! And the church has procedures in place for welcoming 11,000 new members a month!

The Presbyterian Church in Indonesia has also played a significant role in Presbyterianism, accounting as it does for 12% of Presbyterians worldwide, or one in every eight. Its foundation was in the work of Dutch missionaries to their former colony. Its early vitality, like the Korean church's, was seen through the courage of Christians interrogated, tortured or killed by their Japanese captors during the Second World War. Its subsequent growth, across some 35 denominations, has been due to its continuing evangelism, especially successful in some parts of that diverse nation.

5. The *integrity* of Indonesian Christians has been particularly important. The National Monument, with its 13 kilogram solid gold flame ornament at the top, stands in the centre of the capital Jakarta. From its top you get a magnificent view of the largest mosque in Asia (which is next to Jakarta Cathedral, minute by comparison), which was built by a Christian architect because the Muslims wanted someone they could trust 'to build a thoroughly well-designed functional building.'

FIGURE 5.11
The largest Mosque in Asia: Jakarta, Indonesia

So what does all this mean?

Presbyterianism is an expression of the Christian faith which has spread worldwide, and today is especially strong in Asia. It has grown over 50 years, both where it is weak (in South America) and where it is strong (in South Korea and Africa).

However, it has not kept pace either with Christendom or with the world's population in North America, and has declined in Europe mainly because of its fall in the Netherlands.

Its phenomenal growth in Korea, and to a lesser extent in Indonesia, are important as examples for major institutional growth. It is suggested that this growth has come about through having:

- A high profile focus and commitment to prayer
- Clear vision
- A large amount of mission activity as witnessed numerically by the numbers of Korean missionaries sent overseas
- Major evangelistic events within Korea strengthened by good retention procedures of converts
- Publicly affirmed integrity of Christian people, both through their behaviour during wartime and since.

NOTES

1. *Orthodox News,* London, UK, Volume 10, Number 5, 1996, Page 2.
2. *Forbidden Revolutions*, Professor David Martin, SPCK, London, UK, 1996, Page 34.
3. 'The Sunday Review', *Independent on Sunday*, London, UK, 4th January 1998, Page 10.
4. Ibid.
5. Article on 'Luther, Martin' in *The New International Dictionary of the Christian Church*, edited by J D Douglas, Paternoster Press, then of Exeter, Devon, UK, 1974, Page 609.
6. *Christianity in Europe*, MARC Monograph Number 22, 1989, MARC Europe, London, UK, Pages 45 and 47.
7. *The Lutherans in Australia*, Maurice E Schild and Dr Philip J Hughes, Australian Government Publishing Service, Canberra, Australia, 1996, Page 23.
8. Ibid, page 41.
9. Ibid, page 37.
10. *Eurostat Yearbook '95,* Brussels, Belgium, available from The Stationery Office.
11. *Strukturbedingungen der Kirche anf längere sicht*, [Long-term structural requirements for the church], EKD, Germany, 1985.
12. Op cit (Item 5), article on 'Presbyterianism', Page 800.
13. A brief description of this event may be found in the leading article 'A Church for Every People' in *Quadrant,* Christian Research, London, UK, July 1995, Page 1.

14. See, for example, *The Fourth Dimension*, by Dr Paul [he has since changed his name to David] Yonggi Cho, Church Growth international, Seoul, Korea, 1979.
15. Ibid, Page 4.
16. *Too Valuable to Lose*, Exploring the Causes and Cures of Missionary Attrition, edited by Dr William Taylor, William Carey Library, Pasadena, California, USA, 1997, Page 94.

6

THE CHARISMATIC CHURCHES: PENTECOSTAL AND INDIGENOUS

The *World Churches Handbook* has two denominational groups which are entirely or largely charismatic: Pentecostals, and Indigenous Churches. This chapter looks at these two groups.

What does being Charismatic mean?

This question is being answered in statistical not theological terms! But the evidence to be given in this chapter suggests that Charismatics:

- Are part of a growing global network. They have seen much more rapid growth than other denomination, especially in the 1980s. It is likely to continue in the 1990s, and then slow down a little in the first decade of the 21st century.

- Expect, not want, to see God at work in their churches. They see Jesus literally healing people's bodies and souls.

- Community is very important for them. They are therefore more likely to be autonomous and independent. Whilst they do have some worldwide denominations, many are associated with single congregations functioning individually.

- Their churches are on average the smallest in the world, but they keep starting new ones! Attendance may well be higher than formal membership, however.

- Their leaders are frequently visionary evangelists, who get the people in. They may lose them again, but to this we return in a later chapter.

THE PENTECOSTAL CHURCHES

Very rapid growth

The Pentecostal Churches are a 20th Century phenomenon. The Pentecostal community was 1% of the world's Christendom in 1960 but will have grown to 8% by the year 2010 if present trends continue. This phenomenal growth is unprecedented for any other group in worldwide Christianity. It is an increase from 12 million people in 1960 to over 150 million by 2010, a rapid and meteoric growth.

Many denominations

The Pentecostals are several separate denominations with similar theology which are grouped together under the name 'Pentecostal'. Their origins date to the early twentieth century (1901 in Kansas, United States, and 1906 in Azusa Street, Los Angeles[1]) and they have since spread across the world. The main denominations are the Assemblies of God in at least 121 countries, the Church of God of Prophecy in at least 72, the Church of God (Cleveland) in at least 71, the Apostolic Church in at least 43 countries, the Church of God (Anderson) in at least 32, the Elim Pentecostal in at least 18 countries, and so on. Even these groups are not

122 FUTURE CHURCH

always just one denomination: thus there is an Apostolic Church but there is also the Apostolic Faith Church, the Apostolic Christian Church, the Apostolic Church of Faith in Christ Jesus, the Apostolic Church of Pentecost, etc.

There are thousands of small Pentecostal denominations worldwide: the main ones, together with their Community in 1995 are as follows, listed in order of their size rather than geographical spread:

TABLE 6.1
The main Pentecostal denominations in 1995

Name	Number of countries	1995 Community	Largest individual country with community
Assemblies of God	121	22,140,000	Brazil: 13.0 million USA: 2.5 million Zimbabwe: 0.8 million
Universal Church of the Kingdom of God	1	7,000,000	Brazil: 7.0 million
Church of God in Christ	7	6,052,000	USA: 6.0 million
Christian Church	6	3,576,000	Brazil: 3.4 million
God is Love	2	3,230,000	Brazil: 3.2 million
Brazil for Christ	1	2,550,000	Brazil: 2.6 million
Apostolic Church	43	2,620,000	Nigeria: 1.0 million South Africa: 0.6m
Church of God (Cleveland)	71	2,289,000	USA: 1.1 million India: 0.2 million
Christ Apostolic Church	3	1,474,000	Nigeria: 1.4 million
Church of God Mission International	2	1,223,000	Nigeria: 1.2 million
Nigeria Christian Fellowship	1	1,040,000	Nigeria: 1.0 million
Church of God of Prophecy	72	689,000	USA: 144,000 Dominican Rep.: 67,000
Elim Pentecostal	18	683,000	Kenya: 310,000 UK: 100,000 Uganda: 98,000
Deeper Life Church	5	681,000	Nigeria: 660,000
Church of God (Anderson)	32	495,000	USA: 260,000
Church of God	16	458,000	Kenya: 210,000 Mexico: 160,000
Total	—	56,200,000	Brazil: 29.2 million in those listed above

These 16 denominations, or groups of denominations, account for 53% of all the Pentecostals in the world, showing how many other smaller groups there are.

Pentecostalism by Continent

Across the world, the number of Pentecostals has changed as shown in Table 6.2. The final line is the percentage of the 2010 figure.

TABLE 6.2
The growth of the Pentecostal Community by continent 1960–2010

Year	Africa	Europe	Oceania	North America	Asia	South America	World
1960	100	100	100	100	100	100	100
1970	264	156	272	145	248	275	203
1980	516	217	501	257	461	587	385
1990	1001	307	919	478	741	1233	729
2000	1205	327	1295	646	1029	1739	1003
2010	1814	383	1665	773	1280	2259	1262
1960	1.7m	1.1m	0.1m	5.3m	1.4m	2.6m	12.2m
2010	31.4m	4.3m	1.1m	40.9m	17.6m	58.2m	153.6m
% of total	20%	3%	1%	27%	11%	38%	100%

FIGURE 6.1
Proportions of Pentecostal Community by continent 2010

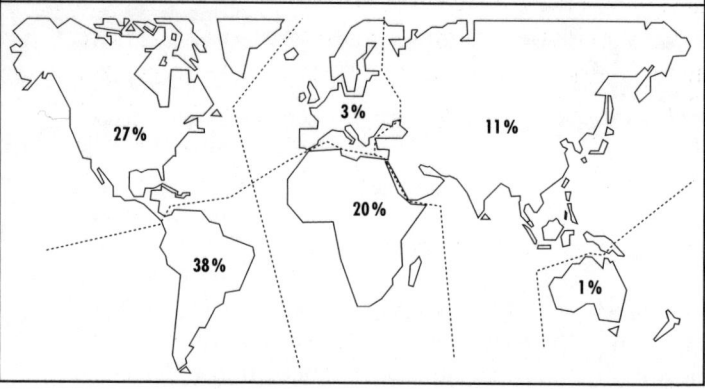

- 27%
- 3%
- 11%
- 20%
- 38%
- 1%

FIGURE 6.2
Growth of Pentecostal Community by continent 1960–2010

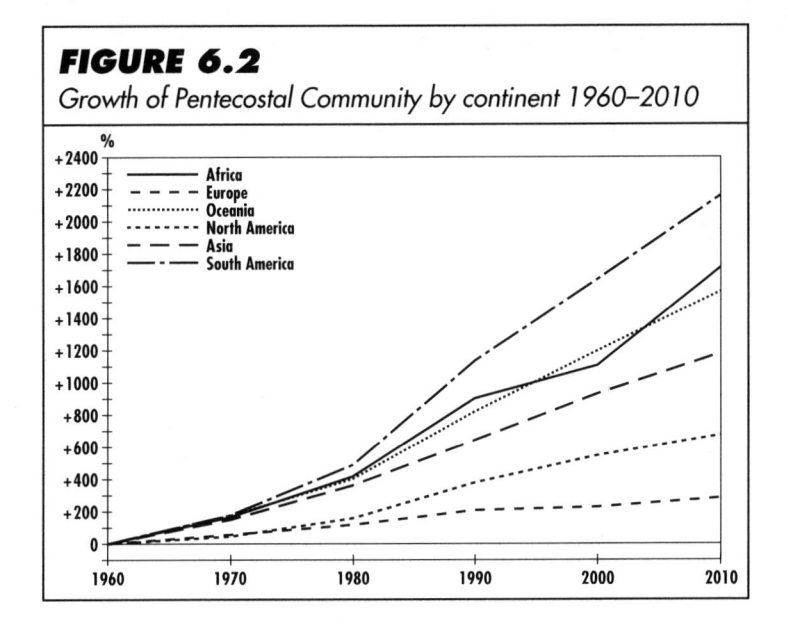

By any kind of reasoning, the growth depicted above is extraordinary. To grow from 2.6 million in 1960 in South America to over 58 million 50 years later is a story of God's amazing grace in a nutshell. No wonder the institutional churches, especially in this case the Roman Catholic Church, have found the Pentecostal churches so hard to cope with!

It is fascinating that the biggest jump in numbers occurred across *every* continent in the 1980s. The main reason world Christianity had its revival in the 1980s was the huge upsurge in the number of Pentecostals around the world. While doubtless some moved from other, often the institutional, churches, this kind of growth could only be because literally millions of outside people were drawn in. 42 million Pentecostals in those 10 years joined the existing 46 million at the start of that decade. Certainly not in recent history, and maybe never since the first century, have proportionally so many joined a church in so short a period in so many continents.

Europe and Oceania

European Pentecostals lag behind. Not only are their numbers small, but growth is patchy. The country with the largest Pentecostal community in Europe is the United Kingdom, with 749,000 in 1995, as Table 6.3 shows, with the six other major European countries:

TABLE 6.3
Pentecostals in Europe in 1995

Country	Community
United Kingdom	749,000
Ukraine	731,000
Italy	410,000
Romania	361,000
France	222,000
Spain	210,000
Germany	195,000

These 7 countries account for 86% of Europe's Pentecostals. Scandinavian countries are noticeably absent. It is interesting that three countries with a strong Roman Catholic presence (Italy, France and Spain) and two with a strong Orthodox Community (Ukraine and Romania) are among the top seven Pentecostal countries in Europe. Germany also has a strong Catholic Community but an equally strong Lutheran Community. Is this suggesting that institutional churches frustrate some believers who find a totally different, freer kind of worship much more acceptable?

In the United Kingdom Pentecostals are the fastest growing church in proportion to their size. In the year 1992/93 their numbers increased by 7.1%, almost three times faster than the next denomination, the Baptists at 2.6%[2]. It was also true that they lost people the fastest, but at a rate of 2.4% there was still a considerable margin of growth, and by far the biggest margin of all denominations.

The other continent with few Pentecostals is Oceania. Papua New Guinea with 352,000 in 1995 and Australia with 222,000 account for 76% of all in this area.

Africa and Asia

In both these continents, Pentecostal growth has exceeded total world Pentecostal growth, only just in Asia but much greater in Africa. In Asia 4 countries account for 89% of all Pentecostals, given in Table 6.4, and in Africa 7 countries account for 83%, given in Table 6.5:

TABLE 6.4
Pentecostals in Asia in 1995

Country	Community
Indonesia	5.7 million
India	2.4 million
Philippines	1.7 million
Korea	1.3 million

TABLE 6.5
Pentecostals in Africa in 1995

Country	Community
Nigeria	6.7 million
Zaïre	3.5 million
South Africa	2.8 million
Kenya	1.5 million
Zimbabwe	1.1 million
Ghana	1.0 million
Ethiopia	0.7 million

North and South America

Pentecostals have grown in North (and Central) America, but at a much slower rate than anywhere else outside Europe. They are dominated by just 4 countries which together cover 88% of the Pentecostal community, given in Table 6.6, and by one country, the United States, which alone accounts for 77%:

TABLE 6.6
Pentecostals in North America in 1995

Country	Community
United States	23.2 million
Guatemala	1.4 million
Mexico	1.1 million
El Salvador	0.8 million

It is in South America that the Pentecostal phenomena has been greatest in the 50 years 1960 to 2010. The majority of this growth is seen in Brazil, whose 31.0 million Pentecostals account for 81% of all the Pentecostals in South America. The next largest country is Argentina, with 1.8 million, accounting for a further 5%.

The above analysis by continent and country shows that half (51%) of the *world's* Pentecostals live in just two countries – Brazil and the United States. Add in the next largest five countries – Nigeria (6.7 million), Indonesia (5.7 million), Zaïre (3.5 million), South Africa (2.8 million) and India (2.4 million) – and you find 7 countries accounting for nearly three-quarters (71%) of the world's Pentecostals.

Churches

These figures relate to the Pentecostal *community*. In membership terms, only 46% actually belong to a church, but, judging by UK experience, actual attendance usually well exceeds formal membership[3]. Their churches also are the smallest – an average membership of 100, compared say to an Anglican membership of 130, Presbyterian of 200, Orthodox of 1,000 or Lutheran of 500. Indigenous churches have an average membership of 150, and Baptists of 200, Methodists of 150, and Other Churches combined of 110. One reason for the smallness of Pentecostal churches is their philosophy of continually planting new churches.

It is worth repeating a comparison of Presbyterian and Pentecostal themes[4], which perhaps helps to explain some of the differences between institutional Christianity and Pentecostalism, drawn up by a Presbyterian missionary in Taiwan in the 1960s, Don McCall:

TABLE 6.7
Presbyterianism versus Pentecostalism

Theme	Presbyterian	Pentecostal
God	Wholly other	Near, immanent
Holy Spirit	Fruit of Spirit	Power, baptism
Church	Covenant people	Incendiary people
Worship	Order, quiet, awe	Spontaneous, ecstasy
Doctrine	Cognitive, confessions	Experience orientated
Ethics	Personal and social	Personal; little social
Supernatural	Miracles possible	Miracles expected
Satan	Affirmed, not emphasized	Active; powerful
Revelation	Scripture; Christ event	Same but new truth
Evangelism	Some do – mostly pastors	All involved

So what does all this mean?

It is surprising perhaps that so few countries account for so much Pentecostalism. It makes the Pentecostal movement very vulnerable to movements in those countries, especially Brazil and the United States. That these two countries with such different cultures, the one with many denominations and a free-for-all air, the other with a dominance of the Roman Catholic tradition which celebrated 500 years in 1992 from the first discoveries of Columbus, should see major growth is of itself interesting.

In Brazil 19% of the population in 1995 was Pentecostal, one person in five; in the United States the proportion was half that at 9%, or one person in 11. It means that Pentecostalism is not strictly a South American phenomenon, but a Brazilian one. It is not that other countries do not have Pentecostals, but that Brazilian Pentecostalism dominates them. It actually grew faster there in the 1980s than in South America as a whole, from 11.6 million in 1980 to more than double to 25.3 million by 1990.

The obvious question is, 'Why?' David Martin, former Professor of Sociology at the London School of Economics suggests[5] that it is due to the breakdown of the religious and social fabric which were woven together as one in South America. Tracing this desire for 'free space' back to European Calvinism, he sees evangelical Christianity pouring 'in and by its own autonomous native power creat[ing] free social space.' 'Evangelicals constitute a *movement*. . . . Pentecostalism in particular [provides] an atmosphere of hope and anticipation rather than despair.' He goes on to say that even if people leave (which we consider in Chapter 9), 'they still carry the imprint of . . . these concepts and these models with them.' He looks at the Catholic response in the development of Liberation Theology, which is 'a major rival to Pentecostalism, . . . [but] is not so successful a competitor as might be expected.' This, he thinks, is because it is largely led by middle-class men speaking for the poor, and the poor, whilst interested, are largely not wanting to fight more battles, as it were.[6]

1. What, then do the Pentecostals stress especially? I visited Brazil in 1991, and had the opportunity of speaking to a number of pastors. The Pentecostal churches were of course known for their emphasis on speaking in tongues, and the use of other gifts of the Spirit. I found, however, an equally strong emphasis on the *gift of healing*. With no National Health Service, and with medical fees and hospital costs beyond the range of many poor people, where did they go when they experienced pain, or were ill, or had an accident? The answer in many cases was the nearest Pentecostal Church, or rather its pastor. They wanted him/her to pray for them, and as a result many were healed.

    I spoke to one pastor[7] who prayed for a man whose right leg had been badly twisted in an accident and which had needed a steel implant to help straighten it. But it continued to cause him much pain, and he eventually went to the pastor who touched his leg, praying that it might heal and be restored to its former strength. It was, and he then returned to the hospital for the steel implant to be removed – he gave it to the pastor as a token of his thanks!

2. Another reason is the *involvement* of Pentecostals. There are many slums and shanty towns in Brazil, and especially in its major cities of Rio, Belo Horizonte and São Paulo. In many of these desperate groups the only church is a Pentecostal Church. When people need someone to turn to there is the church in their midst, sharing their poverty, miserable buildings, lack of electricity, and all the rest.

The Christian message is literally incarnated in front of them, and incarnation brings visibility, the opportunity to share, and the challenge to join and follow.

3. They are also *independent*. There are few mainline Pentecostal denominations, and even where they exist, central control is minimal. Local churches therefore have the opportunity to adapt to local circumstances, and to start their own branch of a church if they so wish. This is not a master plan being worked out by strategic planners in ivory towers at a denominational headquarters, but pragmatic local church development according to the personality of the individual leader. This approach has its obvious dangers in doctrine (many pastors are untrained), and can allow some to become egocentric (the desire for bigger, better buildings is an obvious danger). But it has many advantages in freedom, fun, and flexibility. Above all it facilitates fast growth.

4. This last comment makes me consider a dimension about which I have no information at all. Are Pentecostal elders more likely to have the *gift of leadership*? The only study that I know on this topic is based on English Pentecostals, who may be untypical of those in South America. For what it is worth, however, this study[8] showed that Pentecostals were particularly strong in two areas, compared with other denominations: the leadership style of their leaders was more likely to be Director (rather than Shaper[9]), and they tended to have more Task people in their teams – people whose prime satisfaction comes from completing something, like building a new church, or sharing the gospel, or organising home groups, or whatever. If universally true, it is easily seen how these could help build spectacular growth. Setting goals, and meeting them, are exactly the standards their leadership profiles yearn for!

THE INDIGENOUS CHURCHES

Who are they?

The smallest 'denominational' grouping in the *World Churches Handbook* is called 'Indigenous Churches'. Doctrinally the large majority of them are indistinguishable from Pentecostal churches. Why then keep them separate? Simply because they *are* different. Denominations are to be found in more than one country. Indigenous churches, however, are mostly confined to one country, and often indeed to one group of people within a country. They are local churches in that they belong to one linguistic, cultural or socio-economic group living in a particular area. While they may plant more than one church, they do not usually become a denomination in the sense of having a hierarchy outside the individual congregation. Often they will have been started by a missionary, who may or may not still be with them. Many have been formed by division from other groups. The name 'indigenous' is not perhaps the most appropriate, and none are designated for the continent of Europe (when it could be argued that the majority are indigenous – it's where Christianity expanded from!).

Professor Oosthuizen's list of indigenous South African congregations among the black people are virtually all Zionist related. They had many fascinating names, which were expanded by the addition of an extra word. Thus you might have the Church of the Cherubim, the Church of the Cherubim International, the Beulah Church of the Cherubim, the Worldwide Cherubim Church, and so on, each of which is only one congregation. Each would have their own distinctive clothing for their leaders, and in each the colouring would signify something. Thus I once watched a group of women dancing. A woman dressed in red danced inside two circles of women dressed in green to symbolise their cleansing by the blood of the Lamb. Red meant blood, green faithfulness, blue love and white purity.

Worldwide, groups like this numbered 7 million in 1960, and, if present trends continue, will grow to 49 million by the year 2010. By then some 70% of the indigenous community will be in Africa. A seven-fold increase is very great, but is still only just over half the growth rate of the Pentecostals!

Indigenous churches by continent

Whilst this growth has taken place across all continents (except Europe), it has been seen especially in Africa and in Asia. Details are in the following Table.

TABLE 6.8
The growth of Indigenous churches by continent 1960–2010

Year	Africa	Asia	Oceania	North America	South America	World
1960	100	100	100	100	100	100
1070	176	188	168	120	117	177
1980	284	332	189	159	131	289
1990	419	555	238	188	173	438
2000	524	766	276	220	196	561
2010	629	1015	317	251	223	692
1960	5.4m	1.4m	0.1m	0.2m	0.0m	7.1m
2010	34.2m	14.0m	0.2m	0.4m	0.1m	48.9m
% of total	70%	29%	0%	1%	0%	100%

THE CHARISMATIC CHURCHES 135

FIGURE 6.3
Proportions of Indigenous Community by continent 2010

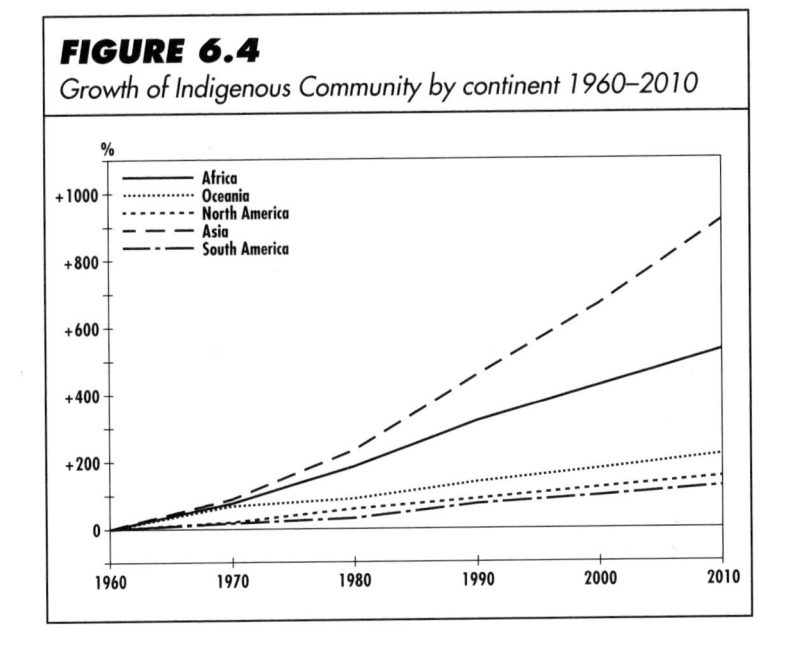

- North America: 1%
- Europe: 0%
- Asia: 29%
- Africa: 70%
- South America: 0%
- Oceania: 0%

FIGURE 6.4
Growth of Indigenous Community by continent 1960–2010

- Africa
- Oceania
- North America
- Asia
- South America

Americas and Asia

Only 1% of Indigenous churches are in the American continents or Oceania. However, they are not a totally African phenomenon, because over a quarter (29%) are in Asia. These experienced growth especially in the 1980s, which is likely to continue in the 1990s and first decade of the 21st century. Of the Asian community 96% were in 3 countries in 1995 – the Philippines with 5.4 million, China with 2.7 million, and India with 500,000. These churches have been formed quite independently and with a totally different ethos from the African churches. All probably relate to specific people groups.

In the Philippines there is an immense archipelago of islands less than 200 miles from the capital Manila on which live a huge variety of tribal peoples, many of whom are still quite under-developed. The island of Mindoro for example has many tribes which are 'simple, peace-loving forest-dwellers, clinging to life through an expert knowledge of jungle law'[10], and it was to these that British missionary Caroline Stickley for example went in the late 1950s to see a church planted amongst the Tadyawan tribes people in the 1960s and 1970s. In the two decades since many of these and other tribes have come to Christ.

Indigenous churches in Africa

Nine countries account for 87% of the Indigenous Churches in Africa:

TABLE 6.9
Indigenous community in Africa in 1995

Country	Community
Nigeria	7.5 million
Zaïre	5.9 million
Kenya	2.3 million
Ghana	1.6 million
Zimbabwe	1.5 million
Malawi	1.1 million
South Africa	1.1 million
Côte d'Ivoire	0.8 million
Zambia	0.5 million

Professor Oosthuizen was well placed to see their growth: by 1994 he had counted over 6,000 such groups of these African Independent Churches (AIC).

They range theologically from evangelical to syncretistic; some groups mix Christian beliefs with ancestor worship and other animistic practices. Almost uniformly, however, a Christian sense of sharing and caring is their distinguishing mark. Many congregations gather in houses, shacks, shelters made from wooden boxes, or in open spaces in the cities and towns. Here the spirit of the traditional extended family finds expression in an ecclesiastical context, along with the basic aspects of traditional culture and religion. The venue is not important so long as there is fellowship, spontaneity in worship, mutual discussion of problems, healing services that provide spiritual and physical refreshment, and empowerment rituals that deal with malevolent social and spiritual forces.[11]

He distinguishes three types of church amongst these 6,000:

- *Ethiopian*, which had reacted in the past to ecclesiastical colonialism, but now the smallest group
- *Zionist*, resulting from contacts with the Christian Catholic Church in Zion City, Illinois, USA, the word 'Zion' appearing in 80% of the names of the AIC churches
- *Apostolic* following the Pentecostal Christianity exemplified by the Azusa Street Mission.

The AIC churches give individual assistance 'on the basis of mutuality within the extended family' which is totally different from the committees of the institutional churches which often do not function well. The AIC focus on 'the sense of community and mutuality.'[12] For immigrants coming from rural areas to informal urban settlements around major cities, their 'money-saving clubs, small businesses, and skills training have much to offer prospective congregants.'[13] The AIC stand for ethnic reconciliation and harmony, and 'demonstrate the power of worship and community life that is existential and holistic.'[14] The consequence of this ethic is powerful, and likely to ensure that these indigenous churches continue for many years yet. It's a question of watching this space!

So what does all this mean?

Indigenous churches are the quintessence of a local church – usually for a local people who will have their own distinctive customs, and traditions, and perhaps language and doctrines. They are growing strongly in Africa and Asia, but are less often found elsewhere in the world. They are Pentecostal in background, and form a special but distinctive addition to the many other Pentecostals in the world.

NOTES

1. Article 'Pentecostal Churches' in *The New International Dictionary of the Christian Church*, edited by J D Douglas, Paternoster Press, then Exeter, Devon, UK, 1974, Page 763.
2. Introductory article, *UK Christian Handbook* 1996/97, edited by Peter Brierley and Heather Wraight, Christian Research, London, UK, 1995, Page 27.
3. See for example the results of the English Church Census in 1989 which suggested attendance could be 40% higher than membership, given in *Prospects for the Nineties*, MARC Europe, London, UK, 1991, Page 36.
4. Quoted from *Pentecost in the Hills in Taiwan*, by Ralph Covell, Hope Publishing Hose, Pasadena, California, USA, 1998, Page 277.
5. *Forbidden Revolutions* by Professor David Martin, SPCK, London, UK, 1996, and his longer earlier book *Tongues of Fire*, The Explosion of Protestantism in Latin America, Basil Blackwell, Oxford, UK, 1990.
6. Ibid (*Tongues of Fire*), Pages 272, 278, 280, 284, 290.
7. Pastor of the Brazilian Central Baptist Church in July 1991.
8. Of members of the Christian Research Association in 1997, and reported in the January 1998 issue of *Quadrant*, Christian Research, London.
9. This terminology comes from *Management Teams*, by Meredith Belbin, Butterworth/Heinemann, London, UK, 1981 but reprinted virtually every year since. Directors and Shapers are both identified as having a prime gift of leadership, though they use it in different ways. Directors are more people orientated and think through *how* a job might be undertaken; Shapers tend to be more achievement or task orientated and consider *why* something must be completed.
10. From the Foreword by A J Broomhall to *Broken Snare*, by Caroline Stickley, OMF Books, London, UK, 1975, Page 8.
11. 'Indigenous Christianity and the Future of the Church in South Africa', by Professor G C Oosthuizen, *International Bulletin of Missionary Research*, New Haven, Connecticut, USA, January 1997, Page 8.
12. Ibid., Page 9.
13. Ibid, Page 10.
14. Ibid, Page 12.

7
THE NON-CHARISMATIC CHURCHES: BAPTIST, METHODIST AND OTHER CHURCHES

In labelling these three denominational groups as 'Non-Charismatic' I do not mean that they have no charismatic churches amongst their number. Far from it! It is simply that the official stance of these denominations is not specifically charismatic, even though in many cases charismatic church life, with all that that means, is welcomed by them. An alternative heading would have been 'The Other Non-Institutional Churches' but that seems even more clumsy than the above, if strictly more accurate!

THE BAPTIST CHURCHES

'The soil out of which the modern Baptist movement arose was that of 17th century English Separatism. . . . in 1612, a small group under Thomas Helwys [formed] the first Baptist church on English spoil, at Spitalfields. They were General (or Arminian) Baptists. The first Particular (or Calvinist) Baptist church came into being between 1633 and 1638. . . . The first Baptist church in mainland Europe was established in Hamburg in 1834 by J G Oncken. . . . Worship is largely nonliturgical, with emphasis on the reading and preaching of the Word.'[1]

A substantial number

In 1995 there were 67 million Baptist people in the world, which is no mean figure! In 1960 they numbered 36 million, and, if present trends continue, will have over 80 million by the year 2010, thus more than doubling in these 50 years. This growth rate is substantial, and is just a little faster than the rate at which Christendom as a whole is growing worldwide (1.6% per annum to 1.4%; the Pentecostal rate is 5.2%!). In 1960 the Baptists were 4% of Christendom, a percentage they should have maintained by 2010; only the Presbyterians kept the same percentage; every other denomination has grown or declined.

Baptists by Continent

The number of Baptists has changed as shown below:

TABLE 7.1
The growth of the Baptist Community by continent 1960–2010

Year	Africa	Europe	Oceania	North America	Asia	South America	World
1960	100	100	100	100	100	100	100
1970	239	107	132	107	152	184	114
1980	533	119	160	127	214	309	145
1990	793	153	211	140	319	486	174
2000	986	163	246	153	427	621	198
2010	1186	182	287	167	508	766	223
1960	1.0m	1.8m	0.2m	30.6m	2.0m	0.5m	36.1m
2010	11.7m	3.3m	0.5m	51.1m	10.3m	3.7m	80.6m
% of total	14%	4%	1%	63%	13%	5%	100%

FIGURE 7.1
Proportion of Baptist Community by continent 2010

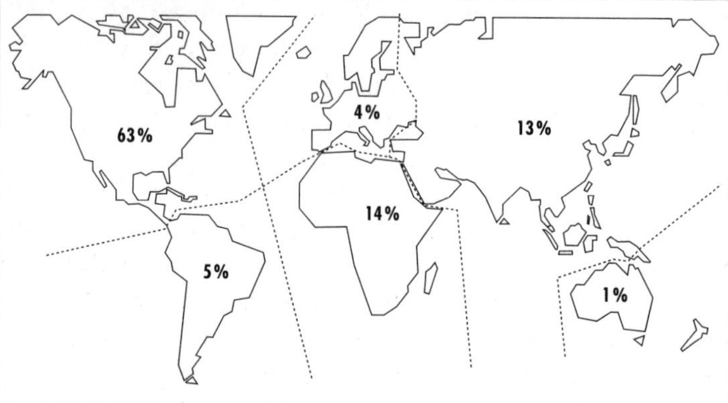

- North America: 63%
- Europe: 4%
- Asia: 13%
- Africa: 14%
- South America: 5%
- Oceania: 1%

FIGURE 7.2
Growth of Baptist Community by continent 1960–2010

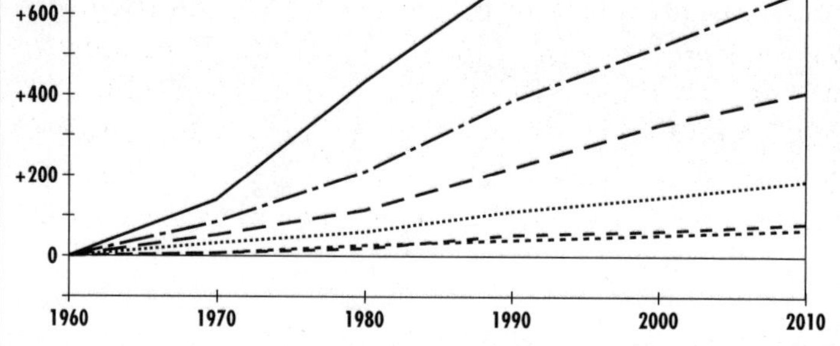

Legend:
- Africa
- Europe
- Oceania
- North America
- Asia
- South America

Baptists have grown very fast in Africa, South America and Asia since 1960 – essentially the Third World continents. They have lagged behind in the Western world, however. The much larger numbers in North America mean that in 2010, five out of every 8 Baptists in the world will be located there.

Although Baptist growth has been significant in Africa, Asia and South America, it has not happened at the same time. The main advance in Africa was in the 1970s, though there was also significant growth in the 1980s. In South America it came primarily in the 1980s, with a significant continuing rapid growth in the 1990s. In Asia there was great growth in the 1980s, but the largest growth anticipated is in the 1990s. It almost reads as if the Baptist growth in Africa sparked the growth in South America which then lit the fire in Asia!

South America

In South America 2.1 million of the country's 2.6 million Baptists in 1995 were in Brazil (81%). There are two Conventions in Brazil – the Baptist Convention with 1.6 million and the National Baptist Convention with 0.4 million. Why do the Baptist churches grow in Brazil? Doubtless for many reasons, but from personal observation, it is because many of the churches care for the suffering. As in the early church, it is not only 'by public witnessing and evangelism or by praying for the lost that the Church grew so rapidly. Rather, it was by their steadfastness in persecution, by seeing people set free from (their) bondages, by seeing their compassionate care for the unwanted and discarded that their witness was most powerful. People became believers because they looked at the lifestyle of Christians, saw how different they were and would then make enquiries.'[2]

Africa

Three-fifths (59%) of the Baptists in Africa are found in three countries: in 1995 there were 2.3 million in Ethiopia,

1.5 million in Zaïre and 1.4 million in Nigeria. Two groups in Zaïre are particularly strong – the River Baptists and the West Baptists, which together account for three-quarters (77%) of the country's Baptists. However, in both Nigeria and Ethiopia the growth is entirely due to two dominant Baptist denominations – the Baptist Convention in Nigeria (97% of all Baptists) and the Kale Heywet Baptist Church in Ethiopia (96% of total).

Asia

In Asia, the largest Baptist country is India with 3.3 million in 1995, which has grown out of William Carey's pioneering missionary work two centuries earlier. The cobbler who reached India in 1792 left a tremendous legacy, recognised by the Indian Government in 1992, his bicentenary, when they issued a stamp in his honour, despite being a largely Hindu country.

The largest Baptist denominations in India are the Council of Baptist Churches of North East India (1.7 million in 1995), the Samavesam of Telugu Baptist Church (0.8 million) and the Baptist Convention in North Circars (0.4 million). The next largest Baptist community in Asia is Myanmar with 1.6 million, followed by South Korea, the Philippines and Russia with 0.7 million each. These five countries account for 89% of Asia's Baptists. In Myanmar, the Myanmar Baptist Convention has 96% of the country's Baptists.

Oceania

In the 50 years from 1960 to 2010 Baptists nearly tripled in Oceania but did not even double in either Europe or North America. Over half (55%) of Oceania's 412,000 Baptists in 1995 were in Australia. Substantial growth in the 1960s was partly due to the Missouri/Australian Crusade in 1964 when 160 Americans arrived for simultaneous crusades in many

Baptist churches. 'While the Billy Graham Crusades in 1959 and 1968 were not exclusively Baptist, the Baptists played a significant role in their organisation and support.'[3] Baptists are especially common in the Northern Territory of Australia, constituting at least 4% of the total population almost throughout the Territory.[4]

Europe

In Europe the largest Baptist country is the Ukraine with 730,000 Baptists in 1995, followed by the United Kingdom with 460,000 and Germany with 330,000. These 3 countries account for 56% of the continent's 2.7 million Baptists.

Baptists in North America

It is in the United States where Baptists dominate. 96% of North America's Baptists are in the USA, where there are many Baptist denominations. The largest (52% of the total) is the Southern Baptist Convention with its 22.5 million adherents, equivalent to 9% or 1 in 11 of the entire population. The Southern Baptists are expanding much faster than the other Baptists in the United States. Between 1960 and 2010 they should increase by 96%, whereas all the others together increase only 39%. The Southern Baptist growth is probably partly fostered by their external emphasis on world mission and internal emphasis on evangelism.

After the Southern Baptists the next three largest groups are the National Baptist Convention of USA (with 8.3 million adherents in 1995, 19% of the total), the rather confusingly named National Baptist Convention of America (with 3.7 million, or 9% of the total), and the American Baptist Churches (with 2.3 million or 5% of the total). These four big Conventions thus account for 85% of the United States' Baptists.

There are other Baptist groups which on the whole are

achieving growth. The Baptist Missionary Association aims to increase from 210,000 to 360,000 over these 50 years, the American Baptist Association from 650,000 to 760,000, the General Association of General Baptists from 90,000 to 104,000, the General Association of Registered Baptists from 200,000 to 245,000, and the Progressive National Baptist Convention from 620,000 to 740,000. All these names start to get confusing!

Not all the Baptist Churches in the USA are growing. The American Baptist Churches is forecast to lose 200,000 of its community between 1960 and 2010. The National Association of Free Will Baptists likewise is expected to lose 40% of its 400,000 strong community (in 1960) by 2010. Likewise the Conservative Baptist Association is dropping from 490,000 in 1960 to 200,000 by 2010, a decline of 60%. The smaller Baptist Church of the Brethren with 280,000 in 1960 is likely to have only 163,000 by 2010, a drop of 40%.

So what does all this mean?

Baptist churches around the world are in fact dominated by the Southern Baptist Convention with 34% of the Baptist community worldwide under its wing in 1995, and by the fact that it is growing quite steadily (1.4% a year). Of every 3 Baptists in the world, 1 is a North American Southern Baptist, 1 is another North American and 1 lives elsewhere in the world.

Or, put it another way: 1 person in 6 in North America is Baptist against 1 in 220 in all the other countries put together. Does the Baptist culture of independence help shape American independence, or does the American independent way of life form a natural fertile soil for Baptistic people?

Baptist churches likewise cannot overlook the fast growth of Baptist churches in the Third World, at 4.1% a year. They may be much smaller but they are growing much faster. Of the 7 largest Baptist Conventions with at least a million adherents, the top 4 are in the USA, but the other 3 are in the Third World, as Table 7.2 shows:

TABLE 7.2
The largest Baptist Conventions in 1995

Convention	Country	Community
Southern Baptist	United States	22.5 million
National Baptist of USA	United States	8.3 million
National Baptist of America	United States	3.7 million
American Baptist Churches	United States	2.3 million
Baptist Churches of North East	India	1.7 million
Myanmar Baptist	Myanmar	1.6 million
Nigeria Baptist	Nigeria	1.3 million

These 7 Conventions account for 5 in every 8 (62%) of the world's Baptists in 1995.

THE METHODIST CHURCHES

Methodism is a 'movement which originated in a search for an effective method to lead Christians toward the goal of scriptural holiness.'[5] John Wesley applied the epithet in his definition in 1729: 'A Methodist is one who lives according to the method laid down in the Bible.' Strictly 'Methodism' refers only to the adherents of Wesley, 'although it is extended to include the followers of (George) N Whitefield and Lady Huntingdon who subscribed to the doctrines of Calvin rather than Arminius.'[6]

Overall numbers

The Methodist Churches are the smallest denomination separately grouped in the *World Churches Handbook*. Smaller denominations are all gathered together as 'Other Churches'. In 1960 the Methodists had a 23 million worldwide community, 3% of the world's Christendom. If present trends continue, they will number 27 million by 2010, but will then be just 1% of Christendom. Their growth rate is very low – 0.3% a year averaged over our 50-year period, compared with 1.4% for Christendom as a whole.

The Methodist community by continent

Methodism is not growing universally: it has declined in the Western world, but grown in the Third World, as the figures below indicate.

TABLE 7.3
Changes to the Methodist Community by continent 1960–2010

Year	Africa	Europe	Oceania	North America	Asia	South America	World
1960	100	100	100	100	100	100	100
1970	133	85	104	94	136	132	101
1980	165	83	31	89	173	175	100
1990	222	80	36	85	231	196	107
2000	275	77	36	83	247	236	114
2010	317	73	38	81	260	270	118
1960	2.9m	2.0m	1.3m	15.6m	1.2m	0.2m	23.2m
2010	9.1m	1.5m	0.5m	12.6m	3.2m	0.5m	27.4m
% of total	33%	5%	2%	46%	12%	2%	100%

FIGURE 7.3

Proportion of Methodist Community by continent 2010

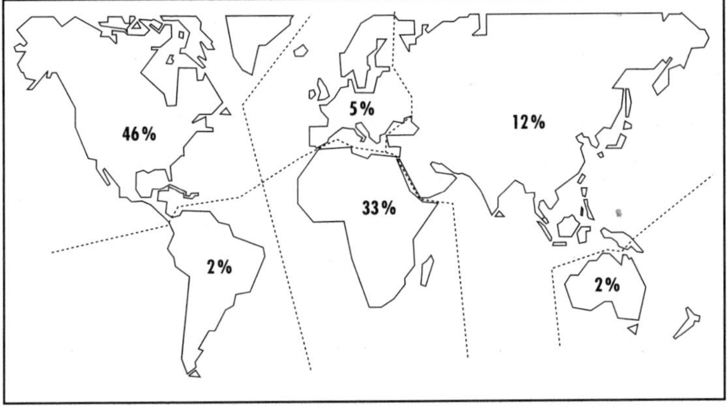
46%
5%
12%
33%
2%
2%

FIGURE 7.4

Change in Methodist Community by continent 1960–2010

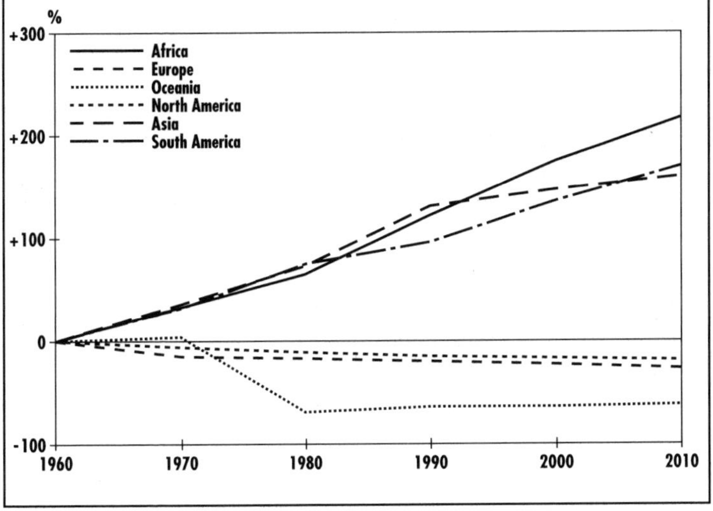
%
+300
+200
+100
0
-100
Africa
Europe
Oceania
North America
Asia
South America
1960
1970
1980
1990
2000
2010

Almost half (46%) the world's Methodists are in North America and a further third (33%) in Africa, which doesn't leave many for the rest of the world!

Europe

By 2010 if present trends continue, only one Methodist in 20 worldwide (5%) will be living in Europe.

Of the 1.6 million Methodists in Europe in 1995 1.3 million (81%) were on the Community Roll of the Methodist Church in Great Britain, which accounts for 95% of the United Kingdom's Methodists. The decline is thus mainly the decline of this church, in many ways the mother church of Methodism! The decline is, however, shared by the other smaller Methodist Churches, except for the Free Methodists, which are very small (2,000 in 1995), but growing.

Africa

Methodism in Africa will have grown three-fold in the 1960 to 2010 period if present trends continue. In 1995 there were 7.0 millions Methodists on the continent, the top 5 countries accounting for 83% of this total.

TABLE 7.4
The largest Methodist Community Rolls in Africa in 1995

Country	Community	Country	Community
South Africa	2,050,000	Kenya	220,000
Nigeria	2,000,000	Angola	180,000
Zaïre	870,000	Côte d'Ivoire	160,000
Ghana	430,000	Sierra Leone	160,000
Zimbabwe	350,000		

Asia

In Asia the key Methodist countries are South Korea and India where there were 1.2 million and 0.8 million Methodists respectively in 1995. Add in the 0.5 million in the Philippines, and you have 78% of Asia's Methodists in 3 countries. The largest Methodist Church in the world is in Seoul, Korea, and has 74,000 members. Bishop Dr Kim began the Kwang Lim Methodist Church in 1972. I have a souvenir mug to prove I was once there, but it is big, like the church, in fact the biggest mug I possess!

South America

In South America in 1995 there were 380,000 Methodists. Two-thirds (66%) of these were in Brazil, with 250,000. The four next largest countries were Argentina with 40,000, Peru with 26,000, Chile with 24,000 and Bolivia with 17,000, adding a further 28% to the total Methodist Community in this continent. The largest branch of the Wesleyan Methodist Church is in Brazil (116,000), though it exists in at least 6 other countries, mostly in the Third World, with a worldwide total of just under 180,000 in 1995.

North America

Virtually all (97%) of North America's 13.1 million Methodists are in the United States, where they exist in at least 10 different denominations. The largest is the United Methodist Church which had 8.5 million on its Community Roll in 1995.

The next largest is the African Methodist Episcopal Church, which had 1.9 million on its roll. This Church exists in some 23 countries around the world, with a total Roll of 2,240,000 but in spite of its name, only 350,000 are outside the United States (the biggest countries being Nigeria with 116,000 and Zambia with 92,000).

The next largest is the African Methodist Episcopal Zion Church, *not* to be confused with the previous church, with 1.3 million in the United States. This, too, is a worldwide church, albeit mostly in the Third World in 10 countries outside the USA. It totals 1.6 million worldwide, the largest countries beyond the United States being South Africa with 92,000, Nigeria with 85,000, Ghana with 72,000 and Jamaica with 26,000.

Methodists in Oceania

There were very few Methodists in Oceania in 1995. The reason is that in June 1977 the Uniting Church of Australia was formed from the Methodist, Presbyterian and Congregational Churches. Unlike the Presbyterian and Congregational Churches, the Methodist had no 'continuing body', that is, a rump of people who did not wish to join the Uniting Church, and formed their own residual denomination instead.

In 1975 there were 980,000 Methodists, 960,000 Presbyterians and 78,000 Congregationalists. The Continuing Presbyterian Church in 1980 had 150,000 people and the Continuing Congregational Fellowship 4,000. Thus the Uniting Church might have expected something like 2,018,000 adherents initially, minus the 154,000 continuants, or a total of 1,864,000. Since the first set of figures are for 1975 and the second set are for 1980 there will never be an exact match because of death, emigration, etc. However, the Uniting Church in 1980 only had 550,000 members, some 1,314,000 short![7]

Some will have joined other churches altogether, but the total Church Community in Australia fell from 10,400,000 in 1975 to 9,500,000 in 1980 according to figures in the quinquennial national population census. So in these five years the Church Community fell by 900,000 people! Almost certainly what happened is that the vast majority of Methodists did not wish to join the new Uniting Church, and did not wish to join any other church either. As the Methodist Church no longer existed a great many of them gave no answer to the 'What is your religion?' question in the census! The figures in Table 7.3 record a unique state of affairs!

A similar, local, phenomenon occurred in Britain in the 1970s and 1980s. The Methodist Church in Cornwall has always been very strong – in 1979 48% of churchgoers there were Methodist[8]. At the same time the Methodist Church in Great Britain had embarked on a policy of closing small churches which were not viable, 'a wholesale closure of chapels' as it has been described[9]. Many of these were in Cornwall. Closing a Church in one village should have meant those members travelling to the next village to go to Church. But they did not do this; instead preferring to leave church altogether! So the 1989 English Church Census recorded a 14% drop in the number of Methodists[10].

So what does all this mean?

Methodism is struggling in its First World context. If present trends continue the numbers of Methodists in the Third World will exceed the First World total by 2020, and will more than double the numbers 20 years after that. What is causing its decline in the West, and its rapid growth in Africa especially?

While official worldwide totals put the number of Methodists in 1996 at 33 million[11], this will include those, like the Australian Methodists who have in effect opted out of the Church, and others 'of whom the church is unaware' as David Barrett described the Anglicans. Notwithstanding, it has links in 108 countries of the world, and when the World Methodist Council next meets in Brighton, England in July 2001 it will have much to discuss. Not least perhaps the results of the conversations about rejoining the Church of England, if the Methodist Conference in June 1998 agrees to go ahead, as the Anglicans have already done.[12]

OTHER CHURCHES

Who are they?

Eight major groups were identified when processing the many denominations for the *World Churches Handbook*: the five institutional churches (Anglican, Catholic, Lutheran, Orthodox and Presbyterian) and three non-institutional (Baptists, Methodists and Pentecostals). This left a host of smaller denominations. Those which tended not to form denominations or move outside their own country were grouped into the Indigenous Churches, but this still leaves many smaller denominations which often are global in coverage. These have collectively been grouped into 'Other Churches'.

The denominations included in this category are some which are truly global churches but which are smaller than the ones treated already. These smaller churches include, for example, the Christian Brethren, present in nearly 100 countries, or the Seventh-day Adventists, active in 170 countries. Others in the 'Other Denominations' category consist of churches special to a particular country but which do not fit into any of the other groups. So, for example, the Church of North India, a million strong in 1995, or the even larger Church of South India are put as 'Other Churches' under India. The very large majority of churches in 'Other Churches' are of this latter type as there are myriads of denominations in the world and most of them are small and particular to just one or two countries. David Barrett estimates there are 25,000 denominations in the world[13] – perhaps fewer than 1,000 of them, other than the major denominations already considered, are global in that they have branches in say 10 or more countries.

Other Churches community by continent

How are the Other Churches spread across the globe and how fast are they growing?

TABLE 7.5
Growth of Other Churches Community by continent 1960–2010

Year	Africa	Europe	Oceania	North America	Asia	South America	World
1960	100	100	100	100	100	100	100
1970	213	100	136	94	149	196	124
1980	354	93	224	98	490	286	210
1990	564	96	212	107	991	508	339
2000	726	95	215	116	1393	621	441
2010	894	97	226	127	1778	753	542
1960	4.8m	3.9m	0.9m	19.3m	6.6m	1.0m	36.5m
2010	43.0m	3.8m	2.1m	24.5m	116.8m	7.8m	198.0m
% of total	22%	2%	1%	12%	59%	4%	100%

FIGURE 7.5
Proportion of Other Churches Community by continent 2010

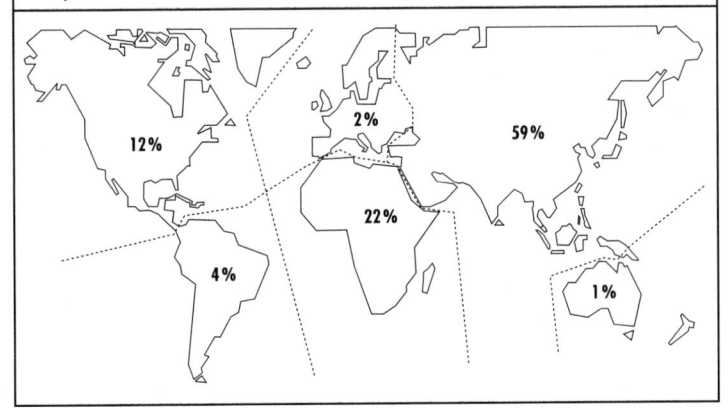

- North America: 12%
- Europe: 2%
- Asia: 59%
- Africa: 22%
- South America: 4%
- Oceania: 1%

FIGURE 7.6

Growth of Other Churches Community by continent 1960–2010

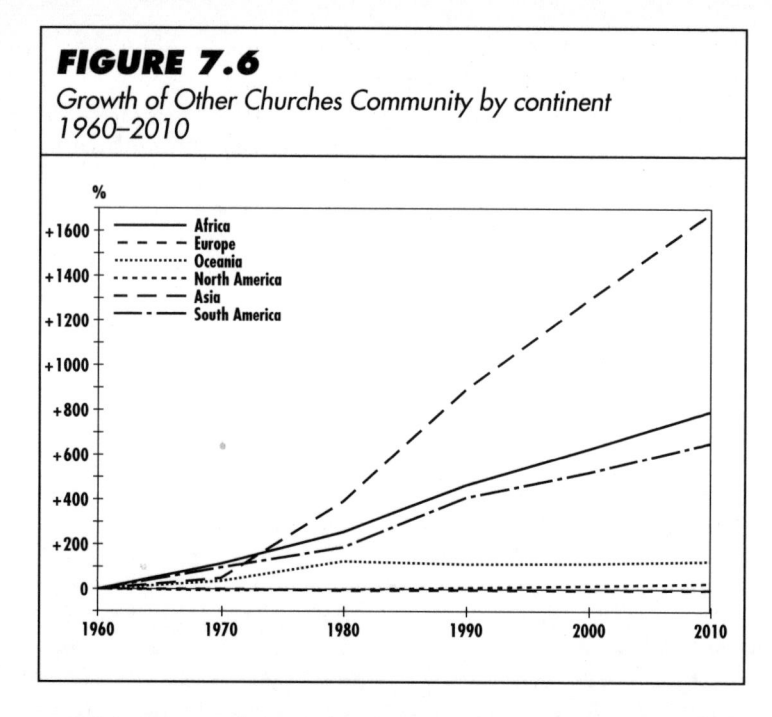

Table 7.5 certainly shows the rapid increase in these Other Churches. The huge growth in Asia is entirely due to the rapid increase in Home Meetings in China, estimated as 240,000 in 1995 with a community of 55 million people. Take this one group out of the numbers, and Asia's figures are then respectively for 1960 to 2010: 100, 141, 208, 360, 451 and 542, that is, a slower rate of growth than in South America or Africa!

The unevenness in some of the changes (for example, Europe goes down, then up, then down and then up again) simply reflects the variations of particular denominations in that continent. The sudden jump between 1970 and 1980 in Oceania, for instance, reflects the formation of the Uniting Church. This is the corollary of the decline in its major merging denominations (Methodist and Presbyterian).

It is clear that the major growth of the smaller denominations are in South America and Africa. Many of these denominations are small charismatic churches, growing like their counterparts in the Pentecostal and Indigenous groupings.

Eight denominations which should have a community of at least half a million by the year 2010 and which exist in at least 20 countries were selected for extra analysis:

- The Christian & Missionary Alliance
- Christian Brethren
- Church of the Nazarene
- Churches of Christ (Instrumental and Non-Instrumental being combined for this purpose)
- Moravians
- The Mennonite groups taken together
- Salvation Army
- Seventh-day Adventists.

To these eight were added the Religious Society of Friends which is in over 20 countries but has a community of less than half a million.

Some worthy other groups get left out. For example, the Disciples of Christ are likely to be 1.8 million strong in 2010 if present trends continue, and are in at least 12 countries. But 93% of their number are in just 2 countries – the United States where they are likely to have 770,000 people (a huge drop from 2.2 million in 1960) and Zaïre where they will have more, 930,000 (a large increase from the 100,000 in 1960). Another such group is the Wesleyan Church and Wesleyan Holiness Church, which are expected to be in at least 28 countries by 2010 with a world community of 470,000, up from 180,000 in 1960.

Nine specific denominations

The total community for these denominations in 1960 and 2010 and the minimum number of countries in which they were represented are given below. They are the minimum because these are simply the number of countries in the *Handbook* which have an entry for a particular denomination. In many cases where this is not known, or the number of people is too small, they will simply be aggregated into a collective 'Other churches' in each country and it is not possible to know which are included in those totals. The final column shows the average percentage increase they experienced *per annum* across this period:

TABLE 7.6
Community in 1960 and 2010 for 9 denominations

Denomination	Minimum countries 1960	2010	Church community 1960	2010	Change per annum
Seventh-day Adventist	144	170	2,036,000	13,467,000	3.9%
Churches of Christ	43	62	5,965,000	7,476,000	0.5%
Christian Brethren	88	98	800,000	3,034,000	2.7%
Salvation Army	63	66	1,422,000	2,613,000	1.2%
Church of the Nazarene	50	90	823,000	2,286,000	2.1%
Mennonites (all groups)	31	45	539,000	1,531,000	2.1%
Christian & Missionary Alliance	26	41	224,000	1,357,000	3.7%
Moravian Churches	21	21	317,000	587,000	1.2%
Religious Society of Friends	23	25	281,000	326,000	0.3%

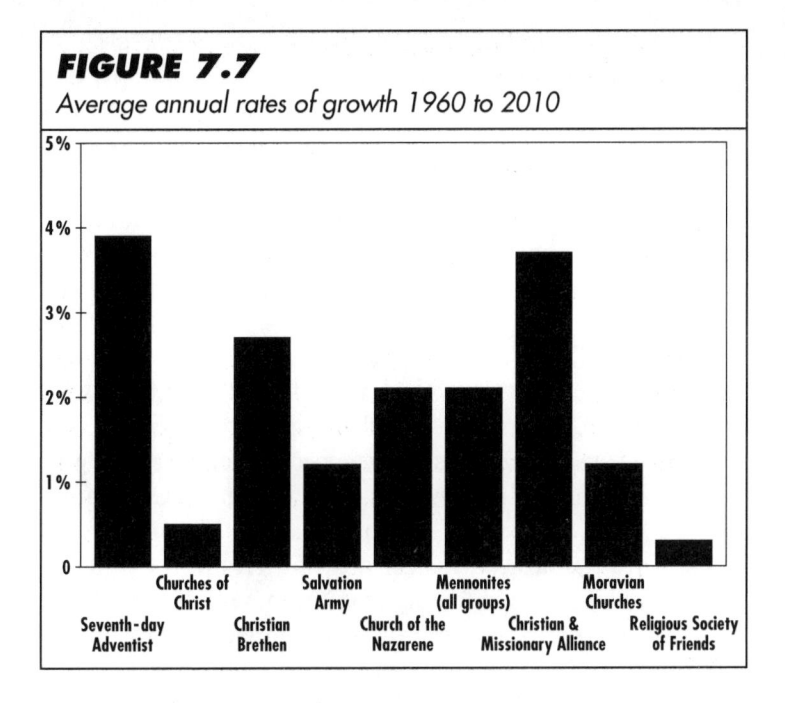

FIGURE 7.7
Average annual rates of growth 1960 to 2010

[Bar chart showing growth rates for: Seventh-day Adventist (~3.9%), Churches of Christ (~0.5%), Christian Brethen (~2.7%), Salvation Army (~1.2%), Church of the Nazarene (~2.1%), Mennonites (all groups) (~2.1%), Christian & Missionary Alliance (~3.7%), Moravian Churches (~1.2%), Religious Society of Friends (~0.3%)]

The fastest growing churches are the Seventh-day Adventists and the Christian and Missionary Alliance (C & MA). Both achieved this growth partly by moving into new countries. Perhaps this strategy is the denominational equivalent of church planting within a country such as the Pentecostals follow with such success! The Adventists especially have opened in more countries in Africa, the C & MA in South America and Europe.

Given that overall the 'Other Churches' category grow at only 3.4% a year, and that is with the Chinese Home Meetings included, the growth of these two denominations is remarkable. However they do not match the growth of the Home Meetings by themselves – 10.1% annually. Without the Home Meetings the Other Churches grow at just 2.3%, still faster than world Christendom at 1.4%.

The group growing third fastest are the Christian Brethren. The numbers above include 84,000 and 101,000 respectively for the Exclusive Brethren, but these numbers are almost certainly too low, because they are extremely difficult to get and are missing for many countries in the *Handbook*. Take them out, however, and the Open Christian Brethren (as they are often called) grow at 2.9% per annum.

Seventh-day Adventists

A church that grew from the work of William Miller who died in 1849, being organised as a church in 1863 in Michigan, USA. Adventists have specific beliefs relating to the second coming, observe the Sabbath day, teach tithing, and follow strict food and health codes.[14]

They are the largest, fastest growing group in the above Table. How they are changing is given in Table 7.7, with the 'Change per annum' column showing the average percentage growth in the community by continent 1960 to 2010:

TABLE 7.7
Seventh-day Adventist Community strength by continent 2010

Continent	Community in 2010	Change per annum	Largest countries in 2010
Africa	5,077,000	4.9%	Zaïre 0.9m, Ghana 0.6m, Tanzania 0.4m, Zimbabwe 0.4m, Kenya 0.4m
S America	3,066,000	5.6%	Brazil 1.4m, Peru 0.7m
N America	2,405,000	2.5%	USA 1.4m, Mexico 0.8m
Asia	1,945,000	4.5%	Philippines 0.8m, India 0.4m, Indonesia 0.3m
Europe	580,000	1.1%	Romania 0.2m, Ukraine 0.1m
Oceania	394,000	2.3%	Papua New Guinea 0.2m, Australia 0.1m
Total	13,467,000	3.9%	Brazil, USA, Zaïre, Philippines

FIGURE 7.8
Where the Seventh-day Adventists are strongest

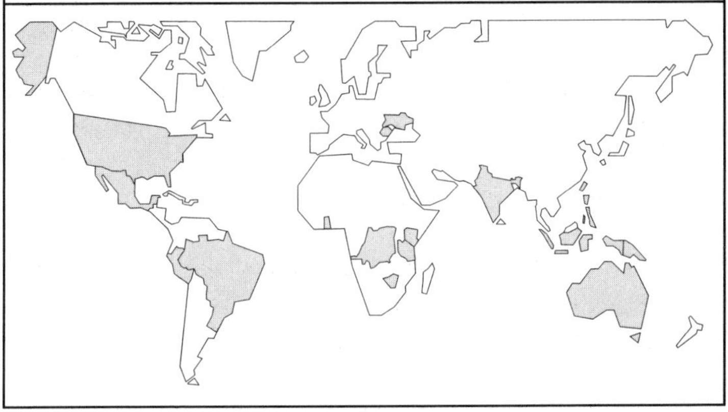

As with other denominations, it is the Third World churches which are growing fastest. It is true also that it is the black Adventist churches in the UK that grow the fastest. How can whites catch the black spirit?!

Christian & Missionary Alliance

This church was begun in 1881 in North America by A B Simpson, and was first called such in 1887. Its early emphasis on sanctification as a crisis-experience 'has been muted' partly by the Calvinistic, Wesleyan, Baptist and pre-millennial groups which have joined it[15].

The C & MA have a definite mission policy built into their basic church policies, so that it is mandatory for C & MA churches to be mission minded. Perhaps that is what has helped it to send so many missionaries overseas, and to work in so many countries.

TABLE 7.8
C & MA Community strength by continent 2010

Continent	Community in 2010	Change per annum	Largest countries in 2010
N America	534,000	2.8%	USA 370,000, Canada 110,000
Africa	350,000	4.4%	Zaïre 160,000, Burkino Faso 70,000, Gabon 62,000
Asia	254,000	4.2%	Philippines 170,000, China 48,000
S America	208,000	4.8%	Peru 65,000, Ecuador 46,000, Colombia 40,000, Chile 32,000
Oceania	7,000	3.7%	Australia 6,800
Europe	4,000	8.6%	Netherlands 2,000, Spain 800
Total	1,357,000	3.7%	USA, Philippines, Zaïre

It is quite remarkable how similar this Table is to the one for the Adventists, especially with very similar largest countries. However, because of their policy of moving into more countries in Europe and Oceania they are becoming less of a Third World denomination in relation to the fastest rates of growth.

FIGURE 7.9
Where the C & MA is strongest

The Christian Brethren

Originally named the Plymouth Brethren because their first church was in this Devonian town in southwest England in 1831. 'The movement was a protest against the prevailing conditions of spiritual deadness, formalism, and sectarianism marking the early years of the 19th century. . . . The meetings were marked by deep devotion to Christ, zeal for evangelism, and a strong leaning toward prophetic studies.'[16]

Today, the Brethren are composed of a number of groups of which the Open or Christian Brethren is the largest. It is their figures which are mostly identified in the *World Churches Handbook*. However, the second largest group worldwide is the Reunited Brethren, who are particularly strong in Europe, Egypt, Zaïre, India, South America and the West Indies[17].

TABLE 7.9
Christian Brethren Community strength by continent 2010

Continent	Community in 2010	Change per annum	Largest countries in 2010
Africa	769,000	6.5%	Chad 370,000, Tanzania 135,000, Zambia 110,000, Zimbabwe 43,000, South Africa 36,000, Nigeria 30,000
N America	606,000	2.7%	USA 250,000, Guatemala 110,000, Honduras 91,000, Canada 93,000
Asia	595,000	3.1%	India 410,000, Pakistan 50,000
Europe	510,000	1.6%	Romania 190,000, UK 153,000, Germany 63,000, Italy 38,000
S America	332,000	2.1%	Argentina 140,000, Brazil 110,000
Oceania	121,000	1.9%	Papua New Guinea 63,000, Australia 36,000, New Zealand 20,000
Total	2,933,000	2.9%	India, Chad, USA, Romania, UK

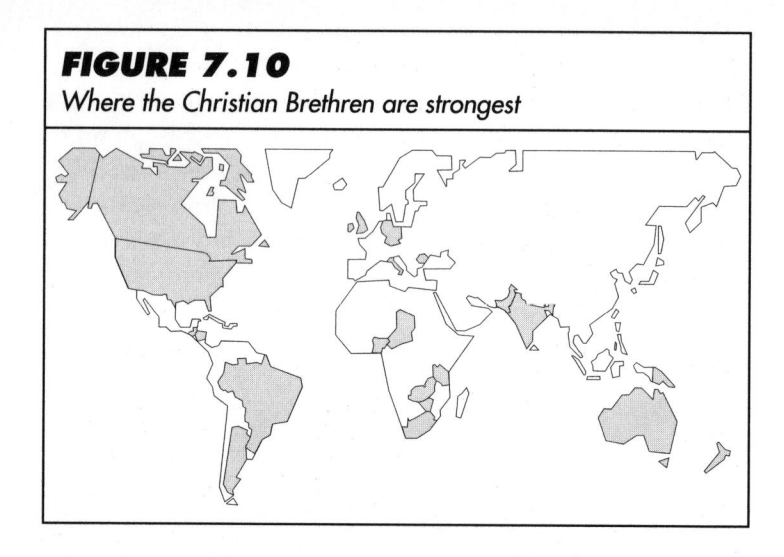

FIGURE 7.10
Where the Christian Brethren are strongest

Africa is becoming increasingly important for the Brethren movement because that is the part of the world where it is growing fastest. Of the five largest Brethren countries in 2010, only two are projected to be in Europe, where the movement began almost two centuries earlier.

The Churches of Christ

The first known church was at Dungannon, Ireland in 1804, and they were organised as a group since 1842. In the United States a similar movement started in 1832 at Lexington, Kentucky, following very closely the doctrinal beliefs of the Disciples of Christ which began in 1811. They follow a congregational pattern of church polity and seek 'to align all church practice and belief with the Scriptures.'[18] They are not to be confused with the Churches of Christ, Scientist.

There are various groupings within the Churches of Christ, and, like others, these are all collated into one here. They are collectively a large group, but with changing fortunes as can be seen from these figures:

TABLE 7.10
The Churches of Christ Community strength by continent 2010

Continent	Community in 2010	Change per annum	Largest countries in 2010
N America	3,804,000	−0.7%	USA 3.6m, Canada 38,000
Africa	2,618,000	4.8%	Nigeria 1.8m, Zimbabwe 220,000, Zambia 200,000, Malawi 160,000, South Africa 135,000
Asia	737,000	3.6%	India 390,000, Philippines 150,000, Myanmar 140,000
Oceania	193,000	1.4%	Australia 100,000
S America	98,000	6.1%	Brazil 70,000
Europe	26,000	0.2%	UK 11,000, Italy 5,000, Spain 3,000
Total	7,476,000	3.7%	USA, Nigeria, India, Zimbabwe

FIGURE 7.11
Where the Churches of Christ are strongest

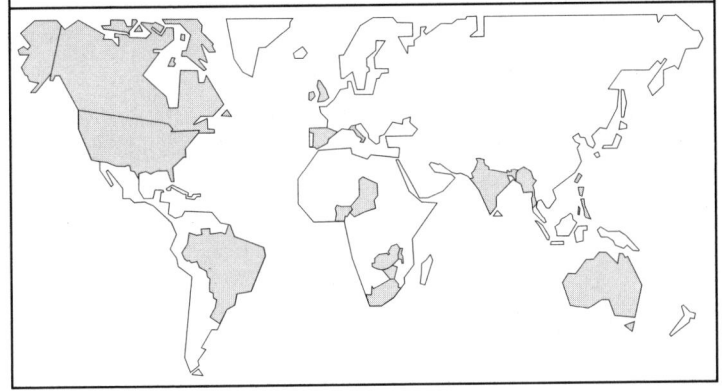

The Churches of Christ have a severe problem. With almost three-quarters (72%) of their community in two countries – the United States and Nigeria – their overall trends are very vulnerable to what happens in them. In Nigeria, as with many parts of Africa, they are growing strongly. But in the United States they are declining: in 1960 there were 5.4 million, which will have shrunk by a third by 2010. In 1960 the Non-Instrumental Churches of Christ were some 3.4 million strong, and the Instrumentals 2.0 million. In 2010 the latter will be about 1.8 million, showing that the Non-Instrumentalists have declined much faster.

Other Churches

Where are the other churches strongest? These are given in the final Table in this chapter:

TABLE 7.11
Community strength by continent 2010

Denomination	Community	Largest countries in 2010
Salvation Army	2,613,000	USA 600,000, India 280,000, Angola 160,000, Korea 140,000, Zimbabwe 130,000, Nigeria 120,000
Church of the Nazarene	2,286,000	USA 1.2m, South Africa 220,000, Haiti 180,000, Peru 71,000, Korea 62,000, Dominican Republic 60,000, Guatemala 59,000, Nigeria 43,000
Mennonites	1,531,000	Zaïre 410,000, India 330,000, USA 260,000, Canada 230,000, Paraguay 83,000, Germany 50,000, Tanzania 31,000, Netherlands 25,000
Moravaians	587,000	Tanzania 286,000, South Africa 89,000 USA 67,000, Suriname 36,000, Germany 29,000, Honduras 17,000, Nicaragua 15,000
Religious Society of Friends	326,000	Kenya 110,000, USA 80,000, Bolivia 33,000, Guatemala 25,000, UK 23,000, Burundi 14,000, Peru 12,000

So what does all this mean?

There are thousands of denominations with tens of thousands of churches spread all over the world. A few denominations span the globe, but most are specific to a country or two. Some are quite large with a community in the millions, others are in the thousands, and others in the hundreds. Some of the larger ones are focused especially on just a few countries.

Some denominations are growing very fast, sometimes because they are starting in new countries, and others are spreading out locally by starting new churches. Many of the latter are charismatic, but not all. In some continents, especially Africa and South America, these new 'plants' are in particularly fertile soil and therefore seem to grow more quickly. Growth in Europe seems hard judging by the experience of both large and small denominations. Perhaps it is time for more new autonomous congregations!

NOTES

1. Article on 'Baptists' in *The New International Dictionary of the Christian Church*, edited by J G Douglas, Paternoster Press, then of Exeter, Devon, UK, 1974, Page 102.
2. Article 'Learning to live and minister in a post-Christendom world' in *DAWN Report*, Colorado Springs, USA, by Lynn Green (Europe, Middle East and Asia Director with Youth With A Mission), Issue No 33, February 1998, Page 7.
3. *The Baptists in Australia*, Dr Philip J Hughes, Australian Government Printing Service, Canberra, 1996, Page 17.
4. Ibid, map showing location of Baptists, Figure 3, Page 41.
5. Op cit (Item 1), article on 'Methodism', Page 652.
6. Ibid, Page 653.
7. A fuller description of the Uniting Church may be found in *The Uniting Church in Australia*, by Peter Bentley and Rev Dr Philip J Hughes, Australian Government Publishing Service, Canberra, Australia, 1996.
8. Results of the 1979 English Church Census, *Prospects for the Eighties*,

Bible Society, London, UK, for the Nationwide Initiative in Evangelism, 1980, Page 56.
9. *1851 Religious Census: West Cornwall and the Isles of Scilly*, Transcribed and edited by J C C Probert, Redruth, Cormwall, UK, 1997, Page 4.
10. *Prospects for the Nineties*, Results of the 1989 English Church Census, MARC Europe, London, UK, 1991, Page 392.
11. News item in *Christianity*, Herald House, Worthing, West Sussex, UK, March 1998, Page 6.
12. Ibid.
13. *World Christian Encyclopedia,* Rev Dr David Barrett, Oxford University Press, Oxford, UK, 1982.
14. Op cit (Item 1), article on 'Seventh-day Adventists', Page 899.
15. Op cit (Item 1), article on 'Christian and Missionary Alliance', Page 220.
16. Op cit (Item 1), article on 'Plymouth Brethren', Page 789.
17. For details of the composition of the Reunited Brethren see Footnote 7 for Table 9.4.4 in *UKCH: Religious Trends* No 1, 1998/99, edited by Dr Peter Brierley, Christian Research, London, and Paternoster Publishing, Carlisle, UK, 1997, Page 9.4.
18. Op cit (Item 1), article on 'Churches of Christ (Great Britain)' and 'Churches of Christ (USA)', Page 227.

8
NOMINALISM AND ITS CONSEQUENCES

So far in this book we have looked at the Christian Community, and in the early chapters, compared it with the overall world population. The one is of course part of the other and may be expressed as in this diagram, where the outer square represents the world population, and the circle, as indicated, the Christian Community.

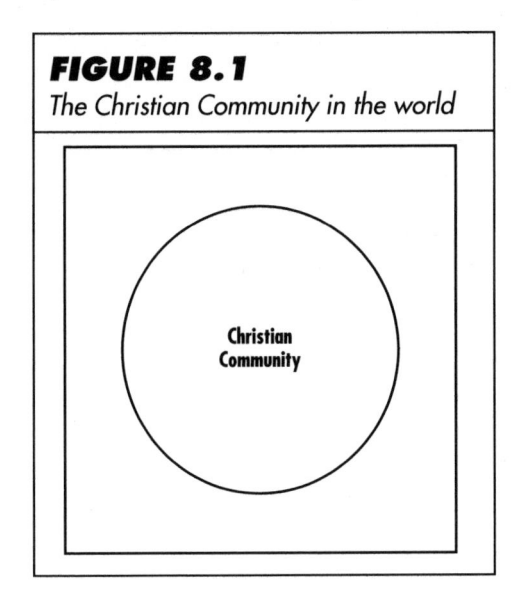

FIGURE 8.1
The Christian Community in the world

Christian Community

But this presentation is too simplistic. There are other concerns. The *World Churches Handbook* gives details of church membership as well as community for each denomination. These have not been analysed in detail primarily because Patrick Johnstone has collected for the different churches their community figure. Membership is in many cases simply a mathematical derivation of that (70% or 60% or 50% etc as is appropriate). An analysis of membership would thus only replicate the findings of the community analysis.

Nominal Christians

There is, however, one more important thing we can do with the figures. In 1995 the world's Christian community stood at 1,615 million people. Membership was estimated at 909 million. Whatever membership may mean, and its strict definition varies with each denomination, that still leaves 706 million people deemed to be part of the Christian community who are not church members. Some may be attending church regularly but who do not wish, or do not wish yet, to become church members. That percentage is likely to be small – in the UK, for example, in 1990 that percentage was just 1%[1] of the entire population. If (and that is a big if!) the same percentage applied universally in 1995, that would still leave of the order of 650 million people who are neither church members nor attending church regularly but who are part of the Christian Community. What do we call such people? The usual name for this category is 'nominal'.

The categories in the previous paragraph may be expressed diagrammatically as:

FIGURE 8.2
Types of religious affiliation

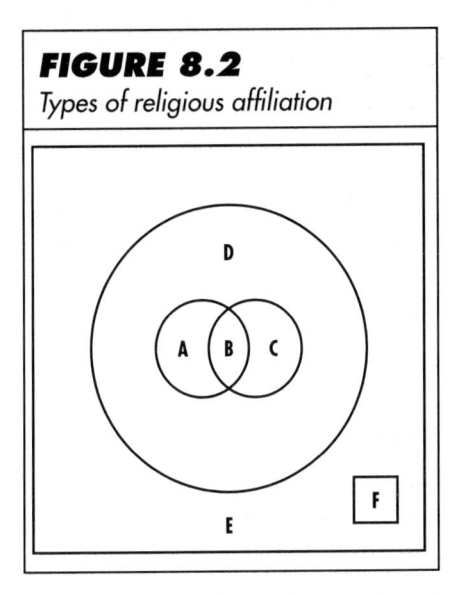

- 'A' = Church attenders who are not church members
- 'B' = Church attenders who are church members
- 'C' = Church members who are not, or not now, regular church attenders
- 'D' = Nominal Christians as defined above
- 'E' = Those who belong to no religious faith
- 'F' = Members of other religions

European nominalism

The figures for all these categories are not available except for 11 countries[2] covering 53% of the population of Western Europe (the largest countries omitted were Italy and Germany)[3]. Inserting the numbers for 1980 and 1990 gives the following:

FIGURE 8.3
Religious composition of 11 European countries 1980 & 1990

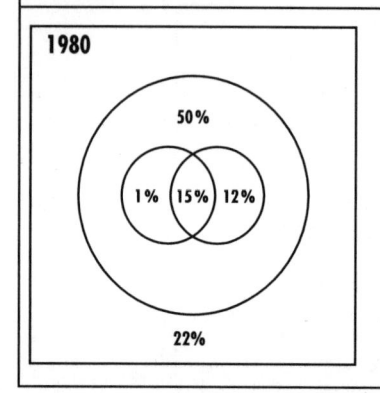

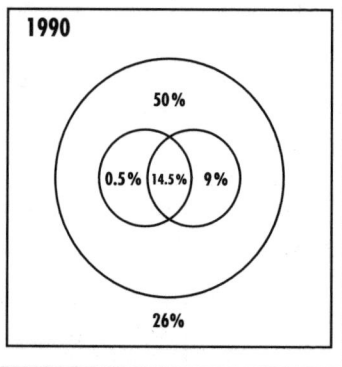

1980
- 50%
- 1% | 15% | 12%
- 22%

1990
- 50%
- 0.5% | 14.5% | 9%
- 26%

This shows that the biggest change across these countries in the 1980s was a decrease in the number of members who did not attend regularly. Perhaps they were ill, or were elderly and were 'promoted to glory' as the Salvation Army say, or lived in rural or other areas where there was no transport. I have sometimes called these 'nominal' Christians and those in Area D (50% in Figure 8.3) 'notional' Christians. By this definition, what happened in Europe in the 1980s was a decline in the number of nominal Christians, that is, as they died off they were not replaced by younger nominal people. It could therefore be argued that this was a good trend!

Worldwide nominalism

The data is not available for an equivalent diagram for world Christianity. This is because:

- Attendance information is not widely available. It is unsafe to extrapolate from the few countries for which it is available to a global figure.

NOMINALISM AND ITS CONSEQUENCES 173

- Even if we did have attendance information, we do not have the overlap of how many *members* attend, which is the crucial 'B' statistic. Without this number we cannot work out the 'C' or the 'A' figures.

We do have the overall figure ('A' + 'B' + 'C' + 'D'), and we do have the total membership figure ('B' + 'C'). It is also possible to get the 'F' figure. This last comes from David Barrett[4] who gives a percentage for the world's other religions as 43%. Thus the best we can construct on the lines used above is:

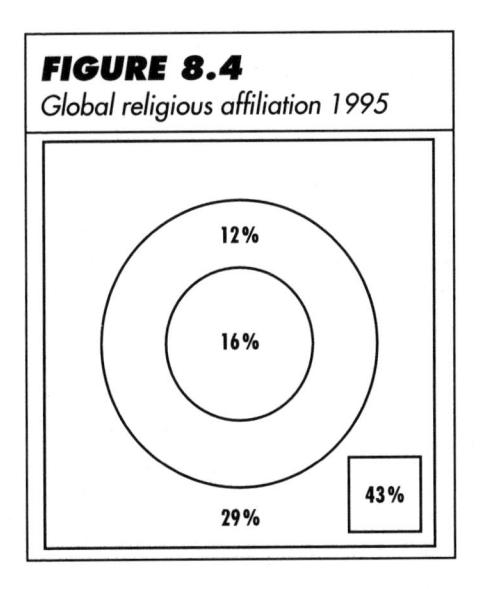

FIGURE 8.4
Global religious affiliation 1995

12%

16%

29%

43%

This shows us:

- Church members account for 16% of the world's population.

- Nominal (or notional) Christians are 12% of the world's population.

- 43% of the world's population belong to religions other than Christianity.

- 29% of the world's population have no religious affiliation, or are officially 'atheists' because they live in a Communist country like China.

It would be quite wrong to suggest that there are no nominal Christians among the 16% who are already church members. Quite the contrary! But we have no means of estimating how many there might be. What we do know is that *at least* 12% of the world's population are nominal Christians. In the UK only about half (47%) of church members actually attended church in 1980, although the percentage had increased to 64% by 1990[5]. If we take from this a rough average of, say, 60% of members who are involved with church, then clearly 40% aren't. Assuming this might apply to the world church, then 40% of the world's 16% of members is a further 6.4%, say 6%, who are nominal. This would mean 10% of the world's population are actively involved with church, and 18% aren't. Whether we take the original 12% (690 million) or the possible 18% (1,030 million) we are clearly talking of a very large number of nominal Christians.

Is it getting better of worse? In his most recent article[6], David Barrett estimates the percentage of the world's population as belonging to other religions as 46% in 1998, with the non-religious decreasing to 26%. In other words, the other religions are gaining some of the non-religious, at the expense of Christianity. The huge number of nominal Christians presumably is not helping Christianity forwards.

What is nominalism? Try the Dictionary!

The Oxford English Dictionary (OED) defines nominalism

as 'existing in name only, not real or actual'. The implication then is that nominal Christians are not real or actual Christians. There are two consequences of such a conclusion:

- We are still describing a static mode. Are nominal Christians in the process of becoming real or actual Christians, that is, are they moving towards something? Or are nominal Christians those who have left an intensity, an involvement, an interest, that is, are they moving away from something? Or, thirdly, are nominal Christians those who have accepted an inadequate or misrepresented form of belief and have no opportunity to move towards something, and are therefore truly static?

- The relationship between belief and behaviour is not apparent. The OED definition probably tends more towards belief than behaviour, but Christian nominalism seems more related to behaviour than belief, even if only defined negatively ('not a regular attender'). The parable of the sower defines the different groups in relation to behaviour, not faith. What nominal Christians might or might not believe is only one part of the equation.

What is nominalism? Try the Bible!

Theologians disagree as to whether Jesus' parable of the sower is 'prescriptive' (saying what will happen when the Gospel is proclaimed) or 'descriptive' (saying what is observed to happen). In either case the four types of soil are not given any kind of quantitative assessment, that is, are the four states equal, or is one group larger than another? The descriptive model suggests that the four modes are fixed; the prescriptive model could suggest that a transition between one type and another might happen.

The parable describes three 'states' – either people are inside the Kingdom, outside it, or somewhere in between. The last tend to degenerate towards those outside because they can't stand the pressure ('when tribulation or persecution arises on account of the word, immediately they fall away.'[7]) or they prefer the alternatives ('the cares of the world, and the delight in riches, and the desire for other things, enter in and choke the word'[8]). In both these cases *other priorities prevailed*. We are seeing exactly the same today certainly in our UK churches. Regular churchgoers, quite apart from occasionally attending members, are attending church less frequently, because they have other priorities on a Sunday than going to church. Are they becoming more nominal as a consequence?

The issue is important. Are nominal Christians a *problem* (something we want to solve or correct) or are they in a *transition* (something that their journey of faith will take them out of in time)?

In some parts of the world second, third and fourth generations of Christians have developed less commitment to the faith, entertain views contrary to the basics of Christianity, and have a lifestyle inconsistent with the teachings of Christ. It may be right to think of nominalism as a problem in these situations. However, even then it is preferable to use less antagonistic language. We are not out to fight nominal Christians but to bring about change, and to win them to a deeper, more relevant, faith.

Even these comments will be interpreted by some as suggesting that change is essential. I believe it is. The New Testament describes the Christian life as one of experiencing forgiveness and a restored relationship with God through faith. Where these fruits are not being evidenced surely we have a duty to encourage their discovery.

What has become clearer since the late 1980s through various research in the Western world is that nominalism is not so much a 'state' (that is, a position which a person permanently holds) than a time of transition, sometimes over many years.

The Centre for the Study of Implicit Religion and Spirituality was inaugurated in Middlesex University in November 1997 with a lecture by its first visiting professor, Rev Canon Dr Edward Bailey. In his address he suggested that implicit religion 'assumes that the religiosity has not been articulated or, perhaps more cogently, has not been understood (or is not conventionally understood) as religious'[9]. Should implicit religion be equated to nominalism? In some senses it should, since both describe something other than full or deep religious or spiritual experience which explicit or non-nominal Christianity knows. But in other ways the two are different in that nominalism can be a reaction from something already known and backed away from, whereas implicit religion (using this definition) relates to something not necessarily known, or at least understood. If this argument is accepted, then nominal Christianity is a wider term than implicit religion and will include the many who have an implicit Christian religion, but not of course those who have an implicit non-Christian religion.

Misconceived nominalism

Someone reading this book well be saying to themselves 'Just a minute! I go to church very regularly, but by your definition I'm a nominal Christian. Please explain!' It is certainly true that some who are 'outside' the church, that is, would be defined as nominal, are far from being so. For example there are regular attenders of the Free Church of Scotland who remain adherents all their life. In that denomination often becoming a member means partaking of Holy Communion, a matter which is taken very seriously. Some people feel unworthy of receiving Holy Communion, so refrain from church membership. They would be counted simply as adherents and therefore by the above definition, outside the church. However, they definitely are not.

In her book *Appalachian Mountain Religion*[10] Deborah McCauley published research on the religion of the peoples living in the Appalachian Mountains (set broadly in North and South Carolina in the south-east of the United States). Groups of people of different religious backgrounds were drawn to this region in the nineteenth century. They mostly lived a tough life and they also built numerous churches, many of which are still standing. The numbers attending church have dwindled considerably in the twentieth century, partly because of a major population decline.

What has this to do with a study of nominalism? Simply many of these people would be defined as nominal Christians. They grew up that way, and were nominal because they had always been so, not because they had dropped out of membership. In other words although their religion played an important part in their life, it was rarely equated to church membership.

Religious life among these mountain people was characterised by being anti-institutional, which while it did not drive them from denominational labels, largely meant that such labels had little significance. They were essentially pietistic, following an intensely personal expression of faith, with an emphasis on the experience of the Holy Spirit, especially in conversion, and a practical understanding of the Bible. These people were also 'oppositive', meaning they defined what they did in opposition to what others did *not* do. Thus they regularly washed each other's feet (which Ms McCauley suggests was a ritual akin to sharing the peace), gave a holy kiss, and refused to take an oath. They emphasised grace and humility, autonomy for the individual but a communal care for each other's needs. They used the picture of the Last Supper by Leonardo da Vinci again and again because it emphasised community and communion. Thus although they might be defined as 'nominal' because they were outside most church structures, in fact they were highly committed, and probably more so than many church members!

Movements into and out of nominalism in the United Kingdom

In 1960 church members were 59% of the world church Community but by the year 2010 that percentage will be 55%. This suggests a slow, but perhaps inexorable, movement towards a greater number of non-members in the church Community, in other words an increase in nominalism. But this is probably too simple as a statement. I say 'probably' because so far most studies of nominalism are based on Western Christianity. How far what is happening to Western Christianity is applicable to the whole of Christendom is not known. Nevertheless, using the situation in the United Kingdom as a case history helps us understand some of the patterns of behaviour and issues which accompany nominalism.

In the 1980s the following pattern could be seen amongst church people[11]:

- 'A' = New Christians who start attending the church coming from either a notional or non-Christian background
- 'B' = Church members who are also church attenders
- 'C' = Nominal, especially older people perhaps, or those who are ill or lack transport
- 'D' = Notional Christians
- 'E' = Not Christian in any category

These categories follow those given in Figure 8.2 except that there is no 'F' category – those in other religions.

FIGURE 8.5

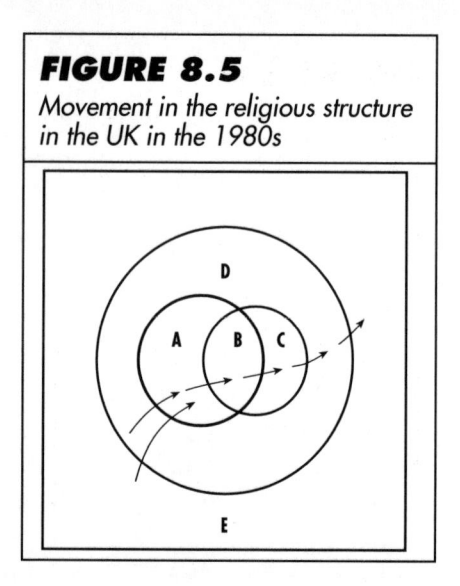

Movement in the religious structure in the UK in the 1980s

The two arrows entering area 'A' represent people attending church coming from a notional or non-Christian background. The arrows ending in area 'B' represents these (new) attenders at some stage joining the church and becoming church members. The arrow ending in area 'C' represents church members no longer able to attend regularly. The arrow ending in area 'D' represents these church members who give up church membership, finally the arrow ending in area 'E' from area 'D' represents the few – the very very few – who give up even notional Christianity.

There is a logical sequence in the above which was perhaps valid for the experience of churchgoing and Christianity in Britain in the 1980s, though not everyone went through every stage. It is, however, now an 'old' model, because it no longer gives the full picture in the 1990s, and has been superseded by a more complicated pattern of changes, which are *additional* to these[12]. These are shown by letters in Figure 8.6, and each letter is then described.

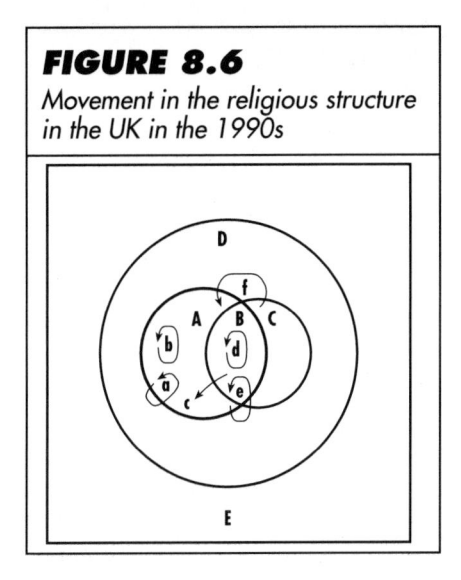

FIGURE 8.6
Movement in the religious structure in the UK in the 1990s

a. Some people have been to church earlier in their lives, but then stopped. They may come back later, but with no interest in becoming members. Some women now living on an estate near Dartford, Kent had attended church before getting married. Their husbands did not wish to look after the children while they went to church, so they no longer attended. The local vicar started a Wednesday morning service, which these women gladly attend while their husbands are at work and their children at school.

b. Others have started going to a church, say Church A. Then after a while they decide to try Church B, and maybe Churches C, D and E as well. They may or may not return to Church A and they don't become a member at any of them. This often happens when churchgoers move house.

My wife, seeing a stranger in our Anglican church leave at the end of the service without speaking to anyone, went out and spoke to her. She came because she 'liked the look of the church when she had driven past it the previous week', and because of a spiritual 'stirring', her mother having recently died. She came the following week 'because she wanted her baby done' but didn't come after that, preferring a nearby Methodist Church instead for the baby's baptism.

c. There are church members who leave their church for some reason, often because they move house, but who do not take up membership of the next church they start attending. This may be because it is, say, a Baptist church and they are Anglican, or it may be because they no longer wish to have the responsibilities of membership. This attitude can easily be encouraged when churches are unable to give good reasons why people should join them. This is the largest group. In 1992/93 in the UK there were 194,000 people who transferred from one church to another, of whom 70,000 did not take out membership[13].

d. Then there are church members who decide to try another church, perhaps only temporarily, or perhaps longer. They may take out membership in their 'new' church without cancelling their old, perhaps because they intend to return eventually, or for sentimental reasons they don't want to completely sever their links. We know several families who have switched churches sometimes for positive reasons (their children enjoy the activities of Church B more than Church A), and sometimes for negative reasons (can't stand the new minister in Church A).

e. There are also church members who drop out of the church scene for some considerable time. They just stop going to church, maybe to have more time for the family, maybe with the intention of returning sometime later.

f. There is yet another group who have stopped attending church, and become essentially nominal in the above sense of the word, but start attending church again, maybe when they've retired and got more time, or because their spouse dies and they want friendship, or other reasons. Churches which run a luncheon club for old people often find some of them start to attend again after years away from church.

Starting, stopping and re-starting church

The above pattern contains a number of elements – not just belonging to a church, but stopping belonging, or at least stopping going, and then maybe starting to go again after a space of several years. One British study *Finding Faith in 1994*[14] has looked at this in some detail. The results are best shown in the following graph:

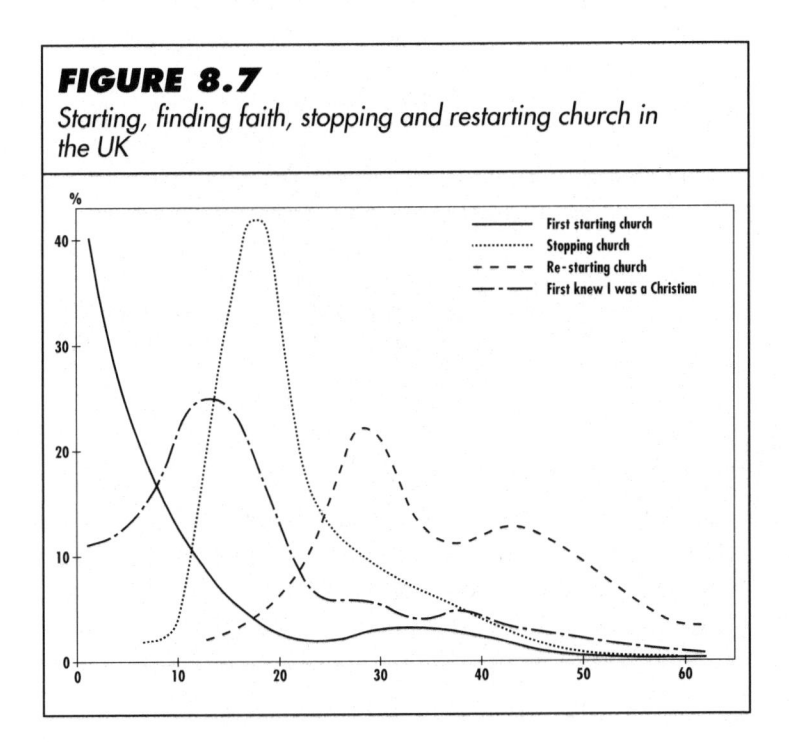

FIGURE 8.7
Starting, finding faith, stopping and restarting church in the UK

- ——— First starting church
- ·········· Stopping church
- – – – Re-starting church
- – · — First knew I was a Christian

This graph shows the following:

- Many people (40%) date when they started church from when they were christened or baptised as a baby. The overall average age is 13.

- The peak age of finding faith is in the mid-teens. 70% of people find their faith by the time they are 20.

- The peak age for stopping church is in the late teens and early twenties, the traditional student ages. Two in five are likely to stop, and to be away for perhaps 8 or 12 years.

- The peak ages for re-starting church are in the late twenties and early thirties, when many, like the person mentioned above, want their baby to be baptised, or want their children to have moral or spiritual teaching.

A report of the Church of England[15], chaired by the Bishop of Rochester, the Rt Rev Michael Nazir-Ali talks of 'drifting belief' in society, 'which is increasingly distant from Christian orthodoxy'. It says, 'The highly privatised culture and proliferation of choice inspire many people to make their spiritual journeys through a pick-'n'-mix approach. The challenge of the Church is to recognise the profile of this kind of burgeoning spirituality and to show how Christianity can meet its needs.'[16]

Worldwide Nominalism

This pattern of nominalism has been found elsewhere. In an international study Rev Dr Eddie Gibbs, Professor of Church Growth at Fuller Theological Seminary, Pasadena, California, has shown[17] that the belief of those who return to church after a time away changes. They still believe in God and accept Jesus as special, but are much less likely to accept the uniqueness of Christianity. He also found that 'those who have left the church at some stage and returned never regain either the depth of their former commitment or their spirituality.'[18]

In Australia 54% of churchgoers have become nominal. A survey[19] summarised the findings:

"Few nominals have totally rejected the Christian faith, but they are far less certain in their affirmation of it than those who attend regularly. In general, they place greater emphasis on faith as supporting moral standards, and comparatively less emphasis on personal access to God."

Eddie Gibbs found five areas in which committed and nominal Christians differ. Committed Christians were much more likely to:

- Be actively involved in their church (such as regular church attendance)
- Attend an event in the church during the week
- Be willing to pray with others
- Talk to others about God
- Sense the presence of God.[20]

Measuring Nominalism

The only measure of global nominalism available is the percentage of the Christian community who are *not* church members. This is not an overly helpful statistic, but worth noting nevertheless. The figures from the *Handbook* are:

TABLE 8.1
Global Nominality 1995 and 1960 to 2010

By Continent		By Denomination		Over time	
Oceania	53%	Anglican	80%	1960	41%
Africa	51%	Pentecostal	54%	1970	41%
Asia	48%	Other Churches	53%	1975	42%
Europe	44%	Presbyterian	51%	1980	43%
N America	39%	Indigenous	50%	1985	43%
S America	38%	Methodist	42%	1990	44%
		Catholic	40%	1995	44%
		Baptist	40%	2000	44%
		Lutheran	38%	2010	44%
World	44%	Orthodox	34%	—	—

This shows that the proportion of nominal Christians has been increasing, albeit very slowly since 1960. There are more nominal than practising Christians in Oceania and Africa! It also shows that the greatest disparity on this issue is not over time nor by continent but by denomination. Four out of five Anglicans are nominal, a percentage no other denomination approaches! But five of the ten denominations' Community is at least half nominal.

Lausanne Congresses on World Evangelization

In 1974 in Lausanne, Switzerland, 4,000 people attended a Congress on World Evangelization. It produced the Lausanne Covenant, a theological statement which showed the Biblical imperative of holistic ministry. It was greatly used by evangelicals – could it have helped the 'revival' which occurred a few years later? A second such Congress, which I also attended, called Lausanne II, was held in Manila in 1989.

These two Congresses classified 'the world population into four categories – the 'committed' (the potential missionary work force), the 'uncommitted' (nominal Christians), the 'unevangelised' (with minimal Christian knowledge) and the 'unreached' (the two million who belong to 12,000 unreached people groups, and who have never heard of Christ).'[21]

This categorisation highlights two things relevant to our discussion – the difference between those who are nominal and those who are not is the difference between the committed and the uncommitted. Secondly, that in Europe at least we are faced much more with the unevangelised, who have minimal Christian knowledge, than the unreached as such.

The 'unchurched'

The 'unchurched' as a label for the uncommitted and unevangelised has been popularised through the work of the highly successful Willow Creek Community Church in Chicago. It is used, for example, in the book *Inside the Mind of Unchurched Harry and Mary*[22]. However, it is misleading in some respects.

The prefix 'un' is a negative, and thus 'unchurched' suggests that a person has never been in a church. That is clearly true for some, but not for all. It would be more accurate to describe those who have attended church regularly and have left as 'dechurched', and when they subsequently returned they might be deemed to be 'rechurched'. The difference is important because we *must* distinguish between the nominal and the unevangelised, as the Lausanne categories do, in order to work through appropriate strategies. 'Unchurched' does not distinguish between them, it is a word describing a previous present state, and gives no hint of their history.

Characteristics

Whether such people are described in Lausanne's terms of

uncommitted and unevangelized, or Willow Creek's unchurched, what are their characteristics? A study by the researcher and author George Barna in the United States[23] found a demographic profile *identical* to a study of those who indicated they 'did not have a religion' in the Northern Ireland Population Census in 1991[24]. They were young, intelligent, hurting (more likely to have been divorced), well off men. They are the hallmark of the next generation who will undoubtedly move into leadership positions in society in the next few years. Yet they are 'unchurched'.

George Barna's study also identified key differences in attitude between the churched and the unchurched. The top three of what church people want in life compared to unchurched people are:

- Having an influence on other people's lives (42% churched to 28% unchurched)

- Living close to one's family (65% to 51%)

- Having a clear purpose for living (82% to 71%).

George Barna also found that the unchurched are more interested in relationships than in receiving information about a church or deity[25]. He found it was better to show them an open heart than to lead them through an open door. The unchurched are looking for a church which emphasises forgiveness rather than righteousness and judgement; they are seeking relevance, not accurate history.

So what does all this mean?

It means that the term 'nominal' is an inexact term covering a variety of spiritual states, from committed in one's own way to being totally non-church. In the Western world it includes stopping and re-starting churchgoing for some. It may have been seen exclusively as a problem in the past, but would now seem to be becoming more of a transitional phase for many. Little firm information is available on what it means outside the Western world, although we will find some clues in the next chapter.

Denominational variations are especially important, as well as focussing on our terminology. Confusing 'nominal' with 'unchurched' does not help, although some nominal are undoubtedly also unchurched. Some people are dechurched, and need to become rechurched. Perhaps a better distinction would be between the 'committed' and the 'less committed'. More actionable variations on this theme need to be researched.

NOTES

1. *UKCH: Religious Trends*, No 1, 1998/99, edited by Dr Peter Brierley, Christian Research, London, and Paternoster Publishing, Carlisle, UK, 1997, Figure 2.2.4, Page 2.2.
2. Austria, Denmark, Finland, France, Great Britain, Northern Ireland, Republic of Ireland, The Netherlands, Norway, Spain and French-speaking Switzerland.
3. Op cit (Item 1), Table 2.4.4, Page 2.4.
4. 'Annual Statistical Table on Global Mission: 1995', by Rev Dr David Barrett, *International Bulletin of Missionary Research*, New Haven, Connecticut, USA, January 1995, Page 25. I have added his numbers for Muslims, Hindus, Buddhists, New Religionists, Tribal Religionists, Sikhs and Jews, and then added the 1995 estimate of the number of Non-Trinitarian Christians from the *World Churches Handbook*.
5. Op cit (Item 1), Figures 2.2.3 and 2.2.4, Page 2.2.
6. 'Annual Statistical Table on Global Mission: 1998', Rev Dr David Barrett, *International Bulletin of Missionary Research*, New Haven, Connecticut, USA, January 1998, Page 27.
7. Mark chapter 4 verse 18.
8. Mark chapter 4 verse 19.
9. Lecture by Professor Rev Canon Dr Edward Bailey 'Implicit Religion: What might that be?' delivered at Lambeth Palace, 12 November 1997 on the inauguration of the Centre.

10. *Appalachian Mountain Religion*, Deborah McCauley, University of Illinois Press, Urbana and Chicago, USA, 1995.
11. *Church nominalism: the plague of the twentieth century?*, by Dr Peter Brierley, MARC Monograph No 2, MARC Europe, London, UK, May 1985.
12. *Nominalism Reconceived: The phenomenon of the 1990s*, by Dr Peter Brierley, Leaders Briefing No 8, Christian Research, London, UK, April 1997, Page 15.
13. *Changing Churches*, An analysis of some of the movements in the contemporary church scene, Leaders Briefing No 3, Dr Peter Brierley, Christian Research, London, UK, 1996, Pages 20, 21 and 23.
14. *Finding Faith in 1994*, Research Report analysing 4,800 questionnaires returned after the ecumenical 1994 Lent Course. The Report, on behalf of Churches Together in England, is available from Christian Research, London, UK, and a summary of its findings was published in *Quadrant*, March 1998, also by Christian Research.
15. *The Search for Faith and the Witness of the Church*, Mission Theological Advisory Group, Church House, 1996.
16. Report in the *Church Times* of 15th November 1996.
17. *Winning Them Back*, Professor Eddie Gibbs, Monarch, Crowborough, East Sussex, UK, 1993, and also available in a separate version in the USA called *In Name Only*, Bridgepoint, USA, 1994.
18. Ibid, Page 293.
19. *Faith Without the Church? Nominalism in Australian Christianity,* Peter Bentley, 'Tricia Blombery and Dr Philip Hughes, Christian Research Association, Victoria and New South Wales, Australia, 1992, Page 33.
20. Op cit (Item 17), Page 290.
21. *Making Christ Known,* edited by Rev Dr John Stott, Paternoster Publishing, Carlisle, Cumbria, UK, 1996.
22. *Inside the Mind of Unchurched Harry and Mary*, Lee Strobel, Zondervan, USA, 1993.
23. *Casting the Net, the Unchurched Population*, George Barna, Barna Research Group, California, USA, 1995, Page 6.
24. *Irish Christian Handbook* 1995/96 edition, edited by Dr Peter Brierley, Christian Research, London, UK, Pages 22 to 26.
25. Op cit (item 23), Page 44.

9
IMPLICATIONS FROM COSTA RICA

A parcel I received from Costa Rica in 1996 turned out to be one of the most interesting documents I have ever read. It was the English version of a doctoral thesis by Jorge Gómez, General Secretary of the International Institute of Evangelism in Depth (IINDEF[1]). He gives an absorbing history of its progress in Central and South America in the introduction to his thesis.

A summary of the research findings has been published in Spanish[2] under the (translated) title of *The Causes of Growth and Desertion in Evangelical Churches in Costa Rica*. This book is unlikely to find its way into many Western church leaders' homes since most, including this author, speak no Spanish. I was therefore delighted to receive the English translation, which I summarise here. What Jorge Gómez found in Costa Rica is applicable on a much wider scale. (The 23,000 square miles of Costa Rica covers 1/24 of 1% of the world's landed surface area).

The problem realised

The *World Churches Handbook* shows Costa Rica as an essentially Christian country with 95% of its 3.42 million people notionally Christian in 1995. They are mostly Catholic – of the 3.26 million church community, 2.94 million were Catholic, leaving just 320,000 Protestants. Of these, just over half (167,000) were Pentecostal and a further 97,000 were Other Churches, leaving very few for the institutional denominations to share between them. The numbers for membership are even more stark – 180,000 Protestant church members, of which 103,000 were Pentecostal and 48,000 Other Churches. How this number had been reached since 1960 is shown below in Table 9.1 which gives total non-Catholic Church membership and the percentage of these which are Pentecostal.

TABLE 9.1
Growth of Protestant church members in Costa Rica 1960–95

Year	Members	Pentecostal
1960	14,000	20%
1965	19,000	28%
1970	30,000	38%
1975	43,000	41%
1980	75,000	44%
1985	113,000	52%
1990	154,000	54%
1995	180,000	57%

FIGURE 9.1
Growth of Protestant church members, Costa Rica, 1960–1995

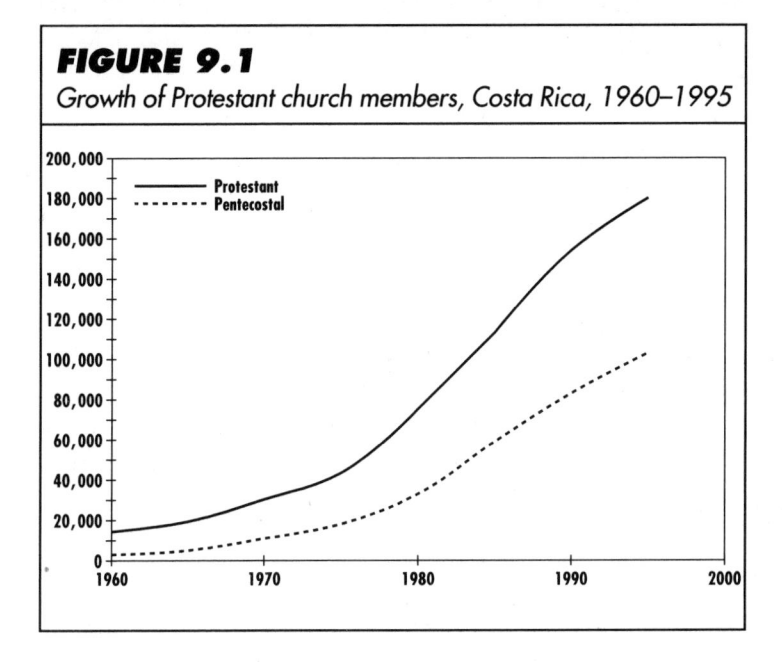

A large increase in the number of Protestants took place each five years between 1975 and 1990, but it slowed down between 1990 and 1995. Much of this increase was in the Pentecostal church which increased its percentage in an already rising total, especially between 1980 and 1985. This is in line with the worldwide 'revival' described in Chapter 1.

The increase had come about because national evangelical leaders took notice of the small numbers in their churches, and realised the need for radical evangelisation. This was undertaken through an Evangelism-in-Depth programme, and was very effective. By the late 1980s many believed that Protestants made up perhaps 16 or 20% of the population. However conversions into the churches were being offset by numbers leaving, so to ascertain the true numbers Dr John Kessler, an acute observer of the Christian scene working in Costa Rica, commissioned a comprehensive survey from

Gallup. This showed that only 8.9% of Costa Ricans claimed to be Protestant, but also revealed that a further 8.1% of the population said they had renounced or abandoned their Protestant church!

Could it be true?

A second survey in 1991 to check these figures showed that 10.6% of Costa Ricans were Protestant, but that 12.1% of the population had deserted the Protestant church. It was immediately apparent that something was going very wrong.

Questions that church leaders needed to find answers for included why people were leaving the Protestant churches, how far desertion was related to the evangelistic message or method, and whether desertion was related to church life, discipleship and discipline. This was the essential research task that Dr Gómez tackled, reported as a substantial part of his thesis.

As part of this work, Gallup were asked for the third time to research church matters with the population. The survey in June 1994 consisted of:

- Asking a random selection of people a set of questions (some of which replicated those asked in 1989 and 1991)
- An additional survey of 5% of the members of a randomly selected group of 50 churches
- A personal interview with the pastor of each of these churches
- A telephone or personal interview with other pastors, denominational leaders or other key people.

This is probably one of the most thorough studies undertaken among church people by a secular company anywhere in the world.

Of the 50 churches selected 35 were Pentecostal and 15 were from traditional/historical churches. These churches spanned 16 denominations: 10 Pentecostal and 6 Traditional. 5 of the Pentecostal and 3 of the Traditional were 'non-independent' denominations, and the other 5 and 3 were from independent denominations.

The overall results showed that 10% of the population belonged to a Protestant church, and 8.6% of the population had left one. All these surveys have a measure of estimation in the final figures, but they show a consistent story of high desertion, as well as a church beginning to not keep pace with the increasing population. The next figure below shows the actual trend in the numbers of the Protestant community (taken as twice the number of members), and the following one the same expressed as a percentage of the population. The importance of comparing numbers with an external reference is readily seen.

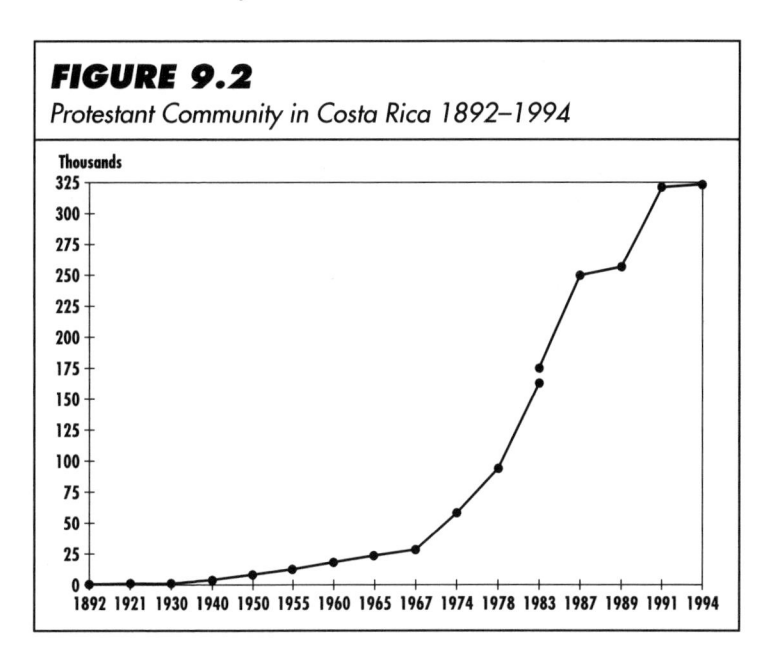

FIGURE 9.2
Protestant Community in Costa Rica 1892–1994

FIGURE 9.3
Protestant community as percentage of Costa Rican population

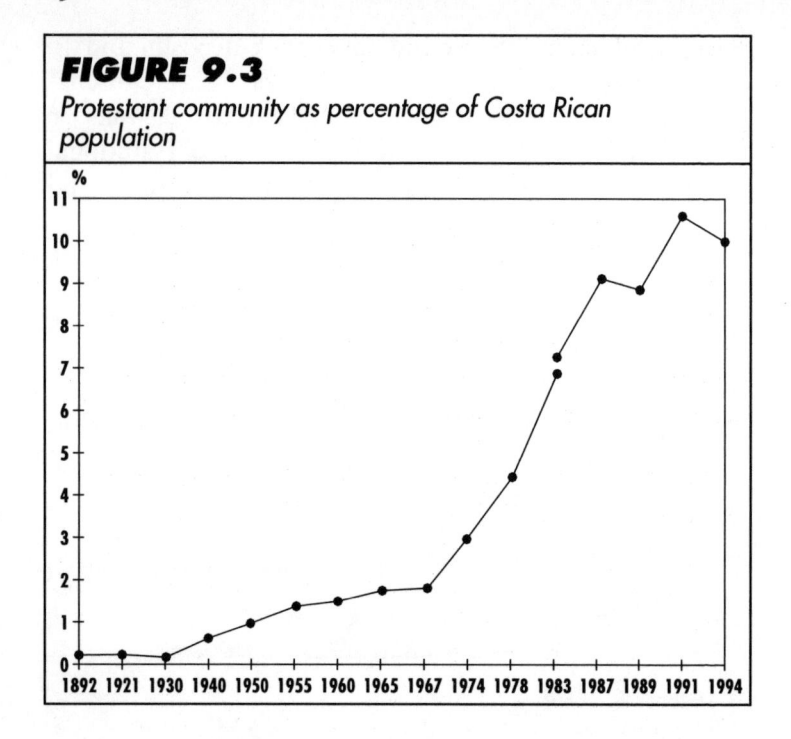

```
%
11
10                                                    •
 9                                              •   •
 8
 7                                         •
 6
 5                                    •
 4
 3                               •
 2                          •
 1              • • • • •
 0 • • •
   1892 1921 1930 1940 1950 1955 1960 1965 1967 1974 1978 1983 1987 1989 1991 1994
```

Reasons for change

The figures show that in the late 1980s and in the early 1990s there was little growth in the Protestant community. Taking into account measurement errors, some estimates showed an actual decline. Certainly as a percentage of the population there are two declines. Why should numbers fall like this? The interviews with the pastors suggested the following:

- Jimmy Swaggart's[3] fall triggered similar falls among other Costa Rican ministers, and the consequential loss of credibility. Jimmy Swaggart's fall 'had far-reaching implications as to the perceived authenticity of the evangelical gospel.'[4]

- A large number of pastors 'had fallen in sin'[5] over the years 1986–1989
- A history of strife between members and leadership in one denomination's largest church.

The decline in the early 1990s appears to have affected more women than men. The number of Protestant men in Costa Rica increased from 289,000 in 1991 to 308,000 in 1994 (although their percentage in the population decreased from 9.3 to 9.2%). However the number of women actually decreased in the same period, from 367,000 to 361,000 (their percentage dropping from 11.8 to 10.8%).

The decline was especially steep among Protestants aged 18 to 24 who went from 255,000 in 1991 to 221,000 in 1994 (8.2% to 6.6%). Those aged 25 to 39 also dropped but not as much, falling from 423,000 to 412,000 in the same period (13.6% to 12.3%). On the other hand numbers of those aged 40 to 59 and 60 and over both increased in this period.

There was also a history of personal desertion. Thus the 1994 survey found that of 34% people interviewed who were born Protestant, 38% were now Catholic, 34% were still Protestant, and 28% had no religion. Were people who were born Protestant more likely to leave Protestant churches in adult life?

The problem of desertion is complicated by the fact that while the Protestant church grew by some 66,000 people from 1989 to 1994 it declined as a percentage in the population. The 66,000 represents a net increase, and the gross increase would be much larger, offset by numbers leaving. Some of the growth would come from Protestants returning to their church after a time away, perhaps exploring 'other religions or stay(ing) without any religious affiliation for a period of time'[6].

Where do people go?

One of the fascinating items arose from the questions about a person's current religion and the length of time they had been a Protestant.

- Those who had been in a Protestant church for less than a year before leaving would most likely go to a Catholic church when they left (57%) or leave religion altogether (36%).

- Those who had a longer exposure to Protestant Christianity (1 to 5 years) were less likely to go to the Catholic church (42%) and more likely instead to join another religion, or the Mormons or Jehovah's Witnesses (8%); half (50%) though would renounce religion altogether.

- Those who stayed at least 5 years in a Protestant church before they left were most likely to leave religion entirely (63%). A quarter would join the Catholic church (24%), and 13% another religion.

This suggests that the longer a person's exposure to a Protestant church, the more likely they are when they leave to choose atheism or another religion rather than join a Catholic church. Protestants thus give some people religion and some people atheism! Is commitment part of the issue here?

The figures in the above paragraphs are summarised in Table 9.2.

TABLE 9.2
Current religion against Time as a Protestant 1994

Time as a Protestant	None	Catholic	Mormon/J Witnesses	Other Religion	Overall
Up to 1 year	36%	57%	2%	5%	47%
1 to 5 years	50%	42%	4%	4%	34%
Over 5 years	63%	24%	5%	8%	19%

Current Religion shown across columns.

How long do they stay?

The next table shows how long Costa Ricans, categorised by age group, stayed in a Protestant church *if they were going to leave*.

TABLE 9.3
Current age against Time as a Protestant 1994

Time as a Protestant	18–24	25–39	40–59	60 or over	Overall
1 month	28%	12%	18%	28%	19%
2–12 months	18%	32%	35%	22%	28%
1 to 5 years	31%	36%	39%	25%	34%
Over 5 years	23%	20%	8%	25%	19%

Current Age shown across columns.

This shows that about half (47%) of those who leave, whatever their age, stay in their church for less than a year. About a third (34%) stay for between 1 and 5 years, and about a fifth (19%) for longer. The difference is in those aged 40 to 59, who tend to stay for shorter periods. Could that be because they have families and are wanting suitable programmes for their children?

If these figures are applicable to all churches, and beyond Costa Rica, it means that the first twelve months (and in reality the first month for younger and for older people) are the critical time to draw people in, ensure that the welcome procedure is followed, that the minister talks with them personally, and perhaps encourage them to join a small group.

Number of churches tried

How many churches had people tried before they left their existing church? Half (54%) had attended just one, and a quarter (26%) two. One in eight (13%) had attended three churches, leaving 7% or one person in 14 who had attended 4 or more.

Again, if these results are applicable globally, it means that the culture of the church people attend first will affect them most strongly as to whether they stay not only in that church, but *in the Christian faith*.

Combining this result with the last we see that about half the people who leave do so within a year of going to a church, and half those who leave do so after trying only one church. So the need to help them in that first year is not so much just to get to know a particular church, but to get to know Christianity.

Men were found to be more likely than women to try more than one church before they left. Younger people were likely to try just one church (60%); those aged 25 to 39 were slightly more inclined to try two (29%).[7]

Type of church attended

What kind of church did people attend before they left? In Costa Rica the main alternatives are Catholicism and Pentecostalism.

TABLE 9.4
Type of church attended against Time as a Protestant 1994

Time as a Protestant	Pentecostal	Other	Don't know
Up to 1 year	58%	9%	33%
1 to 5 years	41%	19%	40%
Over 5 years	53%	24%	23%
Overall	51%	16%	33%

Three-fifths (58%) who left within a year did so from a Pentecostal church, and knew that's what it was. But a third (33%) who left within that period didn't know what type of church it was. Is it good to stress your denomination or not? I know one person who went to a Baptist church who felt it 'so Baptist emphasised' that they didn't want to go there again. But at least that person knew the denomination of that church!

The longer it was before a person left a non-Pentecostal church the greater the likelihood that they would know what kind of church it was. But this still represented only one person in six (16%) who left. A third (33%) never did find out what kind of church they had been attending – even after more than five years! That either is too extraordinary to be true or just might be for the same reason!

Why did people leave?

This in some ways is the key '$64,000' question. The reasons which emerge are interesting. Two-thirds (66%) left for five main reasons. In order they were:

- 'I cannot live up to the demands of the evangelical gospel' (29%)
- 'Bad administration of tithes and offerings' (13%)
- 'Poor behaviour of other church members' (9%)
- 'Poor conduct of the pastor or senior leader' (8%)
- 'Pressure put upon me by my friends and family members' (7%).

Many more minor reasons were given – another religion was more attractive (6%), they had no reason to keep going (5%), personal problems at home (4%), there was no-one able to help them spiritually (3%), pastors not capable of leading (3%), no-one liked them because they had transferred from another church (3%), they had married a Catholic who didn't want them going to a Protestant church (3%), people who wanted to stay as Catholics (2%), they could manage life without religion (1%), sermons were boring (1%), no-one was willing to help them (1%) and other reasons (2%).

The first reason given was more true of men than women (36% to 23%), and so was the second (24% to 14%). Young people (aged 18 to 24) felt more strongly about the second reason (19%). Those who gave the second reason as their main reason gave the top reason as their second reason. So the impact of the first two reasons is in fact very strong. Three people in 7 left the church for one of these reasons. They show the importance of people not having unrealistic expectations, and the importance of the church being seen to control its finances well. The first reason accords with the findings of a UK survey[8] in which those aged 26 to 40 found the problem of living up to one's faith the key reason for not coming to faith.

At the same time as the main survey, the pastor of one large church in the city of Alajuela used the same questionnaire to find out why people were leaving his church. The main reason for almost half his respondents (43%), was the pressure put on them by friends and family. The second reason was their own inability to live up to the gospel standards (13%), and the third reason was the poor sermons (13%)! One hopes he managed to improve his sermons after finding this out!

Did leavers understand the gospel message?

Two-thirds of those who left (68%) said they understood the message of salvation. A further fifth (19%) thought they did, leaving just one person in 8 (13%) who felt that they didn't. Those aged 18 to 24 were much more likely to say that they didn't understand the message (34%).

What do you like most about Protestants?

Remember, this was asked of those who'd *left* the church! A quarter (28%) said 'understanding', and another quarter (23%) said 'kindliness'. These tally with a UK survey in which non-Christians were asked what they thought of Christians. 'They care,' they said[9].

Higher and lower attrition – member's views

The structure of the Gallup survey involved a random selection of churches and then interviews with 5% of their congregations and with all their pastors. In this way two types of church were distinguished – those with a below average rate of attrition for their particular denomination and obviously the remainder which had a higher rate. This second group was divided into two: those who move on to another church or were known to be temporary visitors, or deliberately left to plant new churches; those who left for negative reasons. All told 981 people responded.

The characteristics of these three types of churches were as follows:[10]

TABLE 9.5
Characteristics of different types of church – by members

Characteristic	Lower Attrition	Higher Attrition More mobile	Negative
Average church membership	440	290	46
% male members	44%	36%	38%
% members 18–24	26%	20%	16%
% members 60+	7%	12%	12%
% members with degree	26%	23%	14%
% born Protestant	22%	18%	16%
% new believers	11%	7%	10%
% been a member only this church	47%	49%	53%
% attending at least weekly	81%	79%	76%
% members for over 11 years	19%	31%	25%

The main variations here (taken arbitrarily as where the percentages differ by more than 7%) are that churches with lower attrition tend to:

- Be larger
- Have more men in the congregation
- Have more younger people
- Have more highly educated

- Have fewer long-term members.

The theological beliefs of church members were also evaluated[11]. Those in lower attrition churches were *less* likely to believe that:

- Christians can be saved by good works (32% to 41%)
- At the moment of salvation God transforms our emotions, feelings and mind (58% to 67%)
- The moment a listener raises his hands to receive Christ as Saviour he is saved (54% to 67%)
- It is necessary when explaining the gospel to give a personal testimony (71% to 82%)
- True repentance follows intelligent preaching of the gospel (45% to 63%)
- Praise and worship should motivate the church more than preaching (17% to 25%).

Lower attrition church members were much *more* likely to:

- Believe that their congregations should *always* be trying to evangelise their community (38% to 12%)
- Have access to a personal spiritual counsellor (64% to 46%)
- Be developing more effective programmes for new believers (52% to 12%)
- Apply church discipline when needed (51% to 37%)
- Have been taught how to disciple other believers (49% to 31%).

These findings suggest that lower attrition churches are more:

- Clearly focussed towards their future programme in terms of what they want new believers to be taught
- Involved with their community
- Willing perhaps to keep some of the 'finer edges' of evangelical theology in the background.

Perhaps their philosophy could be summed up as in the slogan, 'Making the main thing to keep the main thing the main thing.'

Higher and lower attrition – pastor's views

Altogether 71 pastors of these churches were interviewed, so the following Table has percentages based on much smaller numbers[12]:

TABLE 9.6
Characteristics of different types of church – by pastors

Characteristic	Lower Attrition	Higher Attrition More mobile	Negative
% pastors 25–39	60%	52%	60%
% pastors with degree	44%	57%	24%
% born Protestant	16%	33%	20%
% evangelical for 15 or more years	48%	76%	64%
% with 2 pastors in last 10 years	48%	52%	32%
% with 4 years theological training	52%	19%	28%

The key factors here for churches with lower attrition would seem to be to have pastors who have:

- More education
- Longer theological training
- Moved around more
- Been evangelical for a shorter period.

This last is interesting – could it mean that those who have been evangelical longer have become more set in their ways, and less able to adapt to new circumstances? Or is it that those pastors who have become evangelical more recently are better able to understand the backgrounds of new converts?

Hindering growth

What caused churches *not* to grow?[13] 'Lack of evangelism,' said the higher attrition churches (36%). 'Lack of personal attention and discipleship,' said the lower attrition churches (40%). Both put as their second reasons what the other had put as their first reason, and both groups agreed on the third major reason – fights, striving and gossip. The pastors generally agreed with these also.

Both groups also agreed with the top three reasons why people left:

- Personal behaviour incompatible with the gospel (34% lower attrition, 45% higher)
- Lack of a personal spiritual counsellor (20% lower, 32% higher)
- Poor conduct of church members (22% lower, 15% higher)

Pastors agreed with these and added a fourth[14] – the poor conduct of pastors or church leaders.

The corollary to these statements was that both groups felt it most important to help people in their individual discipleship and give personal attention to their spiritual walk (62% lower and 57% higher)[15]. After that it was felt good to have a harmonious and loving church (24% lower, 32% higher). Again the pastors agreed with this order. 'A relationship with Jesus' was the key anchor point (29% lower, 35% higher).

Why people change churches

Protestants transfer between churches because of 'a lack of harmony between church members' (33% lower, 36% higher), and because they move house (29% lower, 36% higher)[16]. The pastors agreed with the first reason, but in lower attrition churches added another reason equal with the second – a lack of personal discipleship. In higher attrition churches it was felt that the poor conduct of the pastor or leaders was the second most common reason why people changed.

Another key problem was that a third (36%) of the church members felt that people were so independent that it wouldn't be noticed if they were having spiritual problems[17]. On the other hand, two-thirds (67%) of the Protestants in Costa Rica feel accepted and loved in their churches. Most (64%) felt churches did not show prejudice about a person's social status.

Despite the finding that those in lower attrition churches came out less strongly for motivational singing, about half (48%) of those interviewed said they found praise and worship more motivating than the preaching[18]. This is theory v practice! Half (53%) of church members believed they were affirmed in their faith by the preaching and teaching in their churches. It is what a church teaches (rather than its denomination or leadership or worship times) that attracts people to a church (44%). This and the love and harmony between members (50%)[19].

So what does all this mean?

The huge Costa Rican survey looked at the issues of why people joined, moved or left churches. Their key concern was to find why people were leaving their churches. Many of their findings are much more widely applicable, to other countries and churches.

Some of the important factors found were that people tend to try a new church for up to a year. They are likely to be drawn to it more by what it teaches rather than what denomination it is, its leadership or the type of worship. In that year it is more important to teach them about the Christian faith than denominational distinctives, because if they leave they may try one more church, but if not will lapse back into non-church ways. Men and younger people are more likely to try a second church if they leave their first. For younger and for older people the first month rather than the first year is the most important. In that time they need to be linked up with others.

This suggests that the welcome programmes of churches are extremely important in the retention of newcomers. The *culture* of the church a newcomer tries is critical not only for whether they stay in that church, but whether they continue in the Christian faith. Each church therefore has a wider relevance than just their local expression – newcomers see them as an example of what it means to belong to the Body of Christ.

The example rather than the style of leadership is very important. Poor examples probably put more people off than good examples attract. University educated leaders, with longer theological training, who have moved around a bit and not been evangelical for too long are likely to have lower attrition rates in their churches. Churches which know where they are going especially in helping new people get integrated, and which are highly involved with the community, are likely to have less attrition.

Living up to the demands of the gospel, or rather the inability to do so, is a major reason for leaving. So is the poor administration of finance. These affect men and young people more than women and older people. The Costa Rican survey highlighted the importance of a person's spiritual walk as critical[20] to their leaving not just their church but the faith. At the same time the love and harmony of church members are a huge motivational force to stay[21]. As Jorge Gómez comments, 'This study suggests that many former Protestants rejected the evangelical faith because of those who profess it.'[22]

Isn't all this known already? Some will say it is. But mostly it is known by hearsay, or through opinions gathered by talking to people. Here, perhaps for the first time, are major statements being given a realistic and firm statistical basis because of a high quality, and doubtless expensive, piece of research. It is not so much having the facts, but having the corroboration of the facts that makes this study so relevant to global Christianity.

The message is unequivocal: what Christians believe MUST be worked out in their lives.

NOTES

1. El Instituto Internacional de Evangelización a Fondo, Apartado 168–2350, San Francisco de Dos Ríos, Costa Rica. Phone: (506) 227–9385, Fax: (506) 227–8598, e-mail: iindef@sol.racsa.co.cr
2. *el Crecimiento y la Deserción en la iglesia evangólica costaricense*, Dr Jorge I Gómez V, IINDEF Publications, San José, Costa Rica, 1996.

3. Jimmy Swaggart was an evangelist with an almost worldwide TV gospel outreach. His adultery was widely publicised.
4. *Protestant Growth and Desertion in Costa Rica*, by Dr Jorge Gómez, doctoral thesis Columbia International University, South Carolina, USA, December 1995, Page 169.
5. Ibid, Page 170.
6. Ibid, Page 219.
7. Ibid, page 251.
8. *Finding Faith in 1994*, Christian Research, London, UK 1995, Page 70.
9. *The Ansvar Survey of English Social Behaviour*, research report by Christian Research, London, UK, and published in a special issue of *Quadrant* bulletin, November 1995.
10. Op cit (Item 4), Page 312.
11. Op cit (Item 4), Page 330.
12. Op cit (Item 4), Page 316.
13. Op cit (Item 4), Page 385.
14. Op cit (Item 4), Page 391.
15. Op cit (Item 4), Page 395.
16. Op cit (Item 4), Page 401.
17. Op cit (Item 4), Page 518.
18. Op cit (Item 4), Page 520.
19. Op cit (Item 4), Page 524.
20. Op cit (Item 4), Page 596.
21. Op cit (Item 4), Page 621.
22. Op cit (Item 4), Page 645.

10

CULTURE AND CHURCH LEADERSHIP

Things are certainly happening in this Christian world of ours! Take the Everlasting Dawn Church in Ulaanbaatar, the capital of Mongolia, which in 1997 had to divide into two Sunday morning worship services as there wasn't room for everyone coming. The older group met first – that is, all those aged 23 or over![1]

The 26,000 Toura people live in north west Côte d'Ivoire and until December 1997 had not been reached with the Gospel. A scheme to bring health care by 13 women and 3 doctors treated the sick in the morning, visited homes in the afternoon, and showed evangelistic films in the evening. As a consequence '43 people gave their lives to Jesus' and they 'managed to negotiate with the chief for land where we could build a church'. All in one visit![2] The *JESUS* film had been seen by an estimated 1,120 million people in 219 countries by July 1997 – one-fifth (19%) of the world's population![3]

In 1980 12 people started the Power of Jesus Around the World Pentecostal Church in Uganda. By 1997 there were 66 local churches. In October 1997 'a man dying of cancer was brought forward for prayer. His eyes were sunken, his limbs so thin. God quite remarkably touched and healed him, and ten days later he was discharged from the hospital with

CULTURE AND CHURCH LEADERSHIP 213

medical certification that there were absolutely no traces of cancer in his body.'[4]

These three stories of God at work in the world today could literally be multiplied by the thousand, or even the million! It is estimated that there are 17 million[5] added to the Christian community each year, plus 35 million more born into Christian homes, a total of 52 million people. That's a lot of stories! But 7 million are lost through defection, 21 million die[6], and 5 million more drift away, leaving a net increase of 19 million a year. These stories epitomise the real world and its culture, within which the church has to work.

The model used in Chapter 8 on nominalism needs one further modification, as below:

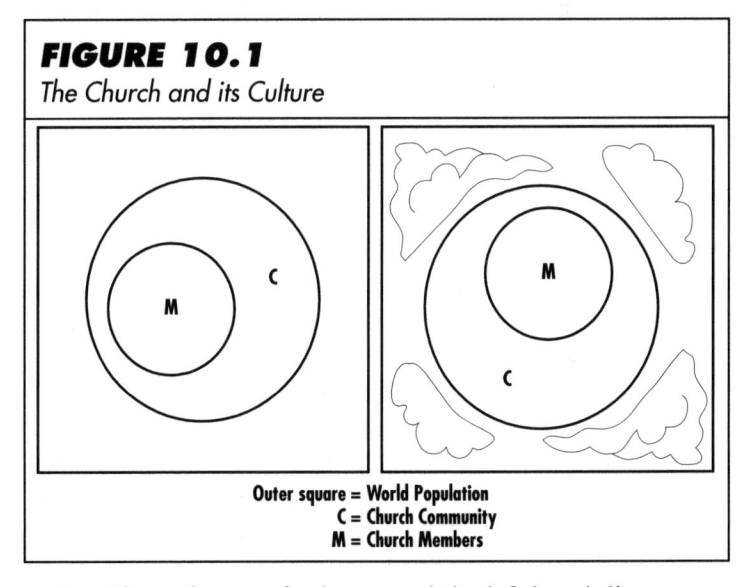

FIGURE 10.1
The Church and its Culture

Outer square = World Population
C = Church Community
M = Church Members

Our discussions so far have used the left hand diagram as their model. But the church does not operate in a vacuum. It operates in the world culture, depicted by the thin, cloud-like lines in the right-hand diagram. (They actually come *within* the church of course as well, but that's part of the story we have already looked at in Chapter 2 on the church in the world). In this final chapter we need to think of the culture within which the church has to live and work, and then to look at some of the implications of that for church leaders.

What is 'Culture'?

Walter Wink is Professor of Biblical Interpretation at Auburn Theological Seminary, New York. In the third volume of his trilogy on the Powers he suggests that culture, or the 'prevailing world-atmosphere', can be defined as that which 'teaches us what to believe, teaches us what to value, and teaches us what to see'[7]. This is useful but gives culture a very high place, almost too high, I believe. It could be taken to mean that in a country with a Christian heritage such as the UK, the culture can in some way make people nominally Christian. If that is what he means, I believe he is elevating culture to make it almost equal with Scripture.

I prefer the definition of Dr Campbell Campbell-Jack, a Scottish clergyman, of culture as 'that complex network of interlocking beliefs, attitudes, shared understanding and history which provides the framework from within which we view ourselves and the world.'[8]

Another definition of culture, from the business world, suggests it is a mix of 'Values, Standards, Expectations and Image'. A study by Kotter and Heskett across 200 companies found, for example, that 'superior long-term profitability' over a 20-year time span correlated with 'corporate cultures which express(ed) the company's purpose in terms of all stakeholder relationships.'[9]

If culture is hard to define, what does it mean in practice? Under the title 'If the 80s were materialism and the 90s are spirituality, then what's next in the CULTURE?' an article in *Netfax* answered, 'Paganism, community, on-line cyberspace, social action, pluralism, globalization, collaboration, a search for traditional values in a culture that has lost its moral and ethical base, the occult moving into the mainstream, stoicism, individualism, experience-based reality, service, relationships, spirituality, continued dysfunction, fragmentation and special interest groups, meaning, indifference to God, tolerance, sub-cultures that are disconnected, a return to the basics, high-tech simplification, confusion, pessimism, complexity, helping and healing, solving world hunger, building houses and world unity.'[10] Oh, was something missed out? Well, now we know where we are, then!

This kind of list may be helpful for some, but what does it mean for the church? They give this answer too! 'If the 80s were church growth and the 90s are church health, then what's next in the CHURCH?' They answer: 'Christian formation and discipleship, community, the learning organization, church planting, church as a safe place, a sanctuary from growing social chaos, a place of authentic community, the integration of growth and health, innovating back to the original stability, mission, global growth, holistic discipleship, identity, indirect influence (as in salt and light), a teacher of religious truth, 'Builders' dead, 'Boomers' retired, 'X'ers' never in church and thousands of small churches dying, social conscience, racial sensitivity, church pruning, church mobilization, substance over style, survival, decentralization, and finally, church intimacy creating villages within large churches.'[11] This is too comprehensive to be really helpful.

Their final question is 'If the role and style of church leadership in the 80s were the pastor as CEO and the 90s team-ministry, then what's next in CHURCH LEADERSHIP?' Their answer is shorter this time! 'Mentors, bearers of identity, the congregation representing the priesthood of all believers, facilitators, models and encouragers, the laity-empowered and mobilized, and finally decentralization and the empowerment of small churches and ministries within the larger churches.' Again, these answers are too wide, so let us narrow the issue down.

Suppose we take a different tack and return to our basic source, the *World Churches Handbook*. Let us look at one aspect of the spiritual horizon which is rarely discussed – the place and growth of what David Barrett calls the 'marginal Protestants' but which I prefer to call the Non-Trinitarian churches. They are one part of the spiritual culture which the church has to meet.

The Non-Trinitarian Community

The *World Churches Handbook* lists the various Non-Trinitarian Churches, but does not include them in its totals. Nevertheless, at 26.5 million they form about 0.5% of the world's population in 1995, or 1.6% of global Christianity. They therefore should not be ignored. They form part of the background culture within which the Trinitarian churches have to work.

The Non-Trinitarian Churches are mainly the Jehovah's Witnesses and the Church of Jesus Christ of Latter-day Saints (or the Mormons) but there are many others, much smaller, in this broad categorisation. All in some way do not accept the historic formulary of the Godhead as the three eternal persons, God the Father, God the Son and god the Holy Spirit, in one unchanging Essence, and the implications that follow from this statement.

Collectively, the Non-Trinitarians have 133,000 churches, on average 200 strong. Membership is 54% of their community, so that each church has on average 110 members. Details of their community follow. The final line is the percentage of the 2010 figure:

TABLE 10.1
The growth of the Non-Trinitarian Community by continent 1960–2010

Year	Africa	Europe	Oceania	North America	Asia	South America	World
1960	100	100	100	100	100	100	100
1970	153	157	142	130	353	295	155
1980	199	203	181	171	395	684	205
1990	305	301	282	254	524	1716	319
2000	387	359	357	326	670	2288	406
2010	461	440	423	401	796	2830	496
1960	0.6m	1.2m	0.2m	4.7m	0.5m	0.2m	7.3m
2010	3.0m	5.1m	0.6m	19.0m	3.8m	4.9m	36.4m
% of total	8%	14%	2%	52%	10%	14%	100%

FIGURE 10.2
Proportions of Non-Trinitarian Community by Continent 2010

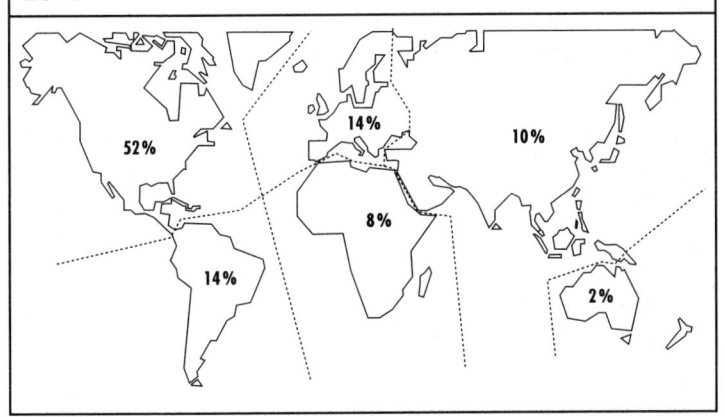

- North America: 52%
- Europe: 14%
- Asia: 10%
- Africa: 8%
- South America: 14%
- Oceania: 2%

FIGURE 10.3
Growth of Non-Trinitarians by continent 1960–2010

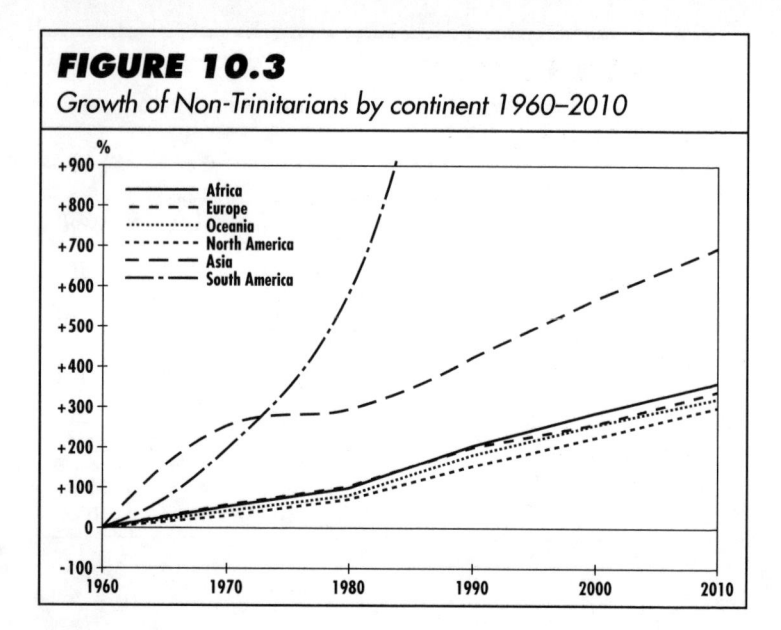

The Non-Trinitarian churches have grown *much faster* than global Christianity. Whereas Christendom has doubled in these 50 years, the Non-Trinitarian community has increased five-fold. It has grown particularly fast in Asia, an eight-fold increase principally due to the rapid expansion of the Unification Church (Moonies) in South Korea. In South America it has exploded, although it began with a very small base in 1960 so that their number in 2010 is not as large as their percentage increase would imply; the increases are largely due to big gains by the Mormons and the Jehovah's Witnesses.

In 1995 the relative strength of the various groups is as given below, with the number of countries in which they were present in the final column. This is as given in the *Handbook*; however, in many countries a small number of Non-Trinitarians have simply been grouped together so that they are present in more countries than shown.

TABLE 10.2
Strength of Non-Trinitarian Churches worldwide in 1995

Church	Community	Countries
Jehovah's Witnesses	10,504,000	208
Mormons	9,040,000	95+
Unification Church	892,000	5+
Unitarians	276,000	10+
Children of God	6,600+	23+
Churches only in one country	768,999+	28
Churches only in two countries	731,000+	7
Churches in other countries	4,244,000	n/a
Total	26,462,000	212

This gives the detail in the *World Churches Handbook*, and shows that the Jehovah's Witnesses are *the* worldwide Non-Trinitarian church – no other has branches in so many countries! The largest countries are the United States with 2.5 million, followed by Brazil and Mexico with 800,000 each, then Italy, Nigeria, the Philippines and Zaïre with 400,000 in each, the UK with 300,000, and then Argentina, France, Germany, Japan, Poland, Spain and Venezuela all with over 200,000 in each country.

The Mormons are in fewer countries and often have a smaller presence than the Jehovah's Witnesses, and are growing slightly slower. By far their largest number, some 5 million, are in the United States. The *Handbook* total concurs with other published information[12]. They have 250–300,000 new baptisms every year, with three-quarters claiming a previous Christian affiliation[13].

The Unification Church is almost certainly under represented in the *Handbook,* as their strength in the United States is not known. Likewise the Unitarians will be much stronger than given here, although their United States figure of 167,000 is included in the total above.

The Children of God, at one time called The Family, is very small, but is present almost certainly in more countries than the 23 given in the *Handbook*. They are particularly strong in Europe and South America. Their number in the United States is not known, but they have over a thousand in Mexico, followed by Venezuela with 600.

Satanists are *not* included in these figures, though would be included in 'Other Religions'. One book suggests that there are 'fewer than 6,000 worldwide'[14], most of whom are male, aged 13 to 30, and who practice Satanism privately. They view Christianity as 'narrow, defeatist, self-abasing and devoid of power'[15]. La Vey's Church of Satan is the most well known.

What Tables 10.1 and 10.2 indicate is that there is a large number of small Non-Trinitarian churches. They exist in most countries and testify to people's spiritual needs. A few are very large, like the Church of Scientology (122,000 in the UK alone in 1995[16]).

The Church of Christ, Scientist does not publish membership figures, but there are perhaps between 180 and 250,000 worldwide, in 2,600 branch churches in 66 countries, plus 270 smaller groups in 20 other countries[17]. The separate Religious Science is larger with a 1991 membership of 600,000 in 180 churches and 52 study groups in the USA and 47 groups in other countries[18]. The Unity School of Christianity had 110,000 members worldwide in 1994 in 300 churches, with an additional 35,000 in 150 informal weekly study groups. A new Unity study group is formed every month. They claim to reach 6 million people in 160 countries through their literature[19].

The various groups of Spiritualist Churches are more

likely to be found in Western countries. One of the largest is the Culte Antoiniste Association in France (58,000 in 1995). Many African countries also have Non-Trinitarian churches, such as the Ashes of Purification Church in Côte d'Ivoire (160,000), the Banzies especially in Gabon (109,000), or the Musama Disco in Ghana (106,000).

They show the importance of teaching new people when they come into our churches as much as possible as quickly as possible, as does the Costa Rican experience described in Chapter 9. Perhaps the popular Alpha courses, 10 week introductory sessions on Christianity[20], and similar courses developed for specific denominations, such as the Emmaus course from the Diocese of Wakefield, can help in this.

A Christian worldview

Another aspect of our culture can be called 'worldview'. If the Non-Trinitarian churches are part of the external church culture, this is part of the internal. Some of the 'atmosphere' in which Christians live is their view of the world as given by the Scriptures and the history of the church. The Very Rev Dr Tom Wright, Dean of Lichfield Cathedral, has tackled this issue very helpfully[21], and Rev Graham Cray, Principal of Ridley Hall, Cambridge often quotes him. As I have heard Graham's exposition of worldview more frequently than I have Tom Wright's, what follows is based on the outline Graham uses!

A worldview has to be able to *answer life's key questions*. These are postulated as:

- *Who are we?* Why are human beings on this planet? What are we supposed to be doing? What kind of being are we really?

- *Where are we?* What is the nature of the world and the universe in which it is placed? How did they get here? Where are they going? Is the scientific answer the only one? If we believe God made the world, does that mean He is the supreme Governor of it?

- *What went wrong?* Why is there so much evil everywhere? Why do I face so many obstacles and problems?

- *What is the solution?* Is there a way out? Christianity has a specific answer on this, but so do many Non-Trinitarian churches, cults and other religions. What needs to be done? What do I have to do?

- *What time is it?* Where are we in the global pattern of time? How does 'now' fit into the picture?

- *The key questions of the day*. These will naturally vary with time. As I write this, the funeral of Diana, Princess of Wales following her death in a car crash on 31st August 1997, took place only 7 months ago. That event drew millions to watch it on television, stopping cities throughout the world, even in Muslim countries. It drew out a new kind of national grieving, hundreds of flower shrines, and books of condolence (messages in the main addressed to Diana). One of the key questions was why the life and death of the young woman attracted such enormous attention. Also, did the reaction to her death reveal a spiritual need?[22]

A second element of a worldview is *the story by which we interpret life*. For Christians this is essentially the Scriptural view with creation, redemption, and ultimate destiny in heaven. Others assume that this life ends with death; there is nothing more. Others believe in conditional immortality. But whatever view we hold, it affects our thinking, and possibly our motivation and actions.

Bishop Lesslie Newbigin, the brilliant ex-Indian missionary who could keep audiences captivated right up to a few weeks before his death in January 1998 at the age of 88, explained the key elements of the Christian story[23]:

- The Bible gives a unique *interpretation* of history
- The Bible gives us the *meaning* of history
- It is the story of *God* not of this world[24]
- It is the story of a *people* God has chosen to be the bearer of His blessing for the whole of His creation.

This leads to the third element. A worldview helps to decide *the way we choose to live*. So, for example, a Christian worldview takes seriously Jesus' words, 'By this all men shall know you are my disciples, if you have love for one another.'[25] The author of a book on vision put this same thought in a different way: 'The organisation must be market oriented, giving customers high priority.'[26]

The fourth and final element of a worldview is *the symbols which represent our culture*. Christians use the Cross constantly as their symbol; Muslims use perhaps the Crescent; Buddhists maybe the Prayer Wheel. The credit card is a universal symbol of the global economy. In Britain the National Lottery's crossed finger logo is a symbol of chance and luck. In China when Mao was alive, the Little Red Book was a symbol of communism. In Africa, the drum is a symbol of communication, used for dancing and initiation rites. And across the world, wherever you go, is the big M for McDonald's, with identical stores and menus. A woman I once met in Greece said, 'Thank goodness there's a McDonald's in Athens, I can be sure the toilets are clean!' These symbols do not just represent our culture, they actually shape it by the image they represent. They are literally a sign. How then should Christians use the Cross?

Mathias Zahniser, Professor of Christian Mission at

Asbury Theological Seminary, Kentucky, has studied symbolism in depth[27], and suggests two types of religious symbols:

- *Dominant* symbols which represent the values most people in a society and/or religious tradition accept as obviously true. The cross or the bread and wine of the eucharist are dominant symbols especially for Roman Catholics and Orthodox Christians.
- *Instrumental* symbols, in contrast, have symbolic significance in specific or limited contexts. He cites as an example a rusty nail a priest handed to everyone coming into his Roman Catholic church one Good Friday.

He suggests that both types have three properties: they *condense* many actions, objects, and feelings into one single symbol; they *unify* things very different; they also *polarise* by holding extreme views together in dynamic tension.

When in the United Kingdom an Archbishop crowns the Sovereign on Coronation Day he is demonstrating that the monarch is not the ultimate ruler, but rules by the authority of God. When the new Chief Minister of Montserrat was sworn in during 1997 by the chief local Justice, he did so holding a Bible because he 'could swear by none higher'. Likewise when the President of the United States is sworn in. These are examples of a worldview being enacted which the majority of (notional) Christians in these three countries will affirm as the right way to do this kind of thing. But the Bible itself has in these instances become a dominant symbol and sign.

> People are searching for a new master story that will give meaning to their own lives. But it will have to be a holistic story, that can inform and inspire every part of life. A faith that is only concerned with what goes on in church

buildings for an hour on Sundays is irrelevant to such people.... At one time people would have dismissed the church as dull, boring, or irrelevant. Today, they are more likely to complain that it is 'unspiritual'. And while they may be unclear as to what 'spirituality' really is, a central part of it is undoubtedly this concern to find a new, all-embracing way of understanding and making sense out of the reality that is modern life.[28]

People want authenticity[29]. Danièle Hervieu-Léger[30] said that modern European societies are anaemic because they cannot recall their religious memory, which is perhaps another way of saying culture or worldview.

Worldview is wonderfully illustrated by the world map as drawn by an Australian given on the next page. Note the caption!

Postmodernism

Why look at worldview in a book looking at the world church? Simply because it describes part of the culture in which the church has to operate. The church has to be conscious both of the external and internal religious culture, and also of the external non-religious culture. This is changing. Peter Drucker, the management guru, whose writings have challenged many organisationally, has written:

> Every few hundred years throughout Western history, a sharp transformation has occurred. In a matter of decades society altogether rearranges itself – its worldview, its basic values, its social and political structures, its art, its key institutions. Fifty years later a new world exists. And the people born in that world cannot even imagine the world in which their grandparents lived and into which their own parents were born. Our age is such a transformation.[31]

226 FUTURE CHURCH

FIGURE 10.4
The World as the Australians see it

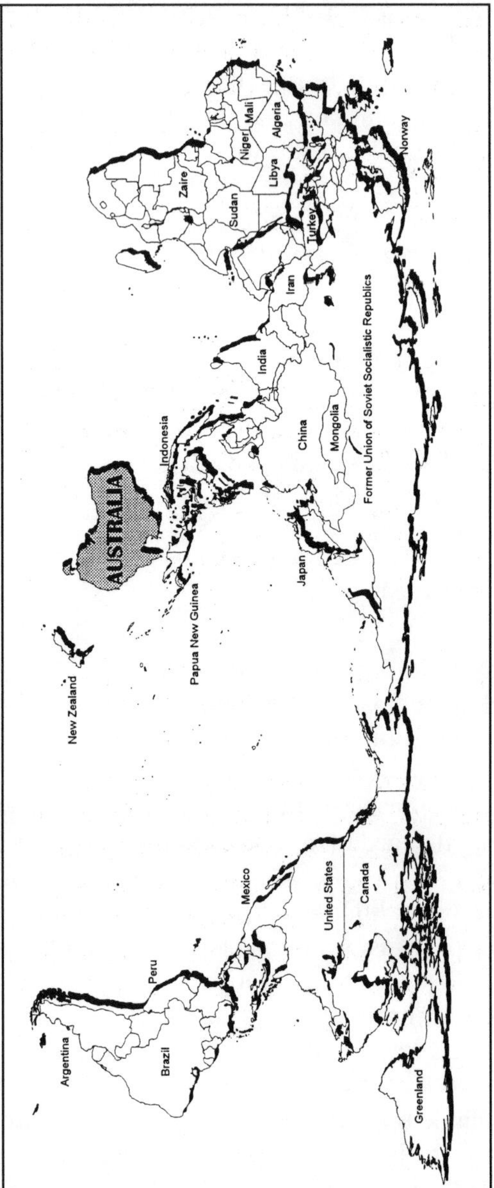

Many books have been written on this topic. One which looks at cultural, economic and political change in 43 societies has this fascinating diagram[32]:

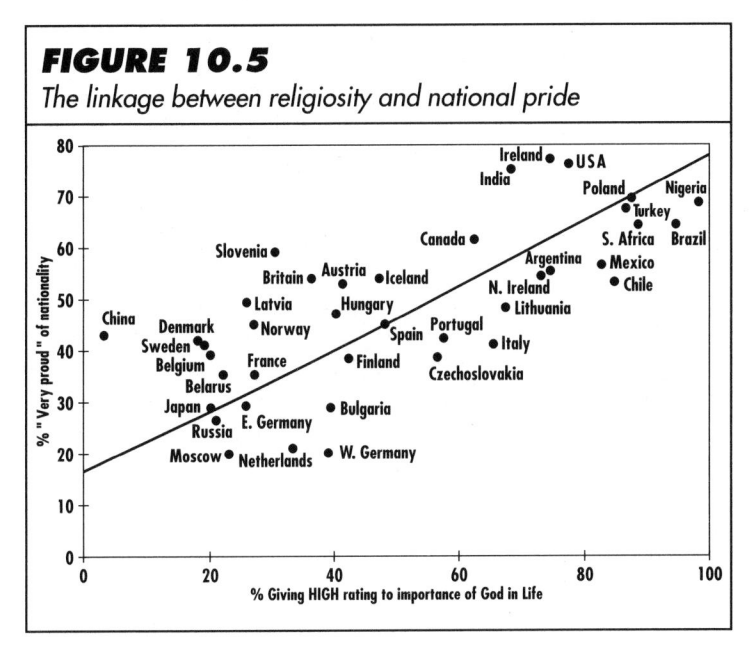

FIGURE 10.5
The linkage between religiosity and national pride

[Scatter plot showing % "Very proud" of nationality (y-axis, 0-80) vs % Giving HIGH rating to importance of God in Life (x-axis, 0-100). Countries plotted include: Ireland, USA, India, Poland, Nigeria, Turkey, Canada, S. Africa, Brazil, Slovenia, Argentina, Mexico, Britain, Austria, Iceland, N. Ireland, Chile, Latvia, Hungary, Lithuania, Denmark, Norway, Spain, Portugal, Sweden, Belgium, France, Finland, Italy, China, Belarus, Czechoslovakia, Japan, Bulgaria, Russia, E. Germany, Moscow, Netherlands, W. Germany. A positive trend line runs through the data.]

This diagram shows that the greater a percentage of people in a country rating God as important in their life the greater the percentage who are very proud of their nationality. National pride and inherent religiosity are correlated.

A useful if simplistic summary was provided by Tom Wolf when he addressed the North American Society for Church Growth, which can be put as a series of contrasts[33]:

Modern world	Postmodern world
Man is a sceptical person	Man is a spiritual person
Natural world	Rediscovery of the supernatural world
Rational authority	Embracing of alternative authorities
Progressive history	Disillusionment of historical progress
Scientific method	Multidimensional methodology
Industrial revolution	Information revolution

For church leaders thinking through the impact this has on their work, I find the summary provided by my colleague Heather Wraight, Assistant Director at Christian Research, the most helpful. She says the postmodern worldview is:

- Spirituality without Christianity
- Environment without a Creator
- Words without meaning
- Individuality without belonging
- The present without a future.

Try using these and wrestling with niche groups and community which is somehow what our churches have to do! Part of our problem, and it is implicit in our focusing throughout this book on the year 2010, is that we 'project the immediate past into the indefinite future. We should remind ourselves that Microsoft did not exist 20 years ago.'[34] Does that mean, as one group trying to think these issues suggested, that 'the institutional churches are too secure to take risk'?[35] But somehow they have to!

An analysis by the Princeton Religious Centre based on their research suggested there were three gaps to cause concern today amongst church people:[36]

- An *Ethics* gap. There is a difference between the way we think of ourselves and the way we actually are. This relates to religious *practice*, or, if you like, concerns the morals of the committed.

- A *Knowledge* gap. There is a gap between stated faith and evidence of the most basic knowledge about that faith. This relates to changing *belief*. Eddie Gibbs explores this to some extent in one of his books.[37]

- A *Behaviour* gap. This is the gap between believers and belongers, and leads to a decoupling between belief and practice. It relates to the third of Durkheim's descriptions of religion, *affiliation*.

Other key elements of global religious culture

It is critical that church leaders consider some of these changes. Professor Parker of the European Institute of Business Administration has analysed statistics across the world by religion.[38] For example, he gives the annual population growth rate in the mid-1990s for Anglican countries as 0.9%, Baptist 1%, Catholic 2%, Indigenous 3%, Lutheran 0.5%, Methodist 1%, Orthodox 0.9%, Pentecostal 1% and Presbyterian 1%, and compares these with Muslim 3%, Hindu 2%, Buddhist 2%, Sikh 2%, and Non-religious 2%, suggesting that the population in Christian countries is increasing slower than in non-Christian countries, and that therefore the church has to grow faster simply to catch up.

Many have written about the impact of secularisation. One of the books which emerged from a detailed analysis of The European Values Study[39], which included questions on religious practice, summarised the results of 'increased individual autonomy' as:

- Many have dissociated themselves from traditional religion

- There is a strong decline in the traditional ways of believing

- People no longer feel the need to explain the cosmos with reference to the supernatural

- The institutional church has lost its dominance in society, and the social power of guiding people's lives

- There has been a decrease in traditional social values, especially in the realm of sexual and civic morality

- The relevance of 'grand worldviews' has diminished and with it the tie between party and voter

- There has been a cultural shift from materialism to post-materialism.

These changes put detail on the culture shift Peter Drucker described. We also need to note other macro changes taking place. He and Lyle Schaller, an American church consultant and author of many books, were together at a church Leadership Network forum in December 1997. They said that 'the biggest issue in every developed country in the next 25 years is not rich or poor but the relationship between young and old'[40]. They also applauded 'the pastoral church, one focused on the congregation and the individual within the congregation, to be the most important social development in the last 25 years.'[41]

Hamish McRae, an economist working with the *Independent* newspaper, gave the following advantages for

Britain in the period 1995–2020[42]:

- It is ageing less quickly than any other large European economy
- It has made the structural adjustment out of mid-technology manufacturing industry more quickly than the rest of Europe
- It has closer relationships with both North America and East Asia than its continental partners.

So, how do the churches take advantage of these factors, or what responsibilities do they give us?

Church and mission

Changing culture affects the church's mission. Why should the churches be involved with mission? Richard Tiplady, Associate Director of the UK Evangelical Missionary Alliance, summarised seven reasons:

- The glory of God
- Need (because people haven't heard the gospel, or are hungry/oppressed)
- Command ('show if you can why you should not obey the last command of Christ')
- Love ('the love of Christ constrains us')
- Identity ('you are a chosen people', that is, the point of being a Christian is to do mission)
- Hope (participating in God's redemptive plan)
- Use of skills/abilities in the service of God.

These are not mutually exclusive, and neither is only one ever operative.[43]

In a major paper for a 'Current Trends in Global Mission' Study Day, Rev Donald Elliott, Secretary of the Churches Commission on Mission for Britain and Ireland suggested that four motivational motifs are operating today among different churches and movements:

- Reaching the Lost
- Empowering the Poor
- Meeting the Stranger
- Planting the Presence

All four motivations are alive and well, he thought, and not now generally regarded as mutually exclusive. Each is rooted in the constraining love of Christ. So co-operation in mission ought to be a good deal easier than it actually is.

He suggested that they could be mapped as follows:[44]

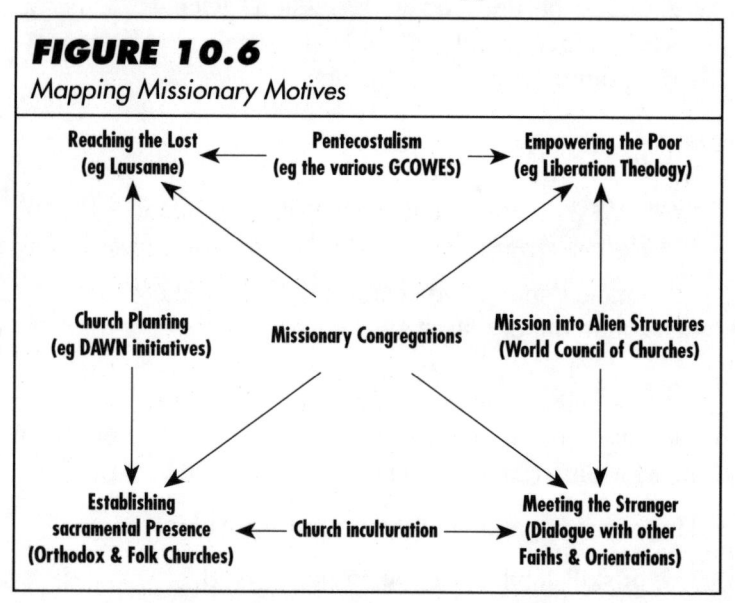

FIGURE 10.6
Mapping Missionary Motives

- **Reaching the Lost** (eg Lausanne) ← **Pentecostalism** (eg the various GCOWES) → **Empowering the Poor** (eg Liberation Theology)
- **Church Planting** (eg DAWN initiatives) — **Missionary Congregations** — **Mission into Alien Structures** (World Council of Churches)
- **Establishing sacramental Presence** (Orthodox & Folk Churches) ← **Church inculturation** → **Meeting the Stranger** (Dialogue with other Faiths & Orientations)

Donald Elliott also identified some of the contemporary major movements for the mission context as follows:

- Christianity is moving south and so is moving *towards the poor*.

- Paradoxically the *mixture of Christian mission and entrepreneurial capitalism* is with us again (for example, Korean missions).

- Christian mission finds itself in an increasingly *competitive religious world*. It is often perceived as a contributor to conflict (for example, Ireland, former Yugoslavia).

- The relation of *gospel and culture* is being re-visited, and the question of *syncretism* re-assessed.[45] Local contextual theologies are proliferating.

- Christianity is also becoming increasingly *Pentecostal and indigenous*[46]. The growth of indigenous missionary movements in the south (for example, India, Brazil) is one of the most striking features of world Christianity today.

- There are worries about these trends *ecclesiologically*. The human condition requires movements of unity and repentance quite as much as movements of identity and creativity. So ecumenism and mission need each other. The New Testament asserts the one Church of Jesus Christ as sign and instrument of God's reconciling purpose for all humankind.

- The cry of *proselytism* is increasingly heard. In many places religious freedom and religious tradition do not sit easily together (for example, Christianity in Russia, Islam in Malaysia).

- *Local churches learning together in mission* is a feature of the European context.

- 'Mission today,' said the Canberra Assembly of the World Council of Churches, 'is not so much into foreign lands as *into alien structures*' (for example, centres of economic power).

Others talk of the 're-emergence of tribalism' with the new break-up of multi-national states[47]. How can the world be organised if there are so many individual units? It can only be by 'federalism', even though it is recognised that this is an unpopular word, and a concept that hasn't a good history of success. Even 'tribalism' is becoming too big a word, and 'niche' is perhaps better. So that, for example, when describing the poor in South America, Doug Petersen, Director of Latin American Child Care, distinguished at least five types of poor in Latin America, all of which need to be addressed, and addressed in their own relevant way: rural Hacienda workers, urban immigrants, women, indigenous peoples and children[48].

The unit church

Culture affects the church's mission. The church's mission impacts each individual church. There are two ideas here, neatly summed up by John Buckeridge, editor of *Youthwork*, when being interviewed in a *Church Growth Digest* article[49]. He said both that 'there is an increasing tendency to work in niche groups' and that 'another key area is relationships'. While he was describing young people's work, it is also true in church management and leadership.

Chris Meyer, Director of Ernst & Young's Centre for Business Innovation in Boston, Massachusetts, talked about 'mastering complexity'. How do you do it? He said, 'you don't start with the factory – you start with the machinery.'[50] There is no point erecting a marvellous building if it cannot house the equipment. For the church, this means the people, but the people *in the context* of the church (or factory).

There is one remaining aspect of the *World Churches Handbook* statistics to consider: the actual number of churches. In 1995 there were 2.3 million churches or congregations in the world, giving an average community per church of 700, and an average membership of 400. The trends by continent are as follows, where k=thousands.

TABLE 10.3
Growth of congregations by continent 1960–2010

Year	Africa	Europe	Oceania	North America	Asia	South America	World
1960	100	100	100	100	100	100	100
1970	168	104	139	109	154	229	126
1980	255	106	155	123	306	367	165
1990	377	108	180	143	511	627	223
2000	463	106	194	159	669	767	263
2010	553	107	207	173	819	915	303
1960	126k	302k	21k	346k	104k	35k	934k
2010	698k	322k	43k	600k	848k	321k	2,832k
% of total	25%	11%	2%	21%	30%	11%	100%

We see that the number of churches has grown much faster proportionately than the number of people (people have doubled in the 50 years 1960 to 2010, churches have trebled). This means that the average church is getting smaller (average membership in 1960 was 590, in 2010 370).

This is true across all continents except in North America where the average church has got bigger! Average North American membership in 1960 was 390, in 2010 410). This could mean that there are so many churches already in North America that church planting on a huge scale simply

FIGURE 10.7
Proportion of individual congregations by continent 2010

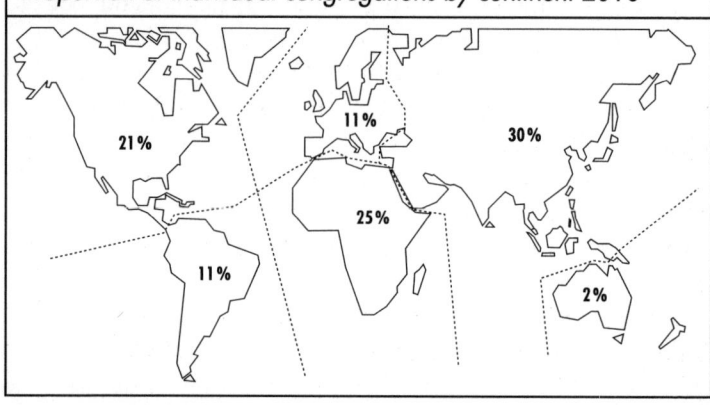

- North America: 21%
- Europe: 11%
- Asia: 30%
- Africa: 25%
- South America: 11%
- Oceania: 2%

FIGURE 10.8
Growth of individual congregations by continent

Legend:
— Africa
– – Europe
⋯⋯ Oceania
- - - North America
– – Asia
–·– South America

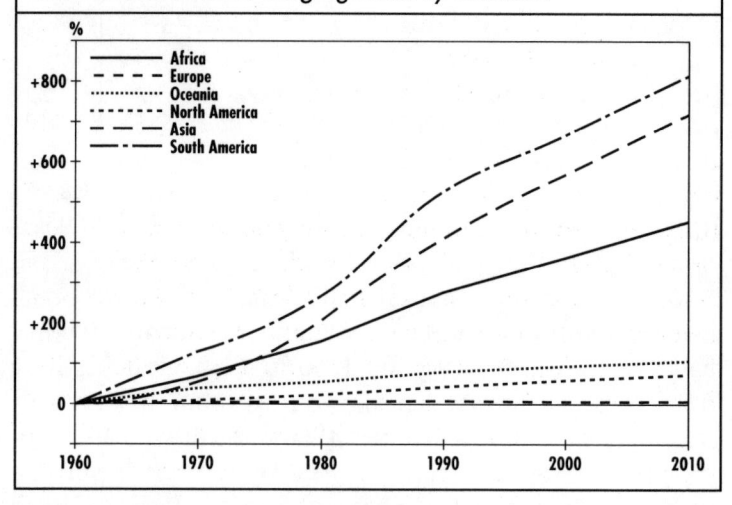

isn't relevant, and the emphasis is on getting larger, not more, churches.

Churches in South America are the biggest in the world – average membership in 1995 was 790. Europe was not far behind with 760; in North America it is 400, in Africa, Asia and Oceania 220 each. This is an interesting divide – Europe and South America don't usually go together, and Africa, Asia and Oceania mix Western and Third Worlds.

By denomination, the Catholics are largest with an average membership per church in 1995 of 1,400, then come the Orthodox with 1,030, Lutherans with 480, Baptists and Presbyterians with 210 each, the Indigenous with 150, Methodists with 140, Anglicans with 130, Other Churches with 110 and the Pentecostals with 100. The Non-Trinitarian churches had 110.

Immediately some of the denominational-continental links explored at the end of the second chapter are seen to be relevant. What do Europe and South America have in common? Lots of Catholics – that is why the average membership is so high when the Catholics have the largest average churches in the world. Why are Asia and Africa and Oceania so small? Because of the huge number of Pentecostal, Indigenous and Other Churches in these continents, not forgetting the many Anglicans in Oceania.

But what are 'churches'? Do we think of them as 'cultures'? For example, as the church developed in Taiwan, could the 'early Taiwanese pastors and missionaries have led (their people) to develop more indigenous forms of church order rather than a rather rigid, clumsy Presbyterian system'[51] imposed by the missionaries? A similar comment could be made of umpteen missionary situations.

How much is Anglicanism, especially in England where 41% of the world's Anglicans live, thought of as 'parishes'? And how much do its Free Church neighbours think of geographical 'areas of influence' as a consequence? How much do they acknowledge the Anglicanism of the 'rulingclasses'? Some divide the church spectrum into sacramental/liturgical, Protestant/evangelical, and Pentecostal/ charismatic[52], though I personally feel this is too compact. Nevertheless, it illustrates the variety of church cultures which exist.

So, finally, what does all this mean?

We have come a long way. Ultimately Christian leaders have to lead today, in postmodern today. What are some of the successful characteristics of successful leadership today?[53]

- *Clarity of vision.* Church leaders must know where they are going. Leaders *lead* people. A visionary leader works in tomorrow as well as living in today, even though postmodernism encourages people to both work and live only in today.

- *Identified values.* A Christian leader needs to know not only what he/she stands for but must be able to identify the relevance of those values and to do so unambiguously. A postmodern society changes values according to the situation in which they have been expressed. Can religious symbols bridge this gap of authenticity?

- *Applied worldview.* Our worldview impinges on our personal culture. Understanding our listener's position as well as knowing ours is critical for leadership else we will be answering questions no-one is asking.

- *High energy.* Leadership has always required energy to be successful, and a postmodern society does not dispute this. There is both physical and mental energy, and there is both positive and negative mental energy.[54]

- *Good relationships.* It used to be said that a gentleman's word was his bond. No longer! The only sure word is legal now. Underpinning the old statement was an implicit trust in the relationship of one person with another. A postmodern society translates trust into a computer printout or an Internet site, and makes personal relationships useful for as long as they are mutually beneficial.

- *Wise decisions.* Leadership requires the ability to judge between different factors, to sift them, identify the pros and cons of each, and decide which path the individual or organisation will follow. In a postmodern society, awash with information constantly being updated, the opportunity to view the total picture is more difficult, sometimes impossible, and can make the decision making process a blur over a period rather than instant in a moment in time.

- *Understood communication.* In a postmodern world communication is 'hot', pervasive and persuasive. Christian leaders have to master these elements knowing that they cannot command attention simply because of their position.

So we need to change. 'The key ingredient for successful change is agreement – teams of committed followers who sacrificially translate the vision into reality.'[55]

And, as hopefully this book has attempted to do, we have to interpret our data and ask ourselves questions like – is it for today or for tomorrow? For my family or my ministry? For a particular group or people generally? For something essential or something of passing interest? For our products or services or our image? For what we do or how we do it?

The ultimate model for change is the incarnation of Jesus Christ. That involved creation and coming, desertion and death, renewal and resurrection. May the Lord help us in whatever part of our journey is mirrored in His journey.

NOTES

1. Prayer letter of two missionaries working with JCS International, January 1998.
2. E-mail message from the Joshua Project Missionary expedition Leader Jeanette Kore, 23/1/98, number INTERNET:AD2000@xc.org
3. *Prayer Track News*, Global Harvest Ministries, AD 2000 & Beyond

Movement, Vol 7 No 1, Jan-Mar 1998, Colorado Springs, USA, Page 2.
4. *InnNews*, quarterly prayer and praise sheet of Inn Christian Ministries, Gillingham, Kent, UK, Winter 1997.
5. David Bogosian of the United States Centre for World Mission, Pasadena, California, estimates this number as closer to 15 million in 1997, 3.4 million in Africa, 3.5 million in Latin America and the Caribbean, 6.4 million in Asia, and 1.6 million elsewhere. E-mail of 19/12/97, number 102671,1724@compuserve. If the 15 million is correct then 3 not 5 million drift away.
6. Op cit (Item 3), Page 3, where I have taken the 53 million stated as a printing error for 35 million.
7. *Engaging the Powers*, by Professor Walter Wink, Fortress Press, Minneapolis, USA, 1992, Pages 53 and 54.
8. Article by Rev Dr Campbell Campbell-Jack in *Whitefield Briefing*, UK, March 1997.
9. Article 'Tomorrow's Company: The Role of Business in a Changing World' in *R Briefing*, Cambridge, UK, 1995.
10. Article 'A Preview of 'What's Next'' in *Netfax*, Number 85, 24th November 1997.
11. Ibid.
12. Such as *Mormonism*, by Kurt van Gorden, Zondervan Publishing Hose, Grand Rapids, Michigan, USA, 1995.
13. Ibid, Page 16.
14. *Satanism*, by Bob and Gretchen Passantino, Zondervan Publishing House, Grand Rapids, Michigan, 1995, Page 10.
15. Ibid, Page 11.
16. *UKCH: Religious Trends* No 1, 1998/99 edition, edited by Dr Peter Brierley, Christian Research, London, and Paternoster Publishing, Carlisle, UK, 1997, Table 10.4.2.
17. *Mind Sciences,* by Todd Ehrenborg, Zondervan Publishing House, Grand Rapids, Michigan, USA, 1995, Page 10.
18. Ibid, Pages 42, 43.
19. Ibid, Pages 62, 63.
20. By the end of 1997 it was estimated that 6,700 Alpha courses had been held in 58 countries; *Alpha* publicity brochure, March 1998.
21. *Jesus and the Victory of God*, Very Rev Dr Tom Wright, SPCK, London, UK, 1995.
22. See *Death of a Princess: Postmodern Spirituality and the Gospel*, Silverfish Creative Marketing, London, UK, July 1998, papers presented at the English Lausanne Committee Consultation, February 1998.

23. Address at the Holy Trinity Brompton Home Focus week, July 1997.
24. Is this why *The Book of God*, by Walter Wangerin, the Bible written like a novel (Lion Publishing, Oxford, UK, 1996), is so popular?
25. John chapter 13 verse 35.
26. From *Lead with Vision*, John L Thompson, International Thomson Business Press, London, UK, 1997, Page 207.
27. *Symbol and Ceremony,* making disciples across cultures, by Professor A H Mathias Zahniser, John Wesley Beeson Professor Christian Mission, E Stanley Jones School of World Mission and Evangelism, Asbury Theological Seminary, Wilmore, Kentucky, USA, MARC, Monrovia, California, USA, 1997, Pages 78 to 83.
28. *Looking at Evangelism from the Inside Out*, by John Drane, Administry, St Albans, UK, Volume 1, Number 5, March 1997.
29. Article 'The Falseness of Society', looking at the 1990s so far and the fragmentation of society, in the 200th issue of the music magazine, *The Face,* January 1997.
30. *Religion as a Collective Memory*, by Danièle Hervieu-Léger, quoted by Grace Davie.
31. Via a talk given by Rev Dr Graham Cray. No other details given.
32. *Modernization and Postmodernization*, by Ronald Inglehart, Princetown University Press, New Jersey, USA, 1997, Page 86.
33. Article 'The Urban Church and the Postmodern World' in *Netfax*, Texas, USA, Number 88, 5th January 1998, Page 1.
34. A fascinating article on looking at the future 'Revising the revolution' by Professor John Kay, in *The Bookseller*, London, UK, 8th August 1997, Page 21, and taken from *The Business of Economics',* Oxford University Press, Oxford, UK, 1996.
35. European Church Growth Association 'Think-Tank' meeting in Bedford, UK, 10th, 11th October 1997.
36. From Gallup's *Religion in America 1996* report, Princeton Religious Centre, New Jersey, USA, and quoted in *MARC Newsletter*, MARC, Monrovia, California, USA, Issue Number 3, 1996, Page 2.
37. *Winning Them Back*, by Professor Eddie Gibbs, USA, published by Monarch Publications, Crowborough, East Sussex, UK, 1993, and by Bridgepoint, USA, 1994 under the title *In Name Only*.
38. *Religious Cultures of the World*, A Statistical Reference, by Professor Philip Parker, Greenwood Press, London, UK, 1997, figures on Pages 77 to 84 used.
39. *The Individualising Society*, edited by Peter Ester, Loek Halman and Ruud de Moor, Tilburg University Press, The Netherlands, 1994, Pages 9 to 11.

40. *Next*, Leadership Network, Dallas, Texas, USA, Volume 4, Number 1, Jan-Feb 1998, Page 1.
41. Ibid.
42. *The World in 2020, by* Hamish McRae, HarperCollins, London, UK, 1995, Page 231.
43. Internal discussion paper *On the Nature of World Mission*, Richard Tiplady, Evangelical Missionary Alliance, Whitefield House, 186 Kennington Park Road, London SE11 4BT, UK.
44. *Charting Mission and Evangelism*, Rev Donald Elliott, Churches Commission on Mission, Council of Churches for Britain and Ireland, Inter-Church House, 35 Lower Marsh, London SE1 7RL, UK, unpublished paper, 1994.
45. As, for example, in the 1997 World Council of Churches Conference in Brazil.
46. In some countries, for example, India, they are becoming 'churches of the dispossessed'. People go the churches because they are disinherited, for personal survival, and with a overt or covert resistance to the powers that be. But some are also white, Anglo-Saxon Protestant!
47. Article 'The Global Paradox – coming soon to a country near you', *Ethos* magazine, London, UK, Issue 6, December/January 1998, Page 16.
48. Article 'Christian relief and development agencies in the twenty-first century' in *Transformation*, Oxford, UK, December 1996, Page 6.
49. Interviewed by Mrs Monica Hill, editor of the British Church Growth Association's *Church Growth Digest*, Bedford, UK, Volume 18, Number 4, Autumn 1997, Page 7.
50. *Management Today*, London, UK, February 1998, Page 34.
51. *Pentecost in the Hills of Taiwan,* by Professor Ralph Covell (Senior Professor of World Christianity at Denver Seminary, USA), Hope Publishing House, Pasadena, California, USA, 1998, Page 266.
52. See *InnNews*, Quarterly Prayer and Praise sheet from Inn Christian Ministries, Gillingham, Kent, UK, Winter 1997, Page 4.
53. This section is considerably expanded in a joint chapter with my colleague Heather Wraight in a forthcoming book by MODEM, The Canterbury Press, Norwich, UK, 1999. This looks also at the converse to this – characteristics of postmodernism which impact leaders.
54. This is worked out in more detail in Chapter 11 'Get up and go!' of *Management and Ministry,* edited by John Nelson, published for MODEM by The Canterbury Press, Norwich, UK, 1996, Page 125.
55. Article 'A time for change' by Brian Molitor, in *Ethos,* London, UK, Issue 6, December/January 1998, Page 10.

INDEX

Abortion, anti- 73
Active involvement 185
Adelaide's Lutherans 102
Administration of church poor 202
Africa
— Anglican growth 82, Tables 4.2, 4.3, 4.7, Fig 4.3
— Baptist growth 143, Table 7.1, Fig 7.2
— Catholic growth 62, Table 3.2
— Christian and Missionary Alliance churches Table 7.8, Fig 7.9
— Christian Brethren Table 7.9, Fig 7.10
— Church community 36, Tables 2.2, 2.3
— Church growth 20, Tables 2.4, 10.3, Figs 2.4, 10.8
— Churches of Christ Table 7.10, Fig 7.11
— Indigenous churches Table 6.8, Fig 6.4
— Lutheran change 101, Table 5.2, Fig 5.5
— Methodist growth 150, Tables 7.3, 7.4, Fig 7.4
— Nominal Christians Table 8.1
— Non-Trinitarian growth Table 10.1, Fig 10.3
— Orthodox growth 97, Table 5.1, Fig 5.2
— Other Churches growth Table 7.5, Fig 7.6
— Pentecostal growth 127, Table 6.2, Fig 6.2
— Presbyterian growth 111, Table 5.4, Fig 5.9
— Seventh-day Adventist churches Table 7.7, Fig 7.8
African Independent Churches 137, 138
African Indigenous churches 53
African Methodist Episcopal Church 151
African Methodist Episcopal Zion Church 152
Ageing society 231
Agenda for the Third Millennium 75
Alban, Father 98
Alexandrine Uniates 18
Alien structures 234
Alpha courses 221, 240
America, *see* North America or South America
American Baptist Association 146, Table 7.2
American Lutheran Church 102
Anglican
— Church 76f
— church size 89, 129, Table 4.7
— churches 89
— community Table 2.5
— continent, by 46, Tables 2.7, 2.8
— culture 90, 237
— grouping 18
— growth 78, Tables 2.6, 4.1, Fig 4.1
— membership 88
— Nominal Christians Table 8.1
— population growth rate 229
Anglican Renewal Ministries 90

Anglicans in Australia 92
Anglicans in Oceania 53
Angola
— Catholics Table 3.3, Fig 3.6
— civil war 83
— Methodists Table 7.4
— Salvation Army Table 7.11
Ansvar Survey of English Social Behaviour 211
Antiochene Uniates 18
Apostolic Christian Church 122
Apostolic Church 121, Table 6.1
Apostolic Church of Faith in Christ Jesus 122
Apostolic Church of Pentecost 122
Apostolic Faith Church 122
Apostolic Independent Churches, Africa 138
Appalachian Mountain Religion 178, 189
Argentina
— Catholics 68, Table 3.5, Fig 3.8
— Christian Brethren Table 7.9, Fig 7.10
— Jehovah's Witnesses 219
— Methodists 151
Armenian Apostolic Church 94
Armenian Baptists 140
Arnott, John 23
Ashes of Purification Church 221
Asia
— Anglican growth 84, Tables 4.2, 4.4, 4.7, Fig 4.3
— Baptist growth 144, Table 7.1, Fig 7.2
— Catholic growth 71, Table 3.2
— Christian and Missionary Alliance churches Table 7.8, Fig 7.9
— Christian Brethren Table 7.9, Fig 7.10
— Church community 36, Tables 2.2, 2.3
— Church growth 20, 21, Tables 2.4, 10.3, Figs 2.4, 10.8
— Churches of Christ Table 7.10, Fig 7.11
— Indigenous churches 136, Table 6.8, Fig 6.4
— Lutheran change 102, Table 5.2, Fig 5.5
— Methodist growth 151, Table 7.3, Fig 7.4
— Nominal Christians Table 8.1
— Non-Trinitarian growth Table 10.1, Fig 10.3
— Orthodox growth Table 5.1, Fig 5.2
— Other Churches growth Table 7.5, Fig 7.6
— Pentecostal growth 127, Table 6.2, Fig 6.2
— Presbyterian growth 112, Table 5.4, Figs 5.9, 5.10
— Seventh-day Adventist churches Table 7.7, Fig 7.8
— Small denominations 52
Assemblies of God 23, 121, Table 6.1
Atlas of World Christianity 9, 29, 33, 54, 75
Attrition characteristics Tables 9.5, 9.6
Australia
— Anglicans 84, Tables 4.4, 4.6, Fig 4.4
— Baptist churches 144
— Christian and Missionary Alliance churches Table 7.8, Fig 7.9
— Christian Brethren Table 7.9, Fig 7.10
— Churches of Christ Table 7.10, Fig 7.11
— Congregationalists 152
— Lutherans 102
— Methodists 152
— Nominals 185
— Oceania, in 19
— Pentecostals 127
— Presbyterians 152
— Seventh-day Adventists Table 7.7, Fig 7.8
— Worldview Fig 10.4
Austrian Catholics Table 3.6, Fig 3.9
Azusa Street, Los Angeles 121

Bailey, Prof Canon Edward 177, 189
Banzies Church, Gabon 221
Baptist
— Church size 129
— Churches 140f
— Community Table 2.5
— Continent, by 46, Tables 2.7, 2.8
— Growth 78, Table 2.6
— Nominal Christians Table 8.1
— Population growth rate 229
Baptist Church of the Brethren 146
Baptist Churches of North East India Table 7.2
Baptist Convention 143, 144
Baptist Missionary Association, USA 146
Baptist Union of Great Britain 14, Fig 1.2
Baptists in Australia 167

INDEX 245

Baptists in North America 48, 49, 51, Fig 2.7
Barna, George 188, 190
Barrett, Rev Dr David 17, 31–33, 54, 76, 88, 94, 153, 154, 168, 173, 174, 189, 216
Barrow, Simon 55
Behaviour Gap 229
Belarus 20
Belbin, Meredith 139
Belgium Catholics Table 3.6, Fig 3.9
Bentley, Peter 167, 190
Biafran war 84
Bible and authority 224
Bible and history 223
Births into Christian homes 213
Black, Tony 29
Blombery 'Tricia 92, 190
Bogosian, David 240
Bolivia
— Catholics Table 3.5, Fig 3.8
— Methodists 151
— Religious Society of Friends Table 7.11
Book of Common Prayer 90, 108
Book of God, The 241
Bookseller 241
Boredom 163, Fig 1.6
Born into church family Fig 1.5
Brankin, Fr Joe 74
Brazil
— Assemblies of God Table 6.1
— Baptists 143
— Catholics 68, Table 3.5, Fig 3.8
— Christian Brethren Table 7.9, Fig 7.10
— Churches of Christ Table 7.10, Fig 7.11
— Jehovah's Witnesses 219
— Lutherans 103
— Methodists 151
— Pentecostal churches 46, 128, 130, Table 6.1
— Presbyterian church 112
— Seventh-day Adventists Table 7.7, Fig 7.8
Brazil for Christ, Brazil Table 6.1
Brethren, see Christian Brethren
Brierley, Dr Peter 28, 29, 54, 75, 190
Brisbane's Lutherans 102
Britain, see United Kingdom
British advantages 231
Broken Snare 139
Brownsville Assembly of God 23
Buckeridge, John 234

Buddhist
— Population growth rate 229
— Symbols 223
Burkino Faso's Christian and Missionary Alliance churches Table 7.8, Fig 7.9
Burundi
— Catholics Table 3.3, Fig 3.6
— Religious Society of Friends Table 7.11
Business of Economics, The 241
Byzantine Uniates 18

Calvin 147
Calvinistic churches 108
Cameroon Catholics Table 3.3, Fig 3.6
Campbell-Jack, Dr Campbell 214, 240
Canada
— Anglicans Tables 4.5, 4.6, Fig 4.4
— Catholics Table 3.4, Fig 3.7
— Christian and Missionary Alliance churches Table 7.8, Fig 7.9
— Christian Brethren Table 7.9, Fig 7.10
— Churches of Christ Table 7.10, Fig 7.11
— Mennonites Table 7.11
Canterbury, Archbishop of 83, 90
Carey, William 144
Caribbean 19
Casting the Net, the Unchurched Population 190
Catholic
— Church 56f
— Church size 32, 72, 89
— Community Table 2.5
— Continent, by 60, Tables 2.7, 2.8, 3.2, Figs 3.4, 3.5
— Grouping 18
— Growth 57, 78, Tables 2.6, 3.1, Figs 3.3, 3.5
— Nominal Christians Table 8.1
— Population growth rate 229
— World church,a 45
Catholic Missionary Education Centre 74
Catholics in Europe 48, Fig 2.7
Catholics in North America 48, 49, Fig 2.7
Causes of Growth and Desertion in Evangelical Churches in Costa Rica 191
Central America 19
Centre for the Study of Christianity in the Non-western World 33

INDEX

Centre for the Study of Implicit Religion and Spirituality 177
Chad's Christian Brethren Table 7.9, Fig 7.10
Chaldean Uniates 18
Changing Churches 190
Charismatic Churches 18, 32, 120f
Children joining as adults 25
Children of God 220, Table 10.2
Chile
— Catholics Table 3.5, Fig 3.8
— Christian and Missionary Alliance Churches Table 7.8, Fig 7.9
— Methodists 151
China
— Catholics Table 3.8, Fig 3.11
— Christian and Missionary Alliance Churches Table 7.8, Fig 7.9
— Church growth 21
— Home Meetings, *see also*
— Indigenous churches 136
China, Premier, State Council, of 56
Cho, Dr David Yonggi 114, 119
Christ Apostolic Church Table 6.1
Christendom size and growth Table 2.1, Fig 2.2
Christened 184
Christian and Missionary Alliance 157, 159, 161f, Table 7.6, Fig 7.7
Christian Brethren 19, 154, 157, 160, 163f, Table 7.6, Fig 7.7
Christian Church, Brazil Table 6.1
Christian Community
— 1960–2010 Table 2.1
— Continent, by Table 2.2
— Worldwide 169
Christian, first knew I was, by age Fig 8.7
Christian Research Association 28, 190
Christianity in Europe 118
Christianity magazine 29, 168
Church culture Fig 10.1
Church future 214
Church growth 21, 27, 34, Fig 1.4
Church Growth Digest 234, 242
Church in the World 30f
Church movements 29
Church nominalism 190
Church of Christ, Scientist 220
Church of England
— England, in 86
— Name 77
— Parish system 44
— *See also* Anglican
Church of England Newspaper 76
Church of God Table 6.1
Church of God (Anderson) 121, Table 6.1
Church of God (Cleveland) 121, Table 6.1
Church of God in Christ Table 6.1
Church of God Mission International Table 6.1
Church of God of Prophecy 121, Table 6.1
Church of Jesus Christ of Latter-day Saints, *see* Mormons
Church of North India 154
Church of Satan 177
Church of Scientology 220
Church of Scotland Presbyterian Church 46
Church of the Nazarene 157, Tables 7.6, 7.11, Fig 7.7
Church size
— Continent, by 89, 236
— Denomination, by 237
Church Times 190
Churches of Christ 157, 164f, Table 7.6, Fig 7.7
Co-Redemptrix, Mary as 73, 75
Coates, Gerald 23
Collins, Tony 9
Colonial heritage 49
Columbia
— Catholics 68, Table 3.5, Fig 3.8
— Christian and Missionary Alliance churches Table 7.8, Fig 7.9
Columbus, Christopher 130
Communication understood 239
Community
— Growth worldwide 213
— Importance 120
— Involvement 206
— Service 131
— Size Table 2.1
Complexity, mastering 234
Congo civil war 83
Conservative Baptist Association 146
Conversions 25
Coomes, Mrs Anne 92
Coptic Orthodox Church, Egypt 97
Cornwall's Methodist church 153
Coronation Day 224
Costa Rica
— Catholics Table 3.4, Fig 3.7
— Churches 191f
Côte d'Ivoire
— Indigenous Churches Table 6.9
— Methodists Table 7.4
— Spiritualist Churches 221
— Toura people, 212
Council of Baptist Churches 144

Counsellor, lack of 207
Covell, Prof Ralph 139, 242
Coxill, H Wakelin 28
Cray, Rev Graham 221
Cross of Christians 223, 224
Cuban Catholics 65, Table 3.4, Fig 3.7
Culte Antoiniste Association 221
Culture
— Anglican 90
— General 214f
Czech Republic Catholics Table 3.6, Fig 3.9

Daily increase to church 21, Table 1.1
Daily increase to world population Table 1.2, Fig 1.7, 27
Danish missionaries in Africa 102
Dartford, Kent 181
DAWN Report 167
DAWN Initiatives Fig 10.6
Dayton, Ed 17
Death
— Drop in churchgoing 25, Fig 1.6
— Princess of Wales 240
— Worldwide 213
Dechurched 187
Decision making 239
Decline of Protestants, Costa Rica 197
Deeper Life Church Table 6.1
Defection worldwide 213
Demands of the church 202
Demands of the gospel 203
Democratic Republic of Congo, see Zaïre
Denmark's Lutherans 103
Denominations by continent 45
Diana, Princess of Wales 222
Director leaders 132
Disciples of Christ 157, 164
Discipleship, lack of 207
Disney Corporation 49
Dominican Republic
— Catholics Table 3.4, Fig 3.7
— Church of God of Prophecy Table 6.1
— Church of the Nazarene Table 7.11
Dorothea Mission 28
Drane, Prof Dr John 241
Drucker, Peter 225, 230
Drum, African communication 223
Durkheim 229
Dutch Reformed Church, South Africa 111

East African Revival 83
Ecuador
— Catholics Table 3.5, Fig 3.8
— Christian and Missionary Alliance churches Table 7.8, Fig 7.9
Education of pastors 207
Egyptian Orthodox 97
Ehrenborg, Todd 240
El Salvador
— Catholics Table 3.4, Fig 3.7
— Pentecostals Table 6.6
Elim Pentecostal 121, Table 6.1
Elliot, Rev Donald 232, 242
Emmaus Course 221
Empires 52, 77
Energy 238
Engaging the Powers 240
English Anglicans Table 4.6, Fig 4.4
Environment without a Creator 228
Ester, Peter 241
Estonia
— Europe, in 20
— Lutherans 104
Ethics Gap 229
Ethiopia
— Baptists 143
— Independent Churches 138
— Lutherans 101
— Orthodox Church 97
— Pentecostals Table 6.5
Ethos magazine 242
Europe
— Anglican growth 85, Tables 4.2, 4.5, 4.7, Fig 4.3
— Baptist growth 145, Table 7.1, Fig 7.2
— Catholic growth 62, 68, Table 3.2
— Christian and Missionary Alliance Churches Table 7.8, Fig 7.9
— Christian Brethren Table 7.9, Fig 7.10
— Church community 36, 37, Tables 2.2, 2.3
— Church growth Tables 2.4, 10.3, Figs 2.4, 10.8
— Churches of Christ Table 7.10, Fig 7.11
— Institutional churches 52
— Lutheran change 103, Tables 5.2, 5.3, Fig 5.5
— Methodist growth 150, Table 7.3, Fig 7.4
— Nominal Christians 171, Table 8.1
— Non-Trinitarian growth Table 10.1, Fig 10.3
— Orthodox growth 96, Table 5.1, Fig 5.2
— Other Churches growth Table 7.5, Fig 7.6

— Pentecostal growth 126, Table 6.2, Fig 6.2
— Presbyterian growth 111, Table 5.4, Fig 5.9
— Seventh-day Adventist churches Table 7.7, Fig 7.8
Europe Without Priests 75
European Ecumenical Assembly, 1997 52
European Values Study 229
Eurostat Yearbook 118
Evangelical Lutheran Church of Germany (EKD) 102, 104, 118
Evangelicals in South America 130
Evangelism-in-Depth 193
Evangelism in South Korea 115
Evangelism, lack of 207
Exclusive brethren 160

Face, The magazine 241
Faith Without the church? 190
Family, The, see Children of God
Family pressure 202, 203
Finding Faith in 1994 183, 190, 211
Finland
— Lutherans 103
— Missionaries in Africa 102
Flower shrines 222
Forbidden Revolutions 118, 139
Fourth Dimension, The 119
France
— Catholics Tables 3.6, 3.7, Figs 3.9, 3.10
— Jehovah's Witnesses 219
— Pentecostals Table 6.3
— Spiritualist Churches 221
Free Church of Scotland 177
Free Methodists, UK 150
Future Church 19

Gabon
— Christian and Missionary Alliance churches Table 7.8, Fig 7.9
— Spiritualist churches 221
Gallup survey 194, 203
GCOWE, Korea, 1995 114, 115
General Association of Baptists 146
General Association of Registered Baptists 146
General Baptists 140
German
— Baptists 145
— Catholics Tables 3.6, 3.7, Figs 3.9, 3.10
— Christian Brethren Table 7.9, Fig 7.10
— Jehovah's Witnesses 219
— Lutherans 46, 103, 104f, Fig 5.6
— Lutherans in Australia 102
— Mennonites Table 7.11
— Missionaries 102
— Moravians Table 7.11
— Pentecostals Table 6.3
Germany, West, population Fig 5.7
Ghana
— African Methodist Episcopal Zion Church 152
— Indigenous Churches Table 6.9
— Methodists Table 7.4
— Pentecostals Table 6.5
— Presbyterian churches 111
— Seventh-day Adventists Table 7.7, Fig 7.8
— Spiritualist churches 221
Gibbs, Prof Eddie 184, 185, 190, 229, 241
Global Mapping International 28
God is Love Church, Brazil Table 6.1
Gómez, Jorge 9, 191, 194, 210
Gorden, Kurt van 240
Greek Orthodox Church 97
Green, Lynn 167
Gross figures 23
Growth of Protestants, Costa Rica Table 9.1, Figs 9.1, 9.2, 9.3
Grubb, Sir Kenneth 28
Guatemala
— Catholics Table 3.4, Fig 3.7
— Christian Brethren Table 7.9, Fig 7.10
— Church of the Nazarene Table 7.11
— Pentecostals Table 6.6
— Religious Society of Friends Table 7.11

Haiti
— Catholics Table 3.4, Fig 3.7
— Church of the Nazarene Table 7.11
Healing ministry 120, 131
Helwys, Thomas 140
Heritage
— Christian 44
— Colonial 49
Hervieu-Léger, Danièle 225, 241
Hierarchical bureaucracy 44
Hill, Dr Clifford 23
Hill, Mrs Monica 242
Hill, Steve 23
Hindu
— Adherents 31
— Population growth rate 229
Holy Spirit 178

Home Meetings in China 37, 45, 52, 156, 159
Honduras
— Catholics Table 3.4, Fig 3.7
— Christian Brethren Table 7.9, Fig 7.10
— Moravians Table 7.11
House Churches, *see* New Churches
House of Lords 44
Hughes, Dr Philip J 118, 167, 190
Hume, Cardinal Basil 40
Hungary
— Catholics Table 3.6, Fig 3.9
— Presbyterians 111
— Reformed Churches 46

Iceland's Lutherans 103
IINDEF 191, 210
Ill-health Fig 1.6
Implicit religion 177
Importance of God Fig 10.5
In Name Only 190
Independence of Pentecostals 132
Independent on Sunday 75, 98, 118
India
— Catholics Table 3.8, Fig 3.11
— Christian Brethren Table 7.9, Fig 7.10
— Church of God (Cleveland) Table 6.1
— Churches of Christ Table 7.10, Fig 7.11
— Indigenous churches 136
— Lutherans 102
— Mennonites Table 7.11
— Methodists 151
— Pentecostals 128, Table 6.4
— Presbyterian churches 112
— Salvation Army Table 7.11
— Seventh-day Adventists Table 7.7, Fig 7.8
Indigenous
— Church size 129
— Churches 133f
— Churches in Africa 48, Fig 2.7
— Community Table 2.5
— Continent, by 46, Tables 2.7, 2.8
— Grouping 18, 19
— Growth 42, 78, Table 2.6
— Nominal Christians Table 8.1
— Population growth rate 229
Individualising Society 241
Individuality without belonging 228
Indonesia
— Catholics Table 3.8, Fig 3.11
— Lutherans 102
— Pentecostals 128, Table 6.4
— Presbyterian churches 112, 116, Fig 5.10
— Seventh-day Adventists Table 7.7, Fig 7.8
Influence on others 188
Inglehart, Ronald 241
InnNews 240, 242
Inside the Mind of Unchurched Harry and Mary 187, 190
Institutional churches 42, 43, 52, 89, Fig 2.5
Instrumental Churches of Christ 157, 166
Integrity of Korean Christians 116
Intercontinental Church Society 87
International Bulletin of Missionary Research 28, 54, 92, 139, 189
Irish Christian Handbook 190
Italo-Greek-Albanian Uniates 18
Italy
— Catholics Tables 3.6, 3.7, Figs 3.9, 3.10
— Christian Brethren Table 7.9, Fig 7.10
— Churches of Christ Table 7.10, Fig 7.11
— Jehovah's Witnesses 219
— Pentecostals Table 6.3

Jakarta
— Cathedral 116
— Mosque Fig 5.11
— National Monument 116
Jamaica's African Methodist Episcopal Zion Church 152
Japan's Jehovah's Witnesses 219
Jehovah's Witnesses 32, 198, 216, 218, Table 10.2
Jesus and the Victory of God 240
JESUS film 212
Jesus' parable on nominalism 175
Johnstone, Patrick 9, 16, 17, 18, 73, 94, 170
Joining the Catholic church 198
Joining the church Fig 1.5, 25

Kale Heywet Baptist Church, Ethiopia 144
Kay, Prof John 241
Kenya
— Anglicans Tables 4.3, 4.6, Fig 4.4
— Catholics Table 3.3, Fig 3.6
— Church of God Table 6.1
— Elim church Table 6.1

INDEX

— Indigenous Churches Table 6.9
— Methodists Table 7.4
— Pentecostals Table 6.5
— Presbyterian churches 111
— Religious Society of Friends Table 7.11
— Seventh-day Adventists Table 7.7, Fig 7.8
Kenya Research Centre 17
Kerkhofs, Jan 75
Kessler, Dr John 9, 193
Kivengere, Bishop Festo 90
Knowledge Gap 229
Knox, John 108
Korea, South, *see* South Korea
Kotter & Heskett 214
Kwang Lim Methodist Church, Seoul 115, 151

Lambeth Conference 76, 80, 91
Latin American poor 234
Latvia
— Europe, in 20
— Lutherans 104
Lausanne Committee 28, 240, Fig 10.6
Lausanne Congresses 186
Leach, Rev John 90, 92
Lead with Vision 241
Leadership disagreement Fig 1.6
Leadership in the Church 214
Leadership Network forum 230
Leadership of Pentecostals 132
Leadership strife, behaviour 197, 202, 208
Leaving the church
— Costa Rica 197, 198, 201
— UK Fig 1.6
Liberation Theology 130, Fig 10.6
Liberian civil war 83
Lifestyle of church members 202, 207
Linear regression 29
Listed buildings 44
Lithuania 20
Little Red Book 223
Living close to family 188
Looking at Evangelism from the Inside Out 241
Lord's Army 96
Loss of faith 25
Luther, Martin 98, 108
Lutheran
— Church 98f
— Church, North America 102
— Church size 89, 105, 129
— Community Table 2.5
— Continent, by 46, Tables 2.7, 2.8
— Decline 98, Table 2.6, Fig 5.3
— Nominal Christians Table 8.1
— Population growth rate 229
Lutherans in Australia 118
Lutterworth Press 28

McCall, Don 129
McCauley, Deborah 178, 189
McDonald's 223
McGrath, Dr Alister 54
McRae, Hamish 230, 242
Madagascar Catholics Table 3.3, Fig 3.6
Making Christ Known 190
Malawi
— Churches of Christ Table 7.10, Fig 7.11
— Indigenous Churches Table 6.9
Malaysian Anglicans 85, Table 4.4
Management and Ministry 242
Management Teams 139
Management Today 242
MARC (International) 17, 28
MARC Newsletter 241
Marcus, John 9
Marginal Protestants 32
Martin, Prof David 118, 130, 139
Melbourne's Lutherans 102
Membership, North America 236
Mennonites 19, 157, Tables 7.6, 7.11, Fig 7.7
Methodist
— Church size 129
— Churches 147f
— Community Table 2.5
— Continent, by 46, Tables 2.7, 2.8
— Growth Table 2.6
— Nominal Christians Table 8.1
— Population growth rate 229
Mexico
— Catholics Table 3.4, Fig 3.7
— Children of God 220
— Church of God Table 6.1
— Jehovah's Witnesses 219
— Pentecostals Table 6.6
— Seventh-day Adventists Table 7.7, Fig 7.8
Meyer, Chris 234
Microsoft 228
Mihoc, Father 96
Miller, William 160
Mind Sciences 240
Missionary motives 233, Fig 10.6
Missouri/Australian Crusade 1964 144
Modernization and Postmodernization 241

INDEX 251

Moldova, Europe, in 20
Molitor, Brian 242
Mongolian church 212
Montserrat, Chief Minister 224
Moravians 157, Tables 7.6, 7.11, Fig 7.7
Mormons 32, 198, 216, 218, 219, 240, Table 10.2
Mosque in Jakarta Fig 5.11
Moving to another area 182, Figs 1.5, 1.6
Mozambique civil war 83
Musama Disco Church, Ghana 221
Muslim
— Population growth rate 229
— Strength 31
— Symbol 223
Myanmar
— Baptist churches 144, Table 7.2
— Churches of Christ Table 7.10, Fig 7.11
Myers, Boyd 5, 9
Myers, Bryant 33

Namibian Lutherans 101
National Association of Free Will Baptists 146
National Baptist Convention
— America 145, Table 7.2
— Brazil 143
— United States 145, Table 7.2
National Lottery 223
National pride Fig 10.5
Nazarene, *see* Church of the Nazarene
Nazir-Ali, Rt Rev Michael 184, 190
Net figures 23
Netfax 214, 240, 241
Netherlands
— Catholics Table 3.6, Fig 3.9
— Christian and Missionary Alliance Churches Table 7.8, Fig 7.9
— Mennonites Table 7.11
— Presbyterians 111
— Reformed Churches 46
New Churches 14, 15, 28, Fig 1.3
New International Dictionary of the Christian Church 29, 118, 139, 167
New Zealand
— Anglicans 85, Table 4.4
— Christian Brethren Table 7.9, Fig 7.10
— Oceania, in 19
Newbigin, Bishop Lesslie 222
News Review 29
Next 242

Nicaragua
— Catholics Table 3.4, Fig 3.7
— Moravians Table 7.11
Nigeria
— African Methodist Episcopal Zion Church 152
— Anglicans 83, Tables 4.3, 4.6, Fig 4.4
— Apostolic Church Table 6.1
— Baptists 144, Table 7.2
— Catholics Table 3.3, Fig 3.6
— Christian Brethren Table 7.9, Fig 7.10
— Christian Fellowship Table 6.1
— Church of the Nazarene Table 7.11
— Churches of Christ 166, Table 7.10, Fig 7.11
— Indigenous Churches 46, Table 6.9
— Jehovah's Witnesses 219
— Lutherans 101
— Methodists Table 7.4
— Pentecostals 128, Tables 6.1, 6.5
— Salvation Army Table 7.11
Nominal Catholics 74
Nominalism 169f
Nominalism Reconceived 190
Non-charismatic Churches 140f
Non-institutional churches 42, 89, Fig 2.5
Non-Instrumental Churches of Christ 157, 166
Non-Trinitarian community 32, 216, Table 10.1
North America
— Anglican growth 85, Tables 4.2, 4.5, 4.7, Fig 4.3
— Baptist growth 51, 145, Table 7.1, Fig 7.2
— Catholic growth 64, Table 3.2
— Christian and Missionary Alliance churches Table 7.8, Fig 7.9
— Christian Brethren Table 7.9, Fig 7.10
— Church community 36, Tables 2.2, 2.3
— Church growth 21, Tables 2.4, 10.3, Figs 2.4, 10.8
— Churches of Christ Table 7.10, Fig 7.11
— Continental definition 19
— Indigenous churches 136, Table 6.8, Fig 6.4
— Lutheran change 102, Table 5.2, Fig 5.5

252 INDEX

— Methodist growth 151, Table 7.3, Fig 7.4
— Nominal Christians Table 8.1
— Non-Trinitarian growth Table 10.1, Fig 10.3
— Orthodox growth Table 5.1, Fig 5.2
— Other Churches growth Table 7.5, Fig 7.6
— Pentecostal growth 128, Table 6.2, Fig 6.2
— Presbyterian growth 111, Table 5.4, Fig 5.9
— Seventh-day Adventist churches Table 7.7, Fig 7.8
Northern Ireland non-religious 188
Norway
— Lutherans 103
— Missionary training 103
Notional Christians 179

Oceania
— Anglican growth 48, 53, 84, Tables 4.2, 4.4, 4.7, Figs 2.7, 4.3
— Baptist growth 144, Table 7.1, Fig 7.2
— Catholic growth 71, Table 3.2
— Christian and Missionary Alliance Churches Table 7.8, Fig 7.9
— Christian Brethren Table 7.9, Fig 7.10
— Church community 36, Tables 2.2, 2.3
— Church growth Tables 2.4, 10.3, Figs 2.4, 10.8
— Churches of Christ Table 7.10, Fig 7.11
— Continental definition 19
— Indigenous churches Table 6.8, Fig 6.4
— Lutheran change 102, Table 5.2, Fig 5.5
— Methodist growth 152, Table 7.3, Fig 7.4
— Nominal Christians Table 8.1
— Non-Trinitarian growth Table 10.1, Fig 10.3
— Orthodox growth Table 5.1, Fig 5.2
— Other Churches growth Table 7.5, Fig 7.6
— Pentecostal growth 126, Table 6.2, Fig 6.2
— Presbyterian growth 111, Table 5.4, Fig 5.9
— Seventh-day Adventist churches Table 7.7, Fig 7.8
Old Believers, Russia 94

Oosthuizen, Prof 53, 133, 137, 139
Open Brethren, *see* Christian Brethren
Operation Mobilization 17
Operation World 9, 16, 17
Orthodox
— Church size 89, 97, 129
— Churches 93f, Fig 10.6
— Community Table 2.5
— Continent, by Tables 2.7, 2.8
— Counting differences 32
— Europe, in 45, 48, Fig 2.7
— Growth 78, Table 2.6
— Nominal Christians Table 8.1
— Population growth rate 229
Orthodox News 54, 93, 118
Other Churches
— 154f
— Asia, in 48, Fig 2.7
— Church size 129
— Community Table 2.5
— Continent, by Tables 2.7, 2.8
— Grouping 18, 19
— Growth 42, 78, Table 2.6
— Nominal Christians Table 8.1
Overseas Missionary Fellowship 85, 139

Pacific islands 85
Pacific territories 19
Pakistan
— Christian Brethren Table 7.9, Fig 7.10
— Presbyterian churches 112, 113
Panama Catholics Table 3.4, Fig 3.7
Papua New Guinea
— Anglicans 85
— Christian Brethren Table 7.9, Fig 7.10
— Lutherans 102
— Pentecostals 127
— Seventh-day Adventists Table 7.7, Fig 7.8
Paraguay
— Catholics Table 3.5, Fig 3.8
— Mennonites Table 7.11
Parker, Prof Philip 229, 241
Passantino, Bob and Gretchen 240
Pensacola 23, 29
Pentecost in the Hills in Taiwan 139, 242
Pentecostal
— Attendance, Costa Rica 193, Table 9.4
— Beliefs Table 6.7
— Church size 129
— Churches 121f

— Community Table 2.5
— Continent, by 46, Tables 2.7, 2.8
— Growth 42, 78, Table 2.6
— Mainline groups 18
— Nominal Christians Table 8.1
— Population growth rate 229
— South America, in 48, 52, Fig 2.7
Persecution 116
Perth's Lutherans 102
Peru
— Catholics 68, Table 3.5, Fig 3.8
— Christian and Missionary Alliance churches Table 7.8, Fig 7.9
— Church of the Nazarene Table 7.11
— Methodists 151
— Presbyterian church 112
— Religious Society of Friends Table 7.11
— Seventh-day Adventists Table 7.7, Fig 7.8
Petersen, Doug 234
Philippines
— Anglicans Table 4.4
— Baptist churches 144
— Catholics Table 3.8, Fig 3.11
— Christian and Missionary Alliance Churches Table 7.8, Fig 7.9
— Churches of Christ Table 7.10, Fig 7.11
— Indigenous Churches 136
— Jehovah's Witnesses 219
— Methodists 151
— Pentecostals Table 6.4
— Seventh-day Adventists Table 7.7, Fig 7.8
Pickering, Bill 90
Pioneer Churches 23
Poland
— Catholics Tables 3.6, 3.7, Figs 3.9, 3.10
— Jehovah's Witnesses 219
Poor, types of, Latin America 234
Pope 56, 64, 65, 73, 90
Pope John Paul II 73, 75
Population
— Comparison 25, Fig 1.7
— World Fig 2.2
Portuguese Catholics Table 3.6, Fig 3.9
Postmodernism 44, 225f
Power of Jesus Around the World Pentecostal Church 212
Poynter, Pam 5, 9
Prayer life in South Korea 114
Prayer Mountain 114
Prayer Track News 239
Praying with others 185

Presbyterian
— Beliefs Table 6.7
— Church 108f
— Church size 89, 129
— Community Table 2.5
— Continent, by 46, Tables 2.7, 2.8
— Growth 78, Table 2.6
— Nominal Christians Table 8.1
— Population growth rate 229
Presbyterian Church of Australia Continuing 111
Present without a future 228
President of India 56
Price, Clive 29
Princeton Religious Centre 229, 241
Priorities 176
Probert, J C C 168
Progressive National Baptist Convention 146
Prophecy Today magazine 23
Prospects for the Eighties 167
Prospects for the Nineties 139, 168
Protestant Growth and Desertion in Costa Rica 211
Puerto Rican Catholics Table 3.4, Fig 3.7
Purpose for living 188

Quadrant 118, 139

R Briefing 240
Rechurched 187
Reformed Churches 46
Relationships 238
Religion as a Collective memory 241
Religion in America 1996 241
Religious Cultures of the World 241
Religious Science Church 220
Religious Society of Friends 157, Tables 7.6, 7.11, Fig 7.7
Religious Trends No 1 1998/99 92, 168, 189, 240
Renewal, Catholic movement 74
Renewal magazine 29, 92
Restarting church by age 184, Fig 8.7
Reunited Brethren 163, 168
Revival? 13, 23, 43, 186
Roman Catholic, *see* Catholic
Romania
— Christian Brethren Table 7.9, Fig 7.10
— Lord's Army 96
— Pentecostals Table 6.3
— Seventh-day Adventists Table 7.7, Fig 7.8

254 INDEX

Russia
— Baptist churches 144
— Orthodox Churches 32, 93, 94

Sabbath day 160
Salvation Army 19, 157, Tables 7.6, 7.11, Fig 7.7
Samavesam of Telugu Baptist Church 144
Satanists 220, 240
Scandinavian missionaries 101, 102
Schaller, Lyle 230
Schild, Maurice E 118
Search for Faith and the Witness of the Church 190
Second Vatican Council 1962–64 73
Second World War 116
Sensing the Presence of God 185
Seventh-Day Adventists 19, 154, 157, 159, 160f, Table 7.6, Fig 7.7
Shaper leaders 132
Sierra Leone's Methodists Table 7.4
Sikh population growth rate 229
Simpson, A B 161
Sine, Tom 33
Size of churches 89, 129, 236
Smeaton, John 75
Somalian civil war 83
South Africa
— African Methodist Episcopal Zion Church 152
— Anglicans Tables 4.3, 4.6, Fig 4.4
— Apostolic Church Table 6.1
— Catholics Table 3.3, Fig 3.6
— Christian Brethren Table 7.9, Fig 7.10
— Church of the Nazarene Table 7.11
— Churches of Christ Table 7.10, Fig 7.11
— Indigenous Churches Table 6.9
— Lutherans 101
— Methodists Table 7.4
— Moravians Table 7.11
— Pentecostals 128, Table 6.5
— Zionist churches 53
South America
— Anglican growth Tables 4.2, 4.7, Fig 4.3
— Baptist growth 143, Table 7.1, Fig 7.2
— Catholic growth 65, Table 3.2
— Christian and Missionary Alliance Churches Table 7.8, Fig 7.9
— Christian Brethren Table 7.9, Fig 7.10
— Church community 36, Tables 2.2, 2.3
— Church growth 21, Tables 2.4, 10.3, Figs 2.4, 10.8
— Churches of Christ Table 7.10, Fig 7.11
— Indigenous churches 136, Table 6.8, Fig 6.4
— Lutheran change 103, Table 5.2, Fig 5.5
— Methodist growth 151, Table 7.3, Fig 7.4
— Nominal Christians Table 8.1
— Non-Trinitarian growth Table 10.1, Fig 10.3
— Orthodox growth Table 5.1, Fig 5.2
— Other Churches growth Table 7.5, Fig 7.6
— Pentecostal growth 52, 128, Table 6.2, Fig 6.2
— Presbyterian growth 112, Table 5.4, Fig 5.9
— Seventh-day Adventist churches Table 7.7, Fig 7.8
South Korea
— Baptist churches 144
— Catholics Table 3.8, Fig 3.11
— Church of the Nazarene Table 7.11
— Methodists 151
— Missionaries 115
— Pentecostals Table 6.4
— Presbyterian churches 46, 112, 113, 114f, Fig 5.10
— Salvation Army Table 7.11
— Unification Church 218
Southern Baptist Convention 51, 145, 146, Table 7.2
Spain
— Catholics Tables 3.6, 3.7, Figs 3.9, 3.10
— Christian and Missionary Alliance churches Table 7.8, Fig 7.9
— Churches of Christ Table 7.10, Fig 7.11
— Jehovah's Witnesses 219
— Pentecostals Table 6.3
Spiritualist Churches 220
Spirituality without Christianity 228
Sri Lankan Catholics Table 3.8, Fig 3.11
Starting church by age 184, Fig 8.7
State churches 44
Stickley, Caroline 136, 139
Stopping church by age 184, Fig 8.7
Story of Christianity 223
Stott, Rev John 190

INDEX 255

Streams within New Churches 28
Strobel, Lee 190
Study of Anglicanism 92
Sudan
— Anglicans 83, Table 4.3
— Civil war 83
Surinam's Moravians Table 7.11
Swaggart, Jimmy 196, 211
Sweden
— Lutherans 103
— Missionaries in Africa 101
Switching denominations Fig 1.5
Switzerland's Presbyterians 111
Sydney
— Diocese 53
— Lutherans 102
Symbol and Ceremony 241
Symbols of culture 223

Taiwan
— Pastors 237
— Presbyterian churches 112
Talking to others about God 185
Tanzania
— Anglicans 83, Table 4.3
— Catholics Table 3.3, Fig 3.6
— Christian Brethren Table 7.9, Fig 7.10
— Lutherans 101
— Mennonites Table 7.11
— Moravians Table 7.11
— Seventh-day Adventists Table 7.7, Fig 7.8
Taylor, Jan 5, 9
Taylor, Dr William 119
Teaching believers 206, 210
Thompson, John L 241
Tiplady, Richard 231, 242
Tongues of Fire 139
Too Valuable to Lose 119
Torch Centre, Seoul 114
Toronto, Canada 23
Transfer between churches 25, 182, 200, 208, Table 9.4
Transformation, age of 225
Transformation magazine 75, 242
Transition? 176

Uganda
— Anglicans Tables 4.3, 4.6, Fig 4.4
— Catholics 73, Table 3.3, Fig 3.6
— Elim church Table 6.1
— Pentecostal Church 212
— Visit of Pope 1993 64
UK Christian Handbook 28, 54, 92, 139

Ukraine
— Baptists 145
— Europe, in 20
— Pentecostals Table 6.3
— Seventh-day Adventists Table 7.7, Fig 7.8
Unchurched 187
Understanding of church members 203
Uniate Catholics 18
Unification Church 218, 219, Table 10.2
Unitarians 220, Table 10.2
United Kingdom
— Anglicans 86, Table 4.5
— Baptist churches 145
— Catholics Table 3.6, Fig 3.9
— Christian Brethren Table 7.9, Fig 7.10
— Churches of Christ Table 7.10, Fig 7.11
— Elim church Table 6.1
— Jehovah's Witnesses 219
— Methodists 150
— Nominals 174
— Pentecostals 126, Table 6.3
— Presbyterians 46, 111
— Religious Society of Friends Table 7.11
United Nations 19, 20, 27, 37, 95
United States
— African Methodist Episcopal Zion Church 152
— Anglicans 86, Tables 4.5, 4.6, Fig 4.4
— Assemblies of God Table 6.1
— Catholics Table 3.4, Fig 3.7
— Christian and Missionary Alliance churches Table 7.8, Fig 7.9
— Christian Brethren Table 7.9, Fig 7.10
— Church of the Nazarene Table 7.11
— Churches of Christ 166, Table 7.10, Fig 7.11
— Disciples of Christ 157
— Jehovah's Witnesses 219
— Mennonites Table 7.11
— Methodists 46, 151
— Moravians Table 7.11
— Pentecostals 128, 130, Tables 6.1, 6.6
— Presbyterian churches 111
— Religious Science 220
— Religious Society of Friends Table 7.11
— Salvation Army Table 7.11

— Seventh-day Adventists Table 7.7, Fig 7.8
Uniting Church, Australia 84, 111, 152, 156, 167
Unity School of Christianity 220
Universal Church of the Kingdom of God Table 6.1
Uruguay Catholics Table 3.5, Fig 3.8
USSR definition change 20, 95

Values identified 238
Venezuela
— Catholics 68, Table 3.5, Fig 3.8
— Children of God 220
— Jehovah's Witnesses 219
Verwer, George 11, 17
Vietnamese Catholics Table 3.8, Fig 3.11
Vinci, Leonardo da 178
Vineyard Christian Fellowship 23
Vision 238
Vision in South Korea 114

Walls, Prof Andrew 33
Wangerin, Walter 241
Wears Valley, Tennessee 51
WEC International 9
Welcome programme 209
Wesley, John 147
Wesleyan Church 157
Wesleyan Holiness Church 157
Wesleyan Methodist Church 151
West Cornwall and the Isles of Scilly 168
Whitefield Briefing 240
Whitefield, George 147
Willow Creek Community Church 187
Wink, Prof Walter 214, 240
Winning, Cardinal Archbishop Thomas 75
Winning Them Back 190, 241
Wittenberg, Germany 98
Wolf, Tom 227
Woodward, Kenneth 75
Words without meaning 228
World Christian Encyclopedia 17, 76, 168
World Christian Handbook 17
World Churches Handbook 5, 18, 31, 76, 77, 88, 111, 120, 133, 170, 191, 216, 219, 235

World Council of Churches Fig 10.6
World Dominion Press 28
World in 2020, The 242
World Methodist Council 153
World Nominalism 172
World population
— Numbers Fig 2.2
— Summit 1995 73
World Vision International 33
Worldview, Christian 221f, 238
Wraight, Heather 5, 10, 28, 29, 33, 54, 75, 228
Wright, Very Rev Dr Tom 221, 240

Yoido Full Gospel Church 114, 116
Youthwork 234

Zahniser, Prof Mathias 223, 241
Zaïre
— Baptists 144
— Catholics Table 3.3, Fig 3.6
— Christian and Missionary Alliance Churches Table 7.8, Fig 7.9
— Disciples of Christ 157
— Indigenous churches 46, Table 6.9
— Jehovah's Witnesses 219
— Mennonites Table 7.11
— Methodists Table 7.4
— Pentecostals 128, Table 6.5
— Presbyterian's churches 111
— Seventh-day Adventists Table 7.7, Fig 7.8
Zambia
— Christian Brethren Table 7.9, Fig 7.10
— Churches of Christ Table 7.10, Fig 7.11
— Indigenous Churches Table 6.9
Zimbabwe
— Assemblies of God Table 6.1
— Christian Brethren Table 7.9, Fig 7.10
— Churches of Christ Table 7.10, Fig 7.11
— Indigenous Churches Table 6.9
— Methodists Table 7.4
— Pentecostals Table 6.5
— Salvation Army Table 7.11
— Seventh-day Adventists Table 7.7, Fig 7.8
Zionist Churches 53, 133
Zionist Independent Churches 138